Revolutionary Theory

Drawing on the work of Marx, Engels, Lenin, Trotsky, Luxemburg, Mao, and other important revolutionaries, this book provides a systematic examination of the full range of modern revolutionary theory. From an interdisciplinary perspective, it looks at theories of the forces that produce revolution and theories of revolutionary organization and mobilization. A final section, devoted to the shaping of the socialist future, comments on unresolved theoretical issues that have emerged as a result of revolutionary transformation.

Revolutionary Theory

WILLIAM H. FRIEDLAND

with Amy Barton, Bruce Dancis,
Michael Rotkin and Michael Spiro

ALLANHELD, OSMUN   **Publishers**

ALLANHELD, OSMUN & CO. PUBLISHERS, INC.

Published in the United States of America in 1982
by Allanheld, Osmun & Co. Publishers, Inc.
(A Division of Littlefield, Adams & Company)
81 Adams Drive, Totowa, New Jersey 07512

Library of Congress Cataloging in Publication Data

Friedland, William H.
    Revolutionary theory.

    Bibliography: p.
    Includes index.
    1. Revolutions.   I. Barton, Amy E.   II. Title.
JC491.F73   322.4'2'01   80-70921
ISBN 0-86598-074-8   AACR2
ISBN 0-86598-075-6 (pbk.)

82 83 84 / 10 9 8 7 6 5 4 3 2 1

Printed in the United States of America

Contents

vi *Contents*

Acknowledgments

This book was read in manuscript by many friends, colleagues, and co-workers, to whom we owe many debts. The authors stand responsible for all of the arguments but we wish to express our gratitude to the many critical readers of the manuscript: Robert Alford, Ken Barnes, Victoria Bonnell, John Borrego, Jan Carr, Richard Flacks, Todd Gitlin, Walter Goldfrank, Seymour Martin Lipset, Barrie Thorne, Jon Turner.

We also are in debt to the Seminar on Comparative History at the University of California, Santa Cruz, for collective critique of several chapters. To an anonymous reader for Cambridge University Press we are especially grateful; his or her comments helped significantly in the initial revision of the manuscript. Finally, we are indebted to John Borrego for helping to revise the figures in Chapter 6; his visual sense aided intellectual clarity.

I wish to acknowledge permission to use material as quoted on page 46 as follows:

"The Times They Are A-Changin'." Bob Dylan. © 1963. Warner Bros. Inc. All rights reserved. Used by permission.

The Jefferson Airplane quote is from the song "Volunteers" by Marty Balin and Paul Kantner, © 1969.

Introduction

Human beings have tried to improve their conditions of life since the beginnings of recorded history. Often this has taken the form of direct conflict with powerful social groups in an entrenched social structure. However, it was not until the rapid rise of capitalism on a global scale in the 18th and 19th centuries that social movements and thinkers emerged who consciously and deliberately developed revolutionary theories. These theories showed how *existing* social forces might be directed toward the creation of a world without scarcity, inequality, domination, and competition, where all individuals might be allowed to develop their full human potential.

At first, plans to build a new social order were based on the construction of model, utopian socialist communities in which the superiority of cooperation over competition would be clearly demonstrated for all the world to see. After the turn of the 19th century, utopians such as Henri Saint-Simon and Charles Fourier in France, Robert Owen in Great Britain, and others spread their ideas and set up their communities, but they had little impact on the existing social order.

In 1848, however, events occurred which rocked the foundations of virtually every country in Europe and began a process of international revolutionary upheaval that has lasted well over a century. The urban working classes created by the development of capitalism took to the streets in violent uprisings against the ruling property owners with whom they had earlier been allied. Although these revolutions failed, they revealed the social tensions that accompanied capitalist society.

Karl Marx and Friedrich Engels, in their world-shaking pamphlet, *The Communist Manifesto*, examined these changing social and economic conditions in Europe. Anticipating the 1848 events, Marx and Engels tried to demonstrate that working-class revolt was rooted in the property and class relations of capitalism. They argued that workers were exploited by the fundamental characteristics of capitalism: the system of production and exchange for profit, wage labor, private ownership of productive property, and economic competition and inequality regulated through a market. Most importantly, Marx and Engels argued that the working class — the proletariat — was the only social group with the potential to both overthrow capitalism and construct another social order that built on capitalism's improvements but eliminated the sufferings caused by capitalism.

The present book is intended neither to demonstrate that the ills of modern society are rooted in capitalism nor to prove that their solution will require a worldwide revolutionary transformation. We hope, however, that by examining revolution in a theoretical manner we can illustrate the kinds of problems that must be confronted *if* revolutionary change is to be undertaken. Our intent is to address those people dissatisfied with existing arrangements who are groping for alternatives, as well as those who are trying to learn something about the phenomena of revolutionary change that has swept the world.

The term revolution as we use it refers to *the structural transformation of society, a popular struggle resulting in the reorganization of the class structure, class relations, consciousness, and the basic institutions affecting daily life.* We are not concerned here with two other forms of change often labeled as "revolutionary:"

1. The seizure of power by small cabals of individuals — often times a military junta — whether on their own behalf or "in the name of the masses." Because they lack a popular base such "palace revolutions" rarely transform the social structure.

2. Dramatic advances in technology such as the "Industrial Revolution" or new "revolutionary" brands of soap. Our focus is limited to revolutions in social relations.

Perhaps one way to clarify the concept of revolution is to briefly compare three different "revolutions" — the American Revolution of 1776, the French Revolution of 1789, and the Russian Revolution of 1917.

The American War of Independence was *not* a revolution as we have defined it since it did not involve any substantial rearrangements in the class structure of the North American continent. Basic class organization remained essentially the same after the colonies liberated themselves from Great Britain. One way in which the distinction is handled between massive political-military events involving no significant change in the social structure and true social upheavals is to refer to the former as *political* revolutions and distinguish them from *social* revolutions. In this book we reserve the unmodified term *revolution* for the latter alone.

The French Revolution of 1789 was, in contrast to the American War of Independence, a social revolution since it involved a reordering of the class structure of France. Until 1789, French society was dominated by a decaying landed aristocracy. A new class, the bourgeoisie (owners of capital), had been growing within the framework of feudalism for several hundred years. The increasing strains in class relationships ultimately led to popular actions that overthrew the old regime, replacing it with a new political system dominated by the bourgeoisie.

Despite the fact that we regard the French case as a true revolutionary transformation, we will not devote any attention to it from here on. The French Revolution did not give birth to systematic revolutionary theory; this occurred only with the writings of Marx and Engels over half a century later. Thus, we will examine revolutions and revolutionary theory from 1848 to the present.

The Russian Revolution of 1917 contained important similarities to the French Revolution. In this case, feudal elements maintained tight political control and permitted only a truncated development of capitalism. The result was that the Russian bourgeoisie was unable to accomplish a transformation on its own behalf. Instead, a combination of proletarian and peasant popular forces, protesting immense injustices, led to a brief but massive action that overthrew the system of czarist controls. What emerged was a new class structure and, consequently, we regard the Russian uprising as a social revolution.

Revolutionary Theory

For over a century, a substantial body of analysis and argumentation has been generated as movements and people sought to make revolutions more effectively. Newcomers to the study of revolution who are interested in learning more about it are often intimidated by the enormous number of books, pamphlets, and articles on the subject.

The central concerns of this book are to order systematically and condense the thinking of revolutionaries about the problems and prospects for making revolutions. The book draws on the experiences of over one hundred years of revolutionary theory and practice. It centers upon the four key intellectual questions which must be dealt with by all revolutionaries:

THEORIES OF THE DRIVING FORCE

Those dissatisfied with society have argued that the inadequacies of a social system are a product of that very system. Social systems produce strains in all groups and strata in society but affect some strata more than others. The revolutionary potential thus created drives some classes toward revolutionary change. The specific location of revolutionary classes has been — and continues to be — a subject of controversy among revolutionaries, but all agree that a potentially revolutionary agent is necessary to produce a revolution.

THEORIES OF ORGANIZATION

Those actively dissatisfied with society must develop ways to organize themselves. These forms of organization must embody theories about how organized and conscious forces — the revolutionaries — will relate to those classes within which revolutionary potential is generated.

THEORIES OF MOBILIZATION

While society generates revolutionary potential, it is usually believed to be insufficient to leave the dynamics of the system to operate without conscious and deliberate intervention. Most revolutionaries believe it necessary to establish distinctive relationships with those social groups who most directly experience the problems of society in order to galvanize them and develop their revolutionary potential. The goal of such mobilization is to develop social and political activities that may be effective in overturning the system and replacing it with a better one. Without such mobilization, revolutionary classes may simply lash out in periodic outbursts without producing effective change. Mobilizational theory seeks to explain how strategies and tactics should be developed to maximize revolutionary energy in particular situations.

THEORIES OF FUTURE ARRANGEMENTS

These theories originate out of the desire among dissatisfied people to know what a new society would look like if present arrangements were ended. In effect, people say: This society is bad and should be changed; what should it be changed to?

Revolutionary Theory and History

This book explores four bodies of theory by utilizing the experiences of the past. Much can be learned from such experience — including the many errors that have been made. In approaching the important revolutionary thinkers who have dealt with the four theoretical areas, we have avoided formulating our own "program" for revolutionary action. Our purpose is to extract a systematic body of theory out of the writings and practice of revolutionary thinkers operating in a wide variety of contexts over the past century.

In extracting this revolutionary theory, however, we have also tried to avoid the abstract and academic quality of much of the current concern with revolution. In this respect *revolutionary theory* should be distinguished from *theories of revolution.* Although both share a common interest in understanding past revolutions, revolutionary theory, as we treat it, is concerned with *effecting* revolutionary transformation. The revolutionary theorists from whom we draw our material were *revolutionaries* first and *theorists* second. "The philosophers have only *interpreted* the world in various ways; the point, however, is to *change* it."*

The study of revolutions *ought* to begin through reading the work of revolutionaries of previous times and examining the historical contexts in which they wrote. The purpose of historical examination is to develop a better understanding of the various elements that constitute successful and unsuccessful transitions. This kind of study requires a great deal of time and energy. In the long run, of course, there are no short cuts to such understanding. Those readers who are serious about the revolutionary process will need to undertake historical analysis while attempting

---

*The citation is from Marx, "Theses on Feuerbach," in Karl Marx and Frederick Engels, *The German Ideology* (New York: International Publishers, 1947), p. 199. All quotations used are provided with a source reference; where we have drawn from other sources, even though no quotation is included, references are provided in the "References" section beginning on page 219. To avoid cluttering the text with reference notations, no numbers or asterisks have been included.

to apply their understanding to current events. Our hope here is to create a jumping-off point for those who wish to study revolutionary theory in a systematic manner.

However, the writings by practicing revolutionaries pose considerable problems for many readers. Consider the following excerpt from Lenin:

> The sentence employed by the authors of the Economist letter published in *Iskra*, No. 12, that the efforts of the most inspired ideologists fail to divert the working-class movement from the path that is determined by the interaction of the material elements and the material environment *is* therefore *tantamount to renouncing socialism*. If these authors were capable of fearlessly, consistently, and thoroughly considering what they say, as everyone who enters the arena of literary and public activity should be, there would be nothing left for them but to "fold their useless arms over their empty breasts" and — surrender the field of action to the Struves and Prokopoviches, who are dragging the working-class movement "along the line of least resistance," i.e., along the line of bourgeois trade-unionism, or to the Zubatovs, who are dragging it along the line of clerical and gendarme "ideology."

The quotation illustrates three major problems for the reader of original revolutionary literature: jargon, polemical style, and immediate (but no longer relevant) context. For revolutionary writers, jargon serves the same function as it does for any specialized body of knowledge such as sociology, mathematics, physics, or music; intended to facilitate communication among experts in a body of thought, it represents a barrier to most other people. Revolutionary jargon is perhaps better known than other jargons since it comes closer to the everyday lives of many people during rapidly changing times. Similarly, while polemical style is accepted by revolutionary writers as a mode of discourse, most ordinary readers often regard it as offensive.

The problem of context originates because revolutionary thinkers are less concerned with writing theory than they are with dealing with immediate issues in immediate ways. Since only the experts know or care about *Iskra* or the Zubatovs, it is necessary to extract key ideas for generalization out of the immediate contexts in which they have been written. We attempt to deal with the three problems by eliminating as much jargon as possible, removing polemical style, and reinserting ideas in *contemporary* experience to establish contexts that will be more meaningful.

A special problem is posed for American readers in that revolutionary experience has been decidedly underdeveloped in this country compared to much of the rest of the world. The successful revolutions, particularly those of world-historical magnitude — Russia, China, Cuba, and Viet Nam — occurred under social conditions very different from those found in the United States. Specific historical facts such as the existence of a massive peasantry do not exist in the United States nor, indeed, in many advanced capitalist countries. Thus, the relevance of revolutionary experience and the analysis conducted by revolutionary theorists is not immediate and direct. Rather, the application of these ideas represents a challenge to evolving revolutionary theory. This is particularly true because the successes of the revolutionary processes have taken place in countries experiencing minimal capitalist development. Where capitalism has been powerful, its successes in maintaining itself often produced demoralization and cynicism among revolutionaries.

The challenge of understanding the historical context of revolution therefore involves understanding the ideas of differing circumstances and seeking to test their applicability in other situations. That there have been no successful revolutions in advanced capitalist countries does not necessarily negate the power or utility of the analysis. Rather, the fact that advanced capitalism continues to generate alienation, dissatisfaction, protest, and revolutionary activity and ideas simply underlines the need to develop the theoretical basis for revolutionary understanding and action.

One final problem of style has been created by virtue of the present historical context: sex-biased terms are almost universal in older theoretical writings. Most older revolutionary writers used terms such as "he" and "his" when referring to both male and female, just as words now recognized as embodying sexual bias — "mankind," "man," "manfully," etc. — were also the norm. This book has sought to avoid the use of such terms. Where they could not be avoided, we have retained quotations from older writers in their original form.

The intent in this work is *not* to substitute for the original materials. Readers interested in the full development of revolutionary theory need to return to the original sources for study. For these purposes, there are a detailed set of references, a bibliography, and a suggested reading list. A chronology of major events and of key people discussed in the book has also been included.

PART ONE

Who To Organize:
Theories of the Driving Force

The most indubitable feature of a revolution is the direct interference of the masses in historic events. In ordinary times the state, be it monarchical or democratic, elevates itself above the nation, and history is made by specialists in that line of business—kings, ministers, bureaucrats, parliamentarians, journalists. But at those crucial moments when the old order becomes no longer endurable to the masses, they break over the barriers excluding them from the political arena, sweep aside their traditional representatives, and create by their own interference the initial groundwork for a new regime. . . . The history of a revolution is . . . first of all a history of the forcible entry of the masses into the realm of rulership over their own destiny.

— Leon Trotsky

Without the involvement of "the masses," there can be no social revolution; without huge numbers of people, revolutions degenerate into simple coups engineered by conspiratorial groups. While conspiratorial seizures of power, of course, have taken place, and while this sort of explanation—the "outside troublemakers" as the cause of revolution—is a favorite in establishment circles, most revolutionaries reject conspiracies as a substitute for mass action. Large-scale popular participation is needed not only to provide adequate strength to overthrow a system, but also to ensure the very goal of social revolution, the involvement of the overwhelming majority of the population in the determination of their own destinies.

For most revolutionaries, the operations of the social system make the populace prone to revolutionary change, whether they consciously desire it or not. The question of *who* to organize is vitally related to the analysis of the contradictions and conflicts between classes in society—how capitalism as an economic and social system produces the drive that leads oppressed classes to take revolutionary action.

1

This is, in fact, the great discovery of marxian analysis. As the concept of *strain*, it is used by many social scientists to understand basic structural processes of society; but, more importantly, as the concept of *contradictions* it fosters an understanding of both the dynamics of capitalism as a system and as a way of defining where the potential for revolutionary change will be concentrated.

The power of marxian analysis rests on the philosophical base of historical materialism; in this way Marx departed from the idealist philosophies of most of the great thinkers who had preceded him. He argued that people, in the process of behaving and serving their own interests, produced ideas; this stood in sharp contrast to those who argued that ideas were created by ingenious individuals.

Although this was a powerful concept, historical materialism has often been self-defeating for revolutionaries. If marxian analysis is correct and a social class such as the proletariat is driven by social forces to revolution, why should revolutionaries consciously intervene in the process? Leave the social process alone, some might argue, and let it produce its own inexorable change. In fact, few major revolutionary theorists have been so determinist. From Marx to Mao, revolutionaries have agreed that the development of consciousness is itself part of material reality. Material conditions—the level and organization of technology, the forms of production, the availability of raw materials—set the *limits* on the possibilities of consciousness and action but they do not determine them completely. It is inconceivable for a member of a simple tribal society to organize a division of labor similar to that found in advanced industrial societies, but this does not preclude the development of a broad variety of descent or kinship systems. Similarly, capitalist social forms such as private ownership of property establish limits on consciousness, but this still permits great variety in social forms under capitalism and even in the development of socialist consciousness.

Within the limits set by capitalism, therefore, revolutionaries can act in ways that affect the material conditions that determine their own way of thinking. Revolutionaries agree that the contradictions which are concentrated in some social classes will produce a driving force for revolution; but conscious intervention is necessary to give shape to the process of change.

The search for the driving force, for the "motive force of history" to use Marx's term, represents one key aspect of revolutionary thinking. In Marx's time, and for three-quarters of a century afterward, the driving force was located within the proletariat. As shall be shown, Marx examined the way in which social forces operated upon the bourgeoisie, the class that owned property and exploited it for profit, to make them a force for revolutionary change. Marx then went on to argue that the working class, the proletariat, would take on a continuously revolutionary role as capitalist society became established.

The proletariat, as the driving force, remained at the center of events and of marxian theory until the two Russian revolutions of 1905 and 1917. Although the working class was vital to both revolutions, two puzzles emerged. The first had to do with the powerful revolutionary energies contributed to both revolutions by the *peasants*. But even more significant was the failure of the "most advanced" proletariats in Great Britain and Germany to make proletarian revolutions, while the "backward" Russian proletariat produced two revolutions.

In the years since the 1917 revolution the puzzle has been compounded by the relative quiescence of the industrial working class in the capitalist countries. The center of revolutionary gravity shifted to underdeveloped countries, in particular China, Indo-China, and Cuba. The very successes of the peasantry created a theoretical difficulty for marxian thinkers. This was because Marx had argued that capitalism constituted a necessary prior stage to proletarian revolution and the establishment of socialism. It was the bourgeoisie, Marx contended, that liberated the forces of production from the stultifying feudal systems, created bourgeois democratic forms of government, and sowed the seeds of its own destruction through the formation of the proletariat. As a result, the shift of revolutionary action from capitalist to peasant societies and underdeveloped colonies represented a major theoretical problem. This intellectual nut, generally referred to as the *theory of stages of development*, was finally cracked theoretically by Trotsky and practically by Mao Zedong. It involved, however, a relocation of the driving force in the peasantry.

This transition from proletariat to peasantry was not an easy one; the proletariat had been vital to marxists for so long that the shift constituted a major intellectual and theoretical trauma. Moreover, the change did not eliminate the continuing importance of the working class to many revolutionary thinkers. In underdeveloped countries with a tiny proletariat, peasants became the driving force along with the workers because they provided the *mass* to the revolutionary drive. The proletariat continued to contribute, according to revolutionaries in these countries, overall leadership and the definition of the revolution's goals. The reason was that peasant revolutions, left to themselves, usually degenerated into political revolutions in which some peasants became the new landlords with the social system remaining intact. Proletarian ideology in terms of defining a socialist goal — a transformation of the social structure, a breakdown of the distinction between town and country, an introduction of the industrial process to agriculture — was seen as vital if a social revolution were to occur.

The theoretical problem of understanding how the dynamics of the social system — the contradictions in society — produce revolutionary energies in the peasantry is a problem that has not yet been fully solved. Marx's analysis of the driving force in the proletariat was more rigorous and intellectually satisfying than his explanations concerning the peasantry. Yet the revolutionary potential of the peasantry can no longer be denied. Chapters 2 and 3 focus on this subject, and we bring together the relevant thinkers who have grappled with the issue. Unlike the treatment of the proletariat, where Marx himself provided so much of the analysis that was accepted by revolutionaries for so long, no single theoretician has provided an explanation of the peasant-as-revolutionary. Although our synthesis of Trotsky and Mao will probably be unwelcome to either trotskyists or maoists, we believe the theoretical requirements for this "marriage" are more important than the conflicts left over from the past.

In recent years there has been remarkable development of revolutionary potential in social groups other than workers or peasants. This includes women, youth, ethnic and racial minorities, and technical and service workers in all advanced capitalist countries. Explanations are necessary as to the structural forces producing this revolutionary potential. In part, the activism of youth and students can be explained by their idealism, their lack of attachment to the social system, and the greater energy levels of the young which have always made them important to revolutionary change. But the political activism of the 1960s and early 1970s requires a deeper understanding. Similarly, racial and ethnic minorities — we treat only blacks because of the larger body of theory about their revolutionary potential — despite constant oppression and occasional upsurges, represent a revolutionary phenomenon of the last several decades. A parallel situation exists with women whose growing militancy is even newer. As for the new working class, or what was misnamed for years as the "new middle class," a reassessment of the changes in modern capitalism is necessary to explain the development of revolutionary potential in a group that was largely ignored by past revolutionaries. The analysis of the effects of the contradictions of society on this new working class of white collar, clerical workers, technicians, sales people, and professional workers constitutes the most recent frontier in the consideration of driving force theory.

*   *   *

In the five chapters of Part I, we examine the location of driving force in different social strata and the structural features creating potential for revolution. Chapter 1 turns to the working class and is based on the theoretical work of Marx. Chapter 2 explains the theory of stages of development. Chapter 3 assembles the relevant analysis of the social forces operating on the peasantry to make them a driving force for revolution. Chapter 4 treats the applicability of driving force theories to women, blacks, and youth. Chapter 5 considers the new working class and "expanded proletariat" theory.

CHAPTER ONE

Classical Marxian Theory:
The Proletariat as the Driving Force

The Philosophical Basis for Revolutionary Action

Marx's* prediction that the proletariat would make the revolution flowed from his analysis of the forces operating throughout human history. The marxist philosophy, *dialectical materialism*,** provided a method for understanding the social forces acting at any time and grasping their implication for the future.

In developing his revolutionary philosophy, Marx had to confront and synthesize two opposing philosophies which dominated his own time and which still prevail in many spheres of modern thought—idealism and materialism. In opposition to idealist philosophies that saw revolutions as made by "ideas whose time has come," marxism accepted the materialist idea of history as an arena within which people satisfy *real, material needs* such as those for food, clothing, shelter, sex and reproduction, etc. In other words, the past—and the present and future as well—cannot be explained by abstract ideas such as the Absolute Mind, Justice, Truth, Progress, or God's Purpose. Rather, one must look to people and the material means and social relations by which they produce the necessities of life.

On the other hand, Marx rejected the deterministic aspect of materialism which left people powerless before the forces of Nature or Society or History. In the place of a crude materialism which saw people as mere reflexes of their environ-

---

*While most references in this chapter and throughout this book will be to Marx, there is no intention to slight his lifetime collaborator Friedrich Engels. Most references to Marx should include, if only implicitly, Engels.

**Marx delineated his philosophical approach initially as *historical materialism*. Engels subsequently renamed the marxian philosophy as *dialectical materialism*. While some distinctions can be made between the two concepts, they will be used interchangeably in this book. For a discussion on this distinction see Baron, 1963 and Levine, 1975.

ment — "you are what you eat" — Marx accepted the idealist notion that people make history. But he insisted that the actors were *real* people acting out of their own felt needs, not simply the instruments of ideas or God, and he rejected the idea that people were fully free to change society as they might wish:

> Men make their own history, but they do not make it just as they please; they do not make it under circumstances chosen by themselves, but under circumstances directly encountered, given, and transmitted from the past.

The dialectical aspect of marxian philosophy requires that phenomena be examined in their dynamic or changing aspects. At early stages of human development needs are limited to the survival and reproduction of the species. The manner in which these needs are satisfied, however, leads to the elaboration or creation of new needs which are no less real than those arising directly out of biological drives. For example, the initial need for food may be met by the invention of hunting technologies (including tools such as bows and arrows and new social forms like hunting bands) which themselves lead to the creation of new needs such as the division of labor within the family or specialization in arrowhead making. "Human nature," the "necessities" of life, and the particular social forms in which people organize themselves are all historically changing realities. The *needs* for which people will make a revolution may seem insignificant or trivial to other people or historical periods.

Marx argued that as history developed, social change, including revolution, could be best understood as a dynamic relationship between the technical *forces of production* and the social *relations of production* under which these forces of production are organized. As technology improves and new systems of production develop, they create new social forms which correspond to the new technical levels. The new *means of production* — the totality of a technological and social system required to produce things to satisfy the material needs of people — is controlled by the new social relationships. The means of production and the controlling social relationships are thus integrated. As the productive apparatus of society develops further, it lays the basis for new changes in social relations.

Each new social form, as it is created, can be seen as having two aspects. In one sense, new social forms are necessary and useful to the operation and further development of the means of production. In another sense, these same social forms are in contradiction to the new means of production and impede their full development. In the early and "progressive" period of a new form of social organization, the "positive" aspects of the social system may predominate, but later more "negative" aspects may take on greater significance. It is the "positive" and "negative" sides of such social relationships that constitute the dialectical nature of Marx's philosophy.

An example can illustrate this dialectical process:

> Under capitalism, a worker's wages are less than the actual contribution that is made to the value of the product produced. The difference between what the worker is paid and the value contributed constitutes a surplus which the capitalist is encouraged to reinvest in new machinery which will cut labor costs and hence increase profits. This reinvestment of surplus can be seen dialectically as having both a "positive" and "negative" aspect. In its "positive" aspect, the reinvestment

of surplus — which the worker might use merely to buy some consumer item — increases society's productivity and overall output of material goods. In its "negative" aspect, the very same social form, the reinvestment of surplus in labor-saving machinery, leads to a decreased need for labor and hence unemployment.

Marxist analysis sees that "good" and "bad" elements of any social system or historical period are integrally tied together and not merely connected in some accidental manner. It is not possible, given the form of private property that exists, to separate the productivity-increasing aspect of reinvestment from the "bad" results of unemployment. The interrelationships between good and bad, positive and negative, constitute the dialectical phases of all social forms.

Not only do the positive and negative aspects of any given set of social relations remain inextricably bound together, but more significantly, they develop together. The *contradiction* between the two parts of any set of social relations is therefore always growing larger. As contradictions grow, it becomes more difficult to maintain equilibrium between them.

For example, increases in productivity and unemployment have always existed side by side in capitalism. Even during the early "progressive" era of capitalism, periods of dramatic economic expansion (and reinvestment of surplus) alternated with deep depressions in which the demand for labor dropped precipitously. But as the capitalist system matures, the "negative" aspects of socially useless labor for growing sectors of the work force and permanent unemployment for others becomes the "side" of the productivity — unemployment dialectic which increasingly dominates social reality and political consciousness.

When the contradiction between the means of production and the social relations of production developed to the point where they became intolerable for the workers, Marx believed they would respond by overthrowing the system of private property and the bourgeois (capitalist) state which protected private property. Marx saw that, in a similar way, the bourgeois class had earlier created the capitalist state as a means of resolving the contradictions that had been generated in the feudal system.

> In the development of the productive forces a stage is reached where productive forces and means of intercourse are called into being which . . . can only work mischief, and which are, therefore, no longer productive, but destructive, forces.

Dialectical materialism, therefore, places great emphasis on the analysis of material conditions to assess the potential for change in any situation. The material conditions of life, according to Marx, decide whether revolutionary convulsions, which appear periodically, will be sufficiently strong to overthrow existing social forms. The material elements for revolution consist, therefore, of productive forces on the one hand and a revolutionary class or population on the other. The revolutionary class revolts not only against specific conditions which it dislikes but against the total activity of society, because society's problems are inextricably bound to the character of production and the nature of the state and other social relations.

For Marx, the vital manifestation of the dialectic took the form of the class struggle. Because various groups of people shared a similar relationship to the means of production — as workers or capitalists — they developed a common experience and world view; such groups constituted a social class. As Marx and Engels pointed out in *The Communist Manifesto*, history is the expression of the dialectic through the contradictions between social classes.

> The history of all hitherto existing society is the history of class struggles.
> Freeman and slave, patrician and plebeian, lord and serf, guildmaster and journeyman, in a word, oppressor and oppressed, stood in constant opposition to one another, carried on an uninterrupted, now hidden, now open fight, a fight that each time ended, either in a revolutionary reconstitution of society at large, or in the common ruin of the contending classes.
> In the earlier epochs of history, we find almost everywhere a complicated arrangement of society into various orders, a manifold gradation of social rank. . . .
> Our epoch, the epoch of the bourgeoisie, possesses, however, this distinctive feature: it has simplified the class antagonisms. Society as a whole is more and more splitting up into two great hostile camps, into two great classes directly facing each other: Bourgeoisie and Proletariat.*

The Contradictions Producing Driving Force

Marx saw four distinct negative manifestations resulting from the contradictions of capitalism: (1) alienation; (2) the concentration of capital in fewer hands and the resulting increase in the number of persons working for wages or salary, the proletariat; (3) the tendency of the rate of profits to fall and the immiseration of the proletariat; and (4) the anarchy of capitalism and the crisis of overproduction. In treating each of these, Marx also showed their contribution to the expansive nature of capitalism. He argued that each contradiction would drive the proletariat toward a resolution of that contradiction through an overthrow of capitalism.

ALIENATION

The most impressive feat of capitalism and its greatest contribution to the growth of society's productive capacity lay in its breaking down of complex production operations into many simpler tasks. This greatly expanded division of labor has increased output for every hour of the worker's time. While there has always been a division of labor, it has generally become more complex in each successive historical period. The major exception to this increasing complexity came in the transition to feudalism following the collapse of the slave system of the Roman empire; in this transition, the relatively more complex division of labor of Roman society was replaced by a less

---

*The concept of the dialectic has posed continuing problems for Marx's successors. An interesting formulation has been made by Mao Zedong, who distinguished between *primary* and *secondary* contradictions (manifested, for example, by the class struggle) and *antagonistic* contradictions and *nonantagonistic* contradictions (as manifested when different classes unite for national liberation despite their class differences). See *On Contradiction*. Mao later applied these ideas to practical (as opposed to philosophical) issues in his *On the Correct Handling of Contradictions Among the People*. This work dealt with the repression of the revolution in Hungary in 1956 when this popular rebellion against the Communist regime was repressed by the troops and tanks of the Soviet Union. In his writings Mao overtly agreed with repression of the revolution. In the text, however, as Mao discussed the various ways to handle contradictions, he attacked the repressive Communist regime in Hungary. He suggested ways in which the Chinese revolution must function to avoid such draconian repression. Both of Mao's works represent an interesting application of the concept of contradictions.

complex division of the manorial system. Capitalism, however, introduced a division of labor of remarkable diversity reducing the amount of skill needed by each worker. As tasks became simpler, it was possible to introduce machines which allowed for even greater productivity. This dynamic increase in productivity was the positive aspect of the capitalist forms of production.

But the division of labor also has negative aspects. In order that the division of labor take place on a significant scale, it is necessary that enough capital be provided to cover (1) the wages of many workers, who have to be paid for a considerable length of time before a return on the whole process manifests itself, and (2) the cost of machinery and other fixed costs. Under bourgeois property relations, expenses could only be covered by the investment of capital. Thus it comes about that the workers trade their productive power for wages. The capitalists make investments only under the assurance that they will receive profits out of the difference between what their workers produce and what has to be paid to them in wages. This difference is known as *surplus value*.

In trading productive power for a wage, the worker enters into an exchange out of necessity as there are no alternative ways to make a living. Consequently, *alienation* arises. Individual workers have only a tiny part in the making of the final product and no control over its disposition. Thus, in the productive process, workers create objects that become alien to themselves.

To explain why the complex division of labor produces the situation in which the very product becomes alien to the producer, we must return to the philosophical basis of marxist thinking, which argues that the material basis of production gives rise to thoughts and ideas. For Marx, human beings were formed and gained their personalities through the very act of production. When an object is created by workers via a process over which they have no control, the workers are alienated not only from the object and the social power it embodies but also from themselves. The more produced for the capitalist, the less the worker controls; and, in this respect, the worker is diminished as a human being. The very act of laboring becomes alienating under capitalism because it is *always* labor for someone else. Workers continually put their lives into objects but then lose those objects to others. Marx explained, their work "is not the satisfaction of a need, but only a *means* for satisfying other needs."

Alienated labor results in a world dominated by objects, where people become auxiliaries to machines and the things they create. Ultimately the process spreads beyond the work place into society at large, where personal relationships get reduced to cash exchanges and where creativity and emotions become things to be bought and sold. Marx saw this deification of *things*, which increasingly characterizes modern life, as rooted in the capitalist labor process. He believed that as workers became aware of this process of alienation and understood its roots in the capitalist system of production they would organize and fight against alienation and the system behind it.

THE CONCENTRATION OF CAPITAL

The size of the capitalist class—those who own the means of production—shrinks as capitalism matures because larger enterprises gobble up their smaller competitors. As businesses grow in size, they invest a greater proportion of their capital in land improvements, plant expansion, modern machinery, and other forms of *fixed capital*. The greater efficiency of large firms and the size of the markets they can reach permits them to drive smaller firms out of business. The smaller enterprises, more dependent on the exploitation of human labor, are driven out because the larger companies can produce cheaper goods. As time passes, it becomes increasingly difficult for a would-be capitalist to enter many markets because the necessary capital is so large. No individual, for example, can amass the capital necessary to produce automobiles today.

In his early writings in the 1840s, Marx gave a relatively simple explanation for the concentration of capital as resulting from the tendency for large capital to accumulate more rapidly than small amounts of capital. Writing twenty years later in *Capital*, Marx explained that the relationship was more complex but essentially the same. Capital was becoming concentrated in the hands of fewer capitalists

> . . . because beyond certain limits a large capital with a small rate of profit accumulates faster than a small capital with a large rate of profit. At a certain high point this increasing concentration in its turn causes a new fall in the rate of profit. The mass of small dispersed capitals is thereby driven along the adventurous road of speculation, credit frauds, stock swindles, and crises.

THE FALLING RATE OF PROFIT AND IMMISERATION

Considerable controversy has been generated about what Marx meant by the falling rate of profit. Many economists, including committed marxists, have argued that it is the weakest, and certainly the most technical and confusing, link in Marx's economic theory. Stated simply, the theory holds that as capitalism develops there will be a *tendency* for the average rate of profit in the economy to decline.* For many marxists, this *tendency* was seen as an inescapable law of capitalist production. It raised apocalyptic visions (and predictions) of the necessary collapse of capitalism as the profit rate approached zero and investments necessary for production and the reproduction of the system halted. Other more subtle marxists argued that the operation of the "law" was manifested and would continue to be manifested in the periodic depressions which had characterized capitalism since its beginnings. Since depressions rest upon the unwillingness of capitalists to invest when the prospects for profits are uncertain, the long-term tendency for the profit rate to fall would, ostensibly, make each succeeding depression more serious.

*In the third volume of *Capital*, Marx argues that the falling rate of profit results from changes in the technical composition of capital. The rate of profit tends to fall because, as stated above, profits depend on the surplus labor of workers. When a company gets larger it employs relatively fewer workers and more machines. Since machines produce no surplus labor, the capitalists get only what they pay for and the rate (percent) of profits to invested capital tends to fall. It is obvious that, as capitalism has developed, prediction about the increase of machinery has been borne out, but many marxists have made the mistake of assuming that this meant the *value* of machinery relative to the *value* of employed living labor has increased. Although many have made the attempt, no one to date has demonstrated convincingly, either theoretically or empirically, the validity of Marx's assumptions or the operation of the law itself.

While Marx devoted considerable analysis to the falling rate of profit, he also was distinctly aware of counteracting influences and devoted two chapters in *Capital* to these. Among these influences Marx included monopoly pricing, foreign trade, and especially trade with underdeveloped colonies.

Part of the problem in dealing with the falling of profits is that it has parallels with another notion developed by Marx, the concept of *immiseration* — or the increasing misery of the proletariat caused by a decrease in their standard of living. Marx related immiseration primarily to the concept of alienation and to the loss by workers of their power to control their own lives. To the extent that immiseration was put in terms of the decline in wages, it had less to do with the falling rate of profits and more to do with simple increases in population and a decline in numbers of people required by the productive process. Marx described the process whereby the proletariat increased in size when actually fewer workers were needed.

> In a society where prosperity is increasing, only the very wealthiest can live from the interest on money. All others must employ their capital in business or trade. As a result the competition among capitalists increases. The concentration of capital becomes greater, the large capitalists ruin the small ones, and some of the former capitalists sink into the working class, which as a result of this accession of numbers, suffers a further decline in wages and falls into still greater dependence upon the few great capitalists. Since, at the same time, the number of capitalists has diminished, the competition among them for workers hardly exists any longer, whereas the competition among workers, on account of the increase in their numbers, has become greater, more abnormal and more violent. Consequently, a part of the working class falls into a condition of beggary or starvation, with the same necessity as a section of the middle capitalists falls into the working class.

> Thus, even in the state of society which is most favorable to the worker, the inevitable result for the worker is overwork and premature death, reduction to a machine, enslavement to capital which accumulates in menacing opposition to him, renewed competition, and beggary and starvation for a part of the workers.

Another aspect of the controversy over immiseration is concerned with the interpretation of Marx's meaning in discussing the concept. Because Marx discussed immiseration in two distinct ways, there has been much debate on whether he meant immiseration to refer to an *absolute* or a *relative* decline in the conditions of life of the proletariat. In several of his earlier works, Marx emphasized the idea of an absolute decline in the material conditions of the workers. That is, he argued that the proletariat was reduced through increased exploitation to lower and lower economic levels. In *Capital*, however, he put the emphasis on a relative decline in the conditions of the workers. The absolute condition of life does not get worse — it may even get better — but it increases nowhere near as rapidly as the condition of life of other social classes, especially the bourgeoisie, and nowhere near as rapidly as it might. In his notes to *Capital*, Marx showed that the appropriation of surplus value allowed for an improvement in the material conditions of workers and capitalists and that there was no necessary connection between the falling rate of profits and the impoverishment of the workers. Thus, despite a potential improvement in the absolute level of material life of the workers, they experience relative immiseration since their conditions do not improve as rapidly as that of others.

Marx thus clearly saw the capitalist system as driving the proletariat toward at least relative deprivation.

The dynamics by which the proletariat is driven to consciousness and revolutionary action are further enforced by the increased proletarianization of the middle class and the internationalization of the proletariat as capitalism spreads from country to country. Workers looked around them and, Marx believed, were more likely to see that they were becoming more numerous all over the world and were being forced into a miserable situation by a decreasing number of capitalists.

THE ANARCHY OF CAPITAL

The competition between the owners of private property makes it impossible to plan production rationally, and this leads to economic disorganization. Marx quoted an early student of capitalism to the effect that

> Competition simply expresses voluntary exchange, which itself is the logical consequence of the individual right to use and abuse the instruments of production. These three economic factors, which form a unity—the right to use and abuse, free exchange, and arbitrary competition—have the following consequences: everyone produces what he will, how, when and where he will, produces well or ill, too much or not enough, too soon or too late, too dear or too cheap. No one knows whether he will be able to sell his product, or how, when, where or to whom he will sell it; and the same applies to purchases . . . The inevitable consequences are continual and widespread bankruptcies, frauds, sudden ruin and unexpected fortunes, commercial crises, unemployment, periodic surpluses or shortages, instability and swallowing up of wages and profits, massive losses or waste of wealth, time and effort in the area of desperate competition.

Marx saw the erratic fluctuations resulting from this anarchy as aggravating the conditions of the proletariat and driving them toward action which would ultimately end the irrational and destructive system in which they lived and labored.

The disorganization of competitive capitalism is but one part of a more pervasive tendency toward the overproduction crisis in capitalism. The overall increases in productivity fostered by capitalism allows for greater quantities of products to be produced by decreasing numbers of workers. It is not that capitalism produces too much for people to consume but that it produces more than they can afford to buy with the share of their productivity their wages represent. This leads to a central contradiction in capitalism between the expanded powers of the proletariat to produce and the limitations inherent in what they can consume because the capitalists' capture the surplus value created by the workers. It is easy to see the difficulty that arises when a group of workers produce commodities but can only afford to buy back half that amount for their own use. Capitalists will only need half the number of previously employed workers to produce the amount they can sell for profit. After laying off half their workers, only a quarter of the initially existing purchasing power exists. The appropriation of surplus value by the individual capitalist entrepreneur ensures that society's power to consume is *always* less than its ability to produce. As a result, capitalism suffers from periodic crises of overproduction.

Marx insisted that the causes of capitalism's repeated crises, which are forcefully evident to workers through massive unemployment, were not fortuitous but were at the heart of the capitalist system of private property.

"The real limitation upon capitalist production is *capital itself*." Ultimately the capitalist goal of expanding production *for profit* comes into conflict with the goal of expanding production for human use. In situations where it is clear that social needs present opportunities for expanding productive activity — food for the hungry, adequate housing for the poor, public transportation for the cities — capital is unable to organize such production *for profit* and hence does not undertake it. In this sense a contradiction becomes apparent between what is possible, given the level of productive capabilities, and the limitations which capitalism places on these potential forces.

The Proletariat: Resolver of Capitalism's Contradictions

Marx argued that the normal operation of the capitalist system would create the objective conditions for the overthrow of the system.

> Communism is for us not a *state of affairs* which is to be established, an ideal to which reality [will] have to adjust itself. We call communism the *real* movement which abolishes the present state of things. The conditions of this movement result from the premises now in existence. Moreover, the mass of *propertyless* workers — the utterly precarious position of labor-power on a mass scale cut off from capital or from even a limited satisfaction and, therefore, no longer merely temporarily deprived of work itself as a secure source of life — presupposes the *world market* through competition.

This focus on how change will grow out of the contradictions of daily life under capitalism is what most clearly differentiates marxism from more utopian forms of socialism. As capitalism develops and grows, it creates within itself the very forces necessary for its replacement.

Of course, the daily experience of exploitation, alienation, and deprivation do not automatically create a revolutionary force. Initially, the contradictions of capitalism are experienced by each person as an individual problem. As we have shown above, the capitalist system creates many conditions which enhance the likelihood of workers to understand their problems in social terms — as stemming from capitalism and as conditions shared in common by all workers.

It is only through common struggle against daily exploitation, however, that workers can begin to understand and act against the broader system in which these specific problems are rooted. This is why Marx and revolutionaries after him have put so much emphasis upon the development of unions, workers' councils and other self-created forms of worker organization. This awareness of *class consciousness* which grows out of the daily struggles of the working class is a crucial — perhaps *the* critical — element in the creation of a proletarian revolution.

Particularly important to this process of developing common understandings and class unification is the way in which capitalism breaks down the traditional differences between workers based on skills. In the early days of capitalism, capitalization was still relatively small and skills were important; differences in skill levels resulting from the long time required to gain proficiency were important to workers. As enterprises got larger, these skill levels were broken down and workers were thrown together in large numbers. In addition, they had fewer prospects of rising above the level of common wage labor, since only simple skills were required by the complex division of labor. These features created an awareness in workers of their common situation—and their common exploitation. Until class consciousness develops, in Marx's terms, the proletariat is a class *in itself* and not *for itself*; it is a class *objectively* but not *subjectively*.

The structural features of capitalism produce a set of contradictions that can only be resolved by ending capitalism. Capitalism begins as a remarkably progressive social system; indeed, Marx attributed to it enormous contributions. The bourgeoisie, said Marx and Engels in *The Communist Manifesto*:

> . . . has played a most revolutionary part . . .
> . . . has pitilessly torn asunder the motley feudal ties that bound man to his "natural superiors" . . .
> . . . has torn away from the family its sentimental veil . . .
> . . . has been the first to show what man's activity can bring about . . .
> . . . cannot exist without constantly revolutionizing the instruments of production . . .
> . . . has given cosmopolitan character to production and consumption in every country . . .
> . . . draws all nations into civilization . . .
> . . . has created enormous cities . . . and has rescued a considerable part of the population from the idiocy of rural life . . .
> . . . during its rule of scarce one hundred years, has created massive and more colossal productive forces than have all preceding generations together . . .

Despite these revolutionizing effects, the contradictions created by capitalism itself become insoluble over time. It was to the proletariat, the working class, that Marx looked for the resolution of the contradictions. As they realize the contradictions of private property, the workers act to abolish it and replace it with socialism—common ownership and control of the means of production. Marx saw the proletariat as the *only* historical force capable of resolving the contradiction between the increasing socialization of the means of production and the limitations imposed by the narrowing basis of its ownership and control. The triumph of the proletarian revolution was to be the final abolition of class society because it would put into political power the class that subsumed all previous classes, the class that would negate the negation of capitalism and resolve its contradictions by "expropriating the expropriators."

CHAPTER TWO

Stages of Development: The Shift in Driving-Force Theory

The concept of stages of development is explicit in revolutionary theory; it began with Marx and has constituted an important theoretical consideration for every revolutionary since. Stated simply, the argument goes: before socialism can be attained, a proletariat is necessary; before a proletariat can exist in adequate numbers, bourgeois society must exist. Ergo, no bourgeois society, no proletarian revolution, and no socialism. Marx also dealt with the stages of development before capitalism itself arose but this will concern us here only marginally.

For Marx, achieving a socialist revolution was an aspect of the dialectical process in which the bourgeoisie, having been created in the feudal period, gives rise to the proletariat. The working class, in turn, is driven to revolt against capitalism. It was this dialectical analysis that led marxists to say that capitalism sows the seeds of its own destruction.

The equally inevitable fact, for Marx, was the need for the bourgeois stage to be passed through. In the early days of capitalism as a worldwide phenomenon this posed no significant problem for Marx. Difficulties arose for Marx's followers because of the spread of revolution to the non-Western and primarily peasant world.

Background to the Theoretical Problem

For years after the theory of stages of development was set out by Marx and Engels, there was no reason to challenge it. The great strength of the working-class movement was concentrated in the advanced industrialized and capitalist nations of the world. Preeminent among these were Great Britain, Germany, France, and the United States. Where capitalism was more primitive in Italy, Spain, and the Balkans, proletarian movements were less developed. All of this fitted perfectly with the theory of stages. There was a small problem in that capitalist industrialism had emerged later in Germany than in Great Britain, yet Germany had moved with greater speed. According to the theory of stages, Britain should have been further along the path to proletarian revolution but the German working class (See Chapter 8) was much more powerfully organized. Such slight imbalances did not significantly disturb the theory.

In 1905 a series of events began which threw the theory of stages into serious doubt. These included the shift in revolutionary activity from the advanced capitalist nations of the West toward the East, with its largely peasant populations. A series of revolutions started that demonstrated the shift in dramatic fashion.

- In Russia in 1905 a sudden and surprising revolution temporarily undermined the autocratic power of czarism. Beginning with the urban proletariat, the revolution rapidly drew in peasants and sections of the peasant-based armed forces, especially sailors, with tremendous revolutionary energies. Although the revolution was suppressed, its near-success raised questions among theoreticians as to why it had occurred in backward Russia.
- In Russia in 1917 another revolution occurred in which the czarist regime was finally overthrown. A coalition of urban workers and peasant soldiers brought about a collapse of czarism in March; in November the provisional government fell to a second revolutionary impulse led by the Bolsheviks. The attainment of a successful proletarian revolution in Europe's most backward country required explanation.
- In the aftermath of the First World War, it was anticipated that the more advanced capitalist nations of Western Europe would experience their own proletarian revolutions. While there were a number of upsurges, none was successful. The failure of the more advanced proletariat of the West contrasted sharply with the success in Russia which had violated the theory of stages of development.
- In 1922–23, a series of events began in China that continued for over two decades. These consisted of the growth of a peasant-based revolutionary movement led by the Chinese Communist Party. Initially holding rural territory against the superior military forces of Chiang Kai-shek, the Communists were dislodged only to shift to a more remote rural territory where they developed an expanding base. Experiencing occasional setbacks, they drove Chiang Kai-shek and the bourgeois Kuomintang from the mainland in 1949. The significance of the Chinese Revolution underscored the earlier importance of the Russian Revolution and the role that the peasantry had played. Both revolutions challenged the validity of the theory of stages of development as originally set forth by Marx and Engels.

These events were sufficient to require examination of the original formulation of the theory of stages. Subsequent developments have further demonstrated the need for new theoretical refinements. This has to do with the continual failures of the proletarians of most advanced capitalist countries to effectively take power despite the size of the working class in revolutionary upsurges in Germany, Hungary, Italy, and elsewhere. Indeed, with the passage of time, the center of revolutionary activity — certainly in terms successfully taking power — moved to countries whose capitalist development was feeble and where colonial oppression of a largely peasant mass characterized society and economy.

The Evolution of Stages Theory

Marx and Engels set out the theory of stages in one of their earliest works, *The German Ideology*. Polemicizing against contemporary German philosophy, Marx and Engels argued that history was the product of the level of development of production and not of the ideas of human beings. The relations of production, in the form of the division of labor, determined the different stages of growth of human societies. Each type of division of labor was defined by different kinds of social relationships. There are four distinct stages:

1. *Tribal ownership* is the earliest, its economy based on hunting, fishing, cattle-herding, and in its most advanced form, agriculture. A very simple division of labor arose which was tied to the patriarchal family. Slavery began in this social form but only developed with an increased population.

2. *Ancient communal and state ownership*, in which private property began to develop, arose with a more advanced division of labor, in particular in distinguishing town from country. Class relationships between citizens and slaves evolved fully.

3. *Feudal and estate property relations* began as a result of the decline of the Roman Empire and were the product of sparse populations spread over vast areas. Here productive relations were based on enserfing the agriculturists by tying them to the land. At the same time, towns rose in which artisans sought to protect themselves against the robber-nobility based on the land. The division of labor was relatively simple.

4. *Capitalist property* relations followed, in which the division of labor moved into an accelerating process through the increase in population density which, in turn, resulted from increased contact between populations. Labor was "freed" from its previous ties of slavery and serfdom so that the costs of maintenance by the owner of capitalist property could be minimized. The introduction of machinery and the advanced technology began as a result of the continual increase in population density.

The final stages of socialism and communism, when human oppression theoretically comes to an end will be discussed in Part IV and need not concern us here. The theory of stages was translated by Marx and Engels into day-to-day political strategies as they engaged in their revolutionary work after 1844. It led them to support all developments of the bourgeois system against earlier stages of development.

This can be seen in two distinct cases. In the Franco-Prussian War of 1870–71, Marx and Engels initially supported the Prussian forces despite emphasizing the identity of interests of the French and German working classes. Nevertheless, since the war was a defensive war by the Prussians and strengthened the development of a German national identity against the feudal Germanic principalities, Marx at first regarded the war as progressive. In the Civil War in the United States, Marx strongly supported the North. This was both because of Lincoln's doctrine on the need to preserve the Union (a bourgeois democratic state is more significant than several underdeveloped countries) and Marx's implacable hostility to slavery and to its dragging effects on the development of bourgeois freedoms in the United States. In both cases, Marx saw the need for the encouragement of bourgeois social, political, and economic forms as a necessary prerequisite for the development of the proletariat. Engels put the case even more definitively when he stated, "Anyone who says that a socialist revolution can be carried out in a country which has no proletariat or bourgeoisie proves by this statement that he has still to learn the ABCs of socialism."

Engels emphasized the importance of stages in one of his early works, *The Peasant War in Germany*, written in 1850. This analysis of the peasant rebellions of the early 16th century showed, Engels wrote, that a revolution could not transcend the class structure dominating society of the time.

> The worst thing that can befall a leader of an extreme party is to be compelled to take over a government in an epoch when the movement is not yet ripe for the domination of the class which he represents and for the realization of the measures which that domination would imply. . . . he necessarily finds himself in a dilemma. What he *can* do is in contrast to all his actions as hitherto practiced, to all his principles and to the present interests of his party; what he *ought* to do cannot be achieved . . . he is compelled to represent not his party or his class, but the class for whom conditions are ripe for domination.

Those who gained from the peasant rebellions were the princes, Engels tells us, because their rule fitted the economic organization of the period.

If Engels was adamant in insisting on the need for a bourgeoisie and a proletariat before socialism can be attained, Marx and Engels recognized, as early as 1846 in *The German Ideology*, that passage through the stages of development might be accelerated under some circumstances. The most common of these circumstances is late development. Marx and Engels cited the case of the United States, a country which never experienced a feudal epoch. They pointed out that innovative individuals from more developed countries brought advanced ideas with them to their new situations so that the new country could accelerate through the various stages. Writing later in 1874, Engels recognized that countries arriving on the scene of capitalism at a late stage would benefit from the experiences of earlier working classes. He notes this in terms of the rapidity of advancement of the German working class, commenting that

> . . . the practical workers' movement in Germany ought never to forget that it developed on the shoulders of the English and French movements, that it was able simply to utilize their dearly paid experience and could now avoid their mistakes, which were then mostly unavoidable. Where would we be now without the precedent of the English trade unions and the French workers' political struggles, and especially without the gigantic impulse of the Paris Commune?

In analyzing the German revolution of 1848, Marx laid the groundwork for a theory of "combining stages" which did not become politically significant until after the Russian Revolution of 1905 when the theme was again taken up by Trotsky and Lenin:

> While the democratic petty bourgeois wish to bring the revolution to a conclusion as quickly as possible . . . it is our interest and our task to make the revolu-

tion permanent, until all more or less possessing classes have been forced out of their position of dominance, until the proletariat has conquered state power, and the association of the proletarians, not only in one country but in all the dominant countries of the world, has advanced so far that competition among the proletarians of these countries has ceased and that at least the decisive productive forces are concentrated in the hands of the proletarians.
. . . Their battle cry must be: The Revolution in Permanence.

But it was, perhaps, the failure of the Paris Commune of 1871, despite its "gigantic impulse," that served as a warning about the dangers of a proletarian revolution occurring before the capitalist stage had reached its full maturity.

The theory of stages was largely accepted by marxist theoreticians until Russia's proletariat began to grow and showed striking revolutionary proclivities after the turn of the twentieth century. The problem of stages had concerned Russia's marxists previously, as revolutionary socialists questioned whether they could support the much-hated bourgeoisie in the accomplishment of *their* revolution, as well as their problems in accepting the idea that the bourgeois stage might last a considerable period of time. Just prior to the 1905 revolution, two of the activists, Parvus and Trotsky, began to articulate a notion of compressing the stages. No significant theory was formulated, however, until after the 1905 events.

1905 also provided a thorough shaking up for Lenin, who immediately recognized the significance of the Russian workers uprising, as well as understanding the powerful but unfocused energies of the peasantry. Before 1905 Lenin adhered to a position shared by all Russian socialists, that the revolution would result in a state under the control of the bourgeoisie. The impact of the events of 1905, however, influenced Lenin's shift, over several years, toward Trotsky's position that historical stages might be compressed or even combined in a Russian revolution. In a pamphlet written during these events, *Two Tactics*, Lenin argued that Russia's bourgeoisie was too weak and cowardly to effect its own revolution. This would be undertaken for them by the proletariat which had the drive and energy to initiate the revolution. Because it was so small, however, the Russian proletariat required allies. These would be found in the peasantry who, while unable to initiate revolution themselves and without direction except for the proletariat, would bring the enormous energies and the breadth of support necessary to topple czarism and install a period of bourgeois democracy. Lenin anticipated a relatively brief bourgeois period after which the proletariat, grown in size and strength, would overthrow the bourgeoisie and set Russia on the road to socialism. "The complete victory of the present revolution," Lenin wrote, "will mark the end of the democratic revolution [e.g., bourgeois democracy], and the beginning of a determined struggle for a socialist revolution." The immediate problem for revolutionaries was to mobilize the proletariat *and* the peasantry to overturn czarism. To this end, Lenin called for "the revolutionary-democratic dictatorship of the proletariat and peasantry."

Lenin made one additional formulation about the character of the 1905 revolution some months later. He wrote: "From the democratic revolution we shall at once, and precisely in accordance with the measure of our strength, . . . begin to pass to the socialist revolution. We stand for uninterrupted revolution. We shall not stop halfway." Lenin thus took the idea of acceleration of stages, developed only briefly by

Marx and Engels, and introduced a further compression, implicitly the idea of a two-stage revolution. This notion was never further developed by Lenin and it was left to Trotsky and Mao to further refine the theoretical notion.

Leon Trotsky was probably the first to work most systematically on the idea of the combination of stages, a concept he referred to as *combined development* and *the permanent revolution*. In 1906 Trotsky introduced the idea that in industrially backward countries the bourgeois and proletarian stages could be combined. The revolution, once begun, would continue "permanently" through its bourgeois phase, directly into the socialist phase.

Trotsky cited as the basis for his argument the rapidity of growth of Russia's urban population in the latter part of the 19th century and the concentration of its labor force. The urban population increased only from 3 percent in 1725 to 4.4 percent in 1812. By 1850, however, it rose to 7.8 percent and in 1897 it reached 13 percent. The concentration of the industrial proletariat is demonstrated in a comparison of the size of industrial enterprises in the United States and Russia in 1914, shown in Table 2.1.

If the proletariat in Russia was highly concentrated and had the capability of initiating revolution, the weakness of the other two classes with stakes in the revolution against the czar must also be noted. First there was the bourgeoisie, in whose name a democratic revolution must ostensibly be made. Then there was the peasantry.

The problem with the bourgeoisie as a revolutionary force originated in the genesis of capitalism in Russia. This stood in sharp contrast to capitalist development in Western Europe, where capitalism grew out of the class of burghers and artisans in the towns. As their strength and significance expanded, they found themselves fettered by the parochialism of the feudal system. It was to deal with this problem that the bourgeoisie initiated their revolution to establish bourgeois democracy. The contrast in Russia was substantial, according to Trotsky, since there was no significant bourgeoisie. Much of Russia's capitalist development occurred under the sponsorship of the czarist regime and was based on investment from abroad. Nor was this

---

Table 2.1. Size of Enterprises, United States and Russia, 1914 (as a percentage of the total number of enterprises).

	United States	Russia
Small (Less than 100 workers)	35.0	17.8
Medium (100–1000)	47.2	40.8
Large (1000 or more)	17.8	41.4

Source: Trotsky, *History of the Russian Revolution*, Vol. 1, Chapter 1

form colonialist,* as was the case in Asia and Africa, since the foreign bourgeoisie was usually invited in by czarist authorities and existed solely at their behest. This weak bourgeoisie depended, therefore, on the czarist order. It was incapable of conducting a revolution that would open Russia to more rapid capitalist development or to the initiation of bourgeois freedoms within which the proletariat could develop as a political force.

Trotsky argued that as a general historical rule, after the proletariat develops, the bourgeoisie becomes incapable of carrying through the bourgeois revolution. In the French Revolution of 1789, the bourgeoisie had been the vital force for revolutionary transition. By the time of the German revolution of 1848, the bourgeoisie was caught between the old feudal order and the ascendant proletariat. It chose to side with the old order. By 1905 the Russian bourgeoisie could no longer attack the czarist order since it perceived czarism as less of a threat than the proletariat. Trotsky therefore argued that, because of the weakness of the bourgeoisie in backward and colonial countries, democracy could only be initiated through the rule of the proletariat. The bourgeois and proletarian stages are combined in backward countries because the proletariat leads both revolutions. "The task of arming the revolution," Trotsky wrote, "falls with all its weight upon the proletariat."

Trotsky saw problems with the peasantry because of its dispersion. Although despoiled by czarism, the peasants were incapable of independent action. Any peasant revolution, left to itself, degenerated into localized quarrels over land grabbing. With the lead taken elsewhere, as it had been by the Russian proletariat in 1905, the peasants would provide a mass base to ensure the victory of the proletarian revolution. For the peasants, "the proletariat in power will appear as its liberator." In the long run, Trotsky noted, the peasants would come to oppose the proletarian revolution since peasants object to its collectivist and international aspects. The solution is to spread the revolution internationally.

Left to itself, Trotsky argued, the working class of Russia would inevitably be crushed by a counterrevolution coinciding with the peasantry turning its back on the proletariat. Nothing would be left to the workers but to link the fate of their own political rule, and consequently the fate of the whole Russian revolution, with that of the socialist revolution in Europe.

Trotsky's contribution to the theory of stages of development can be summed up as follows:

- The normal progression of Russia through a bourgeois phase is impossible since the bourgeoisie is incapable of making a revolution on its own behalf.
- In backward countries, the driving force for revolution is focused on the proletariat because of their concentration and strategic locations in urban centers and despite their overall numerical weakness.
- The peasantry as a class is incapable of autonomous action but has enormous revolutionary potential when the proletariat provides leadership.
- In carrying out the revolution, democracy must be obtained through the dic-

*See Chapter 3 for a discussion of the various forms of imperialism, of which colonialism is but one.

tatorship of the proletariat (e.g., the disenfranchisement of ruling strata) rather than vice versa, as was the case in the early capitalist countries.

- Once the revolution begins, it is permanent or uninterrupted, passing through the bourgeois phase into its socialist phase. This takes the form of alternating civil wars, peaceful realignments, and various forms of struggle.
- This revolution has an international aspect in that support must develop for it in more industrialized societies with larger proletarian classes or the revolution will degenerate into a conflict between proletariat and peasantry.

With these formulations, Trotsky established the theoretical basis for accelerating the revolution *through* the bourgeois democratic stage of development.

In Mao Zedong we find a different operationalization of a similar conception: the notion of the accomplishment of the bourgeois revolution through a bloc of classes which ultimately develops into a socialist revolution occurring under the hegemony, the ideological domination, of the working class. There is considerable irony in this since Mao became important during the period in which Stalin, opposing the views of Trotsky, came to dominate the world communist movement. In Mao we are confronted with a pragmatic theoretician-activist concerned with leading a revolution in one of the most backward — from the viewpoint of marxist analysis — countries in the world. Attacking Trotsky and trotskyism, Mao paid continual obeisance to Stalin and the Communist International but went about the business of making China's revolution in ways that were often contrary to the line to which he ostensibly adhered. This is not to say that Mao did not accept Stalin's domination of the Communist International; yet the line promulgated by Stalin was violated by Mao in case after case.

The most important of these "violations" was Mao's orientation toward the peasantry. After Chiang Kai-shek dealt the Chinese communists a massive setback when he massacred the Shanghai workers in 1927, Stalin continued to insist on an orientation toward the urban working class and on maintaining the bloc between the communists and the Kuomintang. Mao instead turned from the urban proletariat to the peasantry. By arguing that the peasantry constitutes a social base for revolution, Mao demonstrated empirically the possibility that revolution could be made successfully in one of the most underdeveloped countries in the world. In this respect he also differed sharply with Trotsky, who rejected the notion of making a revolution from a peasant base.

During this period in the late 1920s, Mao worked out a theory for the mobilization of the peasantry grounded on his understanding of the exploited condition of the lower strata of the peasant population. Like Lenin, who had also seen the revolutionary potential of the least affluent peasants, Mao argued that the peasants would follow the proletarian leadership of the Communist Party in overthrowing warlords, landlords, foreign exploiters, and the Kuomintang, which was defined as the political agency of the reactionary forces. And, unlike the revolutions of the Western world, which had predominantly been decided in cataclysmic actions on urban streets, revolutionary work in China came to be seen, by Mao, as "protracted war."

Mao's contributions to the theory of stages can be summarized as follows:

- The proletariat resides at the ideological head of the revolution since proletarian revolutionary goals remain the goals of revolutions in backward countries.

- The driving force is based on the peasantry, who constitute a revolutionary force in themselves.
- The elements creating the driving force in the peasantry are based on the exploitative character of imperialism and land relationships. These are not independent forms of exploitation but are integrally related.
- The bourgeoisie remains too weak, by itself, to make its own bourgeois revolution. It vacillates and is uncertain because segments of it are attached to foreign imperialism of which they are the compradors, the local agents.
- The revolution, in the Chinese context, can only be accomplished by a bloc of classes including the proletariat — which provides direction, particularly through its hegemonic agency, the Chinese Communist Party — the peasantry, the petty bourgeoisie, *and* the national, patriotic bourgeoisie. Contention occurs between the bourgeoisie and the proletariat for the direction of the revolution.
- The character of the revolution itself is bourgeois-democratic to begin with, "and we are for the transition of the democratic revolution in the direction of socialism." Mao argued that the type of bourgeois revolution that occurred in the West was obsolete, its place taken by "the new-democratic revolution" of the colonial and semicolonial countries that oppose international capitalism but maintain elements of a capitalist economy. This revolution results in "a dictatorship of the united front of all revolutionary classes under the leadership of the proletariat." Thus the Chinese revolution is accomplished in stages by blocs among classes, all of whom are progressive in the sense that they oppose imperialism. Some classes, such as the proletariat, are more progressive than others in that they move toward the proletarian revolution. Some segments of classes, such as the poor and middle peasants, are more progressive than others such as the rich peasants. But there is a role for all classes except those aligning with imperialism and its agents.

*   *   *

With Mao, we come to the current stage of thinking among revolutionaries about the theory of stages of development. This theory has had an interesting legacy within marxism in that it took a considerable period of time to overcome the primacy which Marx gave to the proletariat. Trotsky's theoretical innovations maintained the focus of revolutionary energies on the working class while explaining the importance of relatively backward and undeveloped capitalist economies. Lenin gave considerable attention to the peasantry as a revolutionary force, but it was Mao who not only provided a theoretical focus on the peasantry but also operationalized the peasants as the primary social base out of which a revolutionary movement could be built. Although Mao emphasized the ideological importance of the proletariat, by demonstrating the revolutionary potential of the peasantry and its capability of being mobilized for socialist revolutions, he opened the way not only to a consideration of the peasantry as a driving force but of other social categories and groups as well.

CHAPTER THREE

Peasants as a Driving Force

[The peasants] went there to find a new parcel of land which they snatched from the state or from some voracious landholder in the hope of making a little money. They struggled perpetually against the demands of soldiers allied to the large landholding power, and their horizon was limited to the hope of securing a property title. . . . the peasantry is more agressive in its love and possession of the land, that is . . . is most strongly imbued with *petit bourgeois* spirit. The peasant struggles because he wants land for himself, for his children; he wants to till it, to profit from it, and enrich himself through his labor. . . . the peasant quickly learns that he cannot satisfy his desire to possess land without first destroying the large land-holding system.

— Che Guevara

While revolutionaries recognized that peasants had an important capacity for rebellion, the view that peasants might overcome orientations toward the personal accumulation of land and property and move toward a revolutionary transformation of society is comparatively new. The quote above represents what has largely been the marxist view of peasants — a view that sees their concerns for personal accumulation becoming radicalized as it is directed against those who possess large land-holdings.

Marx and Engels recognized the revolutionary capacity of the peasantry under certain conditions; Marx also noted that the peasants were capable of progressive rebellions as well as being supportive of the most reactionary classes in decaying feudal society. The prevailing marxist view of the peasants is stated by Marx in his *Eighteenth Brumaire of Louis Bonaparte*:

The small-holding peasants form a vast mass [living] in similar conditions but without entering into manifold relations with one another. Their mode of production isolates them from one another instead of bringing them into mutual intercourse . . . Their field of production, the small holding, admits of no division of labor. . . . and, therefore, no diversity of development, no variety of talent, no wealth of social relationships. Each individual peasant family . . . directly produces the major part of its consumption and thus acquires its means of life more through exchange with nature than in intercourse with society. . . . the great mass of the French nation is formed by simple addition of homologous magnitudes, much as potatoes in a sack form a sack of potatoes. Insofar as millions of families live under economic conditions of existence that separate their mode of life, their interests, and their culture from those of other classes, and put them in hostile opposition to the latter, they form a class. Insofar as there is merely a local interconnection among these small-holding peasants, and the identity of their interests begets no community, no national bond, and no political organization among them, they do not form a class. They are consequently incapable of enforcing their class interests in their own name, whether through a parliament or through a convention. They cannot represent themselves, they must be represented.

While various groups of marxists attempted to work among peasants before the beginning of the 20th century, the most systematic approach to peasant organization was undertaken in Russia by a group known as *Narodniks*. Seeing the existence of a primitive form of communism in communal land-ownership patterns in which land was held collectively by a village and distributed to members according to need, the *Narodniks* believed it possible to organize peasant movements that would establish socialism without passing through a stage of capitalism. To accomplish this end, they "went to the peasants" and lived among them while seeking to organize them. This proved to be unsuccessful; the lesson that passed into the revolutionary movement was to concentrate on the proletariat and ignore the peasantry.

The Russian revolutionary George Plekhanov organized the first marxist group in Russia during the 1880s and provided a focus for the first time on the proletariat as Russia's revolutionary force. Lenin joined this movement later and initially accepted the relatively suspicious attitude prevalent among Russian marxists about the peasantry.

Prior to the 1905 revolution but more clearly afterward, Lenin reversed his position on the peasantry and came to see them as a vital revolutionary force due to the concentration of landownership in Russia.

> The essence of this (the agrarian) question is the struggle of the peasantry for the abolition of landlordism. . . . Ten and a half million peasant households in European Russia own together 75 million dessiatins of land. Such is the main background of the picture.

The peasantry proved their revolutionary potential during the dramatic events of 1917. Initially, the Bolsheviks remained oriented toward spreading their revolution to the more industrialized countries in the West. As early as 1920, however, in a congress held at Baku, interest grew for integrating the revolutionary potential of the peasantry in Asian countries. By 1924 a series of proletarian revolutions and uprisings had occurred *and failed* in Germany, Hungary, Italy, and elsewhere. With these failures, the Bolsheviks turned to the east and to the peasants of Asia.

It was not until the experience of the Chinese Revolution, however, that the peasantry came to be recognized as a vital social class capable of revolutionary action.

Analytic Problems with the Peasantry

A major problem in the analysis of peasant societies originates in the multiplicity of forms they take around the world; the variation in form influences the character of protest and rebellion. The term "peasant" covers a spectrum of rural, agrarian production systems ranging from societies dominated by vast *latifundia* — large-scale agricultural estates — to those where small-scale holdings predominate. This variability has changed over time as capitalism expanded and affected the economies of peasant societies.

In traditional systems, despite their great variety, the force of tradition and the social dependence of peasants on landlords serve to keep such systems in comparative equilibrium. Traditional societies are exploitative of the peasants; the products of their labor go disproportionately to landlords. But exploitation is mediated by various social arrangements in which the landlord is guarantor of the peasants' existence, ensuring them loans and support during the cyclical periods of financial distress.

These social arrangements produce systems of considerable stability which break down, however, from time to time in localized peasant revolts. During such revolts, peasants are capable of considerable disruption, but this rarely takes the form of revolution. In most cases, rebellion occurs locally and is resolved locally. In the few rare occasions where peasant rebellions become more widespread, they tend to be diffused over time without being capable or organizing a systematic attack on the entire system.

It was this isolation of village life and the restricted communications of peasant life that led Marx and Engels to refer to "the idiocy of rural life." Both recognized the rebellious potential of peasants but saw no hope that they could provide the kind of drive necessary for the overthrow of capitalism.

The analysis of the peasantry by Marx and Engels, as a nonrevolutionary and even reactionary force in general, has been largely borne out in the experiences of the United States and the European countries from which they drew their understanding. Under the relatively rapid development of industrialization in advanced capitalistic economies, small, independent agricultural producers have been a rapidly declining force both in terms of their numbers and their political impact. In this sense, with the exception of the short-lived populist movement in late 19th-century America, they have not been capable of playing any dynamic or propelling role in creating a counterforce to capitalist exploitation and development.

Peasants, Imperialism, and Revolutionary Potential

The growth of capitalism as a world system has had a dramatic effect upon the experience and revolutionary potential of peasants in underdeveloped nations.

Most of the less-developed world has been subjected to the economic dominance of capitalism through that phenomenon known as imperialism. Imperialism itself, as noted by Lenin and others, has undergone various phases. In its earliest forms, it was concerned with extracting raw materials and agricultural products from the undeveloped countries and exporting manufactured goods to them; in the exchange, the imperialist power benefitted economically. At a later stage, the export of capital to the less-developed areas provides the basis for additional, more intensive exploitation.

As capitalism has matured as a global system, the interrelations between developed and underdeveloped countries have become increasingly complex. The growth of huge multinational corporations, which often have only nominal allegiance to any individual nation-state, has made it difficult for outsiders to predict with precision the impact of any given investment decision on a particular country. Prices of international commodities such as aluminum, for example, are often as much dependent upon corporate taxes in different countries as supply, demand, or direct production costs.

Despite the complexity of multinational corporations, it is still possible to generalize about the relations between advanced capitalist countries and underdeveloped countries around the world. The advanced capitalist countries have used their superior economic and military power to establish unequal exchange relationships with the underdeveloped countries, which effectively thwarts the underdeveloped areas from controlling the growth of their own economies in their own political societies. This *imperialist* relationship is propelled by the search of private corporations for expanded profits, but this has repercussions far beyond those planned or even desired by particular capitalist corporations.

Historically, unequal economic relations between developed and underdeveloped nations have been maintained by a range of forms of direct and indirect political control:

- In Russia, it took the form of foreign investments in manufacturing and transportation under czarist auspices. The bourgeoisie that came into existence was completely dependent on the czar and did not seek to exercise political hegemony over Russia.
- In China, extensive control was sought over coastal areas and trading centers. There was relatively little alienation of land for agricultural purposes, the focus being on trade rather than industrial development. Direct political control was not sought; the imperialist powers influenced China's political development through indirect means.
- In much of the remainder of Asia and most of Africa and Oceania, imperialism took the form of colonialism. Here the imperial power established direct control over territory and constituted itself as the political power. Indigenous political systems were either destroyed or incorporated as agents of the dominating power.
- In Latin America, imperialism took the form of politically independent regimes economically dominated by the United States. Direct political intervention occurred only when relations with the north were threatened by local forces. In such circumstances, the United States relied on military force ("gunboat diplomacy") or other forms of pressure.

THE DISRUPTIONS OF IMPERIALISM

Traditional social and economic structures become disturbed by the spread of capitalism and the influence of imperialism. This has been particularly true in the later stages of world capitalist development when capital itself and not just marketable commodities have been exported to underdeveloped countries. In its influence on underdeveloped societies, imperialism has had direct effects upon the peasantry as a social group.

When capital is exported to rural societies, an indigenous bourgeoisie and proletariat are created which change the traditional class structure. Where the basis for a market economy already exists, the introduction of capitalism accelerates the consumption capabilities of local ruling groups, which then proceed to exploit the peasants more intensively. Among other results, it often produces heavy concentration of landownership, the beggaring of the small peasantry, and the formation and expansion of a rural, landless proletariat who survive at minimal levels.

Imperialism creates an exploitative system that extracts increasing surpluses from the peasants. Two conditions produce this situation:

1. Surplus in the form of profit on investments is drained from the country by the foreign bourgeoisie in the exchanges between the industrial and agricultural sectors.

2. The upper levels of the local ruling class, the landlords, enter into economic relations with foreign investors. Where there was once relatively limited demand for commodities, the landlords, having greater access to the products manufactured by the bourgeoisie, begin to engage in competition for them. To develop their capacities to consume, landlords are forced to extract more and more from their peasants. This increases the exploitation of the peasants and disrupts the traditional patron-client relations that existed before capitalist forms were introduced.

Variants of the second condition are possible. A segment of the local nobility may ally with the foreign investors and become their local agents in squeezing the landlords who, in turn, increase their pressure on the peasants. Or, in the exchanges with the foreign power, the demand for more agricultural products may increase to the point where a subclass of landlords seeks greater productivity through land consolidation and the introduction of machinery. This leads them to take loans from the foreigners at high rates of interest. These loans can only be repaid by more intensive exploitation of their peasants. Peasants can also be thrown off the land and become an agricultural proletariat seeking seasonal wage employment.

The cause of this exploitation comes with the development of capitalism.

> The process of organizing a modern state and economic life brought many claims from governments and landlords, though it was especially as the Western demand for cereals and the opportunity to export them increased that the rape of peasant land and abuse of the peasants' labor became tempting; as it was only as

the native landed class got control of political power that they were in a position to satisfy that temptation.*

The introduction of capitalism in all of its imperialist variants produces greater exploitation of the peasants and disrupts the relations to which they have been accustomed. Seeing their condition declining and no longer confident of where they stand with their landlords, peasants become prone to join rebellions when revolutionary action has been initiated elsewhere. They rarely initiate such action themselves, because of their localist orientation and their hesitation before the power of the landlords. Once action has begun elsewhere they have a model which gives them courage.

THE EXPLOITATION AND OPPRESSION OF COLONIALISM

In the case of colonialism, imperialism takes on a different guise entirely. In the previous form, the immediate source of exploitation was not seen by the peasantry as foreign; rather, the local landlords and nobility were defined as the exploiters.

In the colonial form of imperialism, there is effectively no local rule since the foreign power sets up a political system controlled and operated by itself. The physical presence of the British, French, Germans, Belgians, or Dutch, for example, creates within the local peasantries a sense of their domination by foreigners. This adds a new dimension to the issue of exploitation through land — that of *nation*.

Before dealing with the national aspects of colonial domination, it is necessary to distinguish the differences that exist in the exploitative character of colonialism. While comparable data that provide an indication of the effects on material conditions of the indigenous population are not available, there can be little doubt about the disruptiveness of colonial social and economic relations. Whereas in the previous case traditional relations between peasant and landlord are disrupted, in the colonial context these relations tend to be shattered completely. Colonialism introduces entirely new relationships with respect to land. When colonial powers establish plantation systems, as was widely done in most countries with the exception of China, land is taken from the peasants, who are then brutally converted into an agricultural proletariat. In many cases, their land is reduced to fringe plots around the great estates and they are forced into laboring for the plantation owners through the establishment of tax systems.

*An *absolute* decline in the material standard of living is shown by data on Rumania and Russia provided by Mitrany. In Rumania, at the beginning of the 19th century before extensive foreign investment had started, the average peasant household kept a dozen or more large animals. When the peasants were emancipated in 1864, most of them were keeping only four animals; by 1906 many kept no animals at all. The per capita consumption of corn, the peasants' staple food, dropped from 230 kilograms in 1890 to 146 kilos in 1903. In Russia, from which grain exports to the West increased enormously, relief for starving villages increased from 1.5 million rubles in 1890 to an annual average of 90 million in the decade 1890-1900. This annual average increased to 118 million rubles between 1901-05. The number of departments for which relief was required increased from eight in 1860s to 31 after 1900. See Mitrany, 1951: 77-78.

Taxes provide the basis for double exploitation. On the one hand, the requirement to pay tax in the form of cash forces peasants either to enter into employment or into agricultural production for the cash market. When they become employees, they are paid minimal wages providing the most meager subsistence. As agricultural producers, the payment that peasants receive for their crops is placed at the mercy of marketing systems controlled by the colonialists and world pricing arrangements that favor the imperial countries. On the other hand, taxes are exploitative since they are used less to provide social services to the population than for the maintenance of imperialist control: government bureaucrats, police, and an army. Most of this personnel, at least its highest-paid segment, comes from the colonial power and is well paid—indeed, better paid than equivalent personnel "at home." Colonialism thereby provides far greater exploitation than simple imperialism in that the peasants are exploited as producers and taxpayers, as well as through the removal of their land.

The foreigners live under far better material circumstances than local people. They are also more prone to utilize naked force to maintain control, justifying such applications by the alleged "backwardness of the natives" while congratulating themselves for their sacrifices in carrying "the white man's burden." Nor are the people of the colonies permitted the quieting comfort of material goods or a psychologically acceptable role like that held by workers in the colonial metropolis. As Fanon points out,

> When the native is confronted with the colonial order of things, he finds he is in a state of permanent tension. The settler's world is a hostile world, which spurns the native, but at the same time it is a world of which he is envious. . . . not of becoming the settler but of substituting himself for the settler.

Of great significance is the *oppression* which develops in colonial situations. Colonial powers are rarely content simply to economically exploit a territory: with it comes a host of practices calculated to inform the indigenous population that they are inferior compared to the "superior" colonialists. The social practices of colonialism inflict on the indigenous people a host of daily indignities. Even where there is no sense of nationhood before the establishment of the colony, colonialism creates it. It accomplishes this by treating all indigenous residents with equal contempt. Where in the past local people may have engaged in parochial battles with one another, they often come to recognize the foreigner as a common enemy. In Africa, for example, no concept of being "African" existed until, through the continued use of the term and its continual denigration, the indigenous population learned they shared their African-ness in common.

The colonialists justify their exploitation and oppression of underdeveloped countries by creating myths about the animal-like qualities of the colonized. And this myth is believed, for a time, by the colonized.

> The most serious blow suffered by the colonized is being removed from history and from the community. Colonization usurps any free role in either war or peace. . . . The colonized . . . is out of the game. He is in no way a subject of history any more. Of course, he carries its burden, often more cruelly than others, but always as an object. He has forgotten how to participate in history . . . all memory of freedom seems distant; he forgets what it costs or else he no longer

dares pay the price of it. How else can one explain how a garrison of a few men can hold out in a mountain post? How a handful of often arrogant colonizers can live in the midst of a multitude of colonized?

But the oppression of the colonized sets up its own contradiction when the "gook," "chink," or "wog" realizes that "he is not an animal; and it is precisely at the moment he realizes his humanity that he begins to sharpen his weapons with which he will secure . . . victory."

The drive for dignity initially is sporadic and takes many localized forms. Once it becomes more general, it often becomes a political quest for land and national self-determination. For the indigenous person in the colonial system, land brings both food and dignity: food with the end of insupportable taxation; dignity with the ousting of the racist invading oppressor.

The violence necessary for the revolutionary upheaval is generated by the excesses of the colonialist order itself. Once the struggle is unleashed, the colonial myths of native cowardice, laziness, and lack of discipline evaporate along with the supposed omnipotence of the foreign oppressor.

And it is clear that in the colonial countries the peasants alone are revolutionary, for they have nothing to lose and everything to gain. The starving peasant, outside the class system, is the first among the exploited to discover that only violence pays. For him there is no compromise, no possible coming to terms; colonialization and decolonialization are simply a question of relative strength. . . colonialism is not a thinking machine, nor a body endowed with reasoning faculties. It is violence in its natural state, and it will only yield when confronted with greater violence.

THE FORMATION OF PEASANT REVOLUTIONS

The fundamental social processes underlying peasant revolution are the intensification of exploitation and the disruption of the traditionally limited exploitative system. As is the case with the proletariat, this takes two possible forms. In some cases there is an absolute decline in the material standards of life. In other cases, material conditions may improve, but at a much slower rate than that of the ruling strata. Relative deprivation occurs when the indigenous people feel that their conditions are worsening because they see others doing much better.

The conditions under which revolutionary outbursts occur among peasants vary. Five distinct features appear to be necessary:

1. Land is always a motive force for rebellion among peasants; capitalist exploitation in all of its forms quickly creates a market in labor and land. Either by directly separating peasants from their control of traditional lands or by taxing land to such an extent that it limits the ability of peasants to survive on the land in traditional patterns, imperialism produces revolutionary potential among peasants in underdeveloped countries.

2. The requirement for a *revolutionary group* which develops a broader sense of *consciousness* is crucial. The ability of such a group to move through the countryside and open communications between local groups of peasants who were

previously aware only of their own conditions is vital for the development of consciousness.

3. Specifically *peasant forms of organization* are necessary to provide devices whereby peasants can coordinate their actions against their oppressors. These may develop spontaneously or be introduced by revolutionary elements. Unless a revolutionary group is present that can give a broader picture of the conditions of oppression, action will consist of rebellion against local oppressors rather than revolution against the class of oppressors.

4. Conditions are necessary in which *the dominators demonstrate that they are not superhuman*. This can occur in a variety of ways: through increased dependence on the imperialized peoples for greater output—as in times of great wars when the colonialists require materials and people from the colony to fight their wars. It can also take place when one imperialist power defeats another, thereby demonstrating the weaknesses of each. It occurs sporadically when small rebellions grow and win interim successes; although these rebellions may be put down, they demonstrate to the oppressed people that it is possible to organize against imperialist or colonial domination.

5. *Action*, when it begins against colonialism, *is not uniformly distributed* through the peasant stratum.

Lenin recognized, immediately after the 1905 revolution, that it was vital that the "peasantry" be differentiated into various subcategories, since some elements of the rural population proved to be revolutionary and others reactionary. Lenin distinguished between poor or "ruined" peasants, middle peasants, well-to-do peasants and capitalist landowners, and feudal landowners and feudal *latifundia*. In addition to these groups there was also the rural proletariat, consisting of former poor peasants who had lost their land because of capitalist development of agriculture in Russia. It was to the rural proletariat and the poor peasants that Lenin turned his attention.

At a later stage, Mao Zedong made an analysis similar to that of Lenin in breaking the rural population of China into a variety of social classes. In March 1927, writing about the peasant movement in Hunan, Mao made distinctions between the poor, middle, and rich peasants. He commented:

> The poor peasants have always been the main force in the bitter fight in the countryside. . . . Without the poor peasant class, it would have been impossible to bring about the present revolutionary situation in the countryside. . . . The poor peasants, being the most revolutionary group, have gained the leadership of the peasant associations. . . . Without the poor peasants there would be no revolution. To deny their role is to deny the revolution.

Other writers agree that privileged peasants are too closely tied to foreigners to undertake revolutionary risks but argue that the lowest level of peasants are too beaten down for such action. According to this analysis (which is based on what Mao Zedong is reputed to have done rather than what he has written), rebellion begins with the middle peasants, who feel themselves most crushed by imperialism. Once begun, the revolution is joined by the poor peasants.

Conclusion

Revolutionaries came to the peasantry with considerable hesitation, believing that the proletariat, because of its concentrated nature, was the significant force for revolutionary action. Since much of the analysis of the peasantry was initially conducted in those countries that were advancing most rapidly into capitalism, it was an understandable tendency to see the peasantry, a declining social category, as potentially more reactionary than revolutionary.

But the experience of the Russian and Chinese revolutions demonstrated how important the peasantry was in unleashing social transformation. Following the success of the Chinese Revolution, other peasant-based revolutions have transformed a number of peasant societies, including those of Vietnam, Cuba, and Algeria.

The significance of the peasantry — and the failure of the proletariats of the advanced capitalist countries — has led some revolutionaries to believe that the prospects for socialism rest almost entirely on the peasants of the underdeveloped world. Whether true or not — an issue which can only be determined as history unfolds — there can no longer be any doubt that the peasantry constitutes a significant force for revolution in those countries that remain undeveloped.

CHAPTER FOUR

New Revolutionary Groups: Women, Blacks, Youth

Emergent Revolutionary Potential

Traditional marxian analysis has been based on the central importance of *social class*. For marxists, the proletariat and the peasantry were viewed as key driving forces for revolution because of their exploited place in the capitalist division of labor. By emphasizing social class, however, the potential significance of other social relations has been de-emphasized or overlooked. As a result, elements of life beyond the work place or the land — family, community, and distinctive conditions such as gender, race, ethnicity, and age — were not treated with the same seriousness in marxist theory.

Yet what distinguishes revolutionary theory from social theory in general is that revolutionaries are concerned with changing the world in which they live, not simply understanding it. For revolutionary theory to have any lasting meaning, it must be adaptable to changing circumstances and new forces at work in society. Marx, for example, would not have been able to locate the driving force for revolution in the proletariat had not (1) capitalism created an exploited and alienated proletariat which (2) demonstrated through its actions a propensity and ability to make revolution. Similarly, marxian analyses of the peasantry's revolutionary potential only developed in conjunction with successful efforts to organize and mobilize peasants in revolutionary movements.

During the 20th century, as women, racial and ethnic minorities, and youth organized to play important roles in movements for social change, revolutionary theorists have attempted to analyze these developments. The potential significance of race and ethnicity first emerged as an important question during the 1920s, initially in the context of the Soviet Union's turn toward Asia following the failure of the working classes in capitalist countries to make successful revolutions. Later, as a

34

result of the growth of the civil rights and black-power movements and the urban rebellions of the 1960s, race and ethnicity were recognized as significant contributors toward the potential development of revolutionary action. The importation of large numbers of Third World workers into European countries has raised the question of racism in that context as well.

Similarly, the emergence of an activist women's movement in most advanced capitalist countries during the 1960s and 1970s led some theorists to examine gender as a factor producing revolutionary propensities. And, because young people as a distinct social category played such a crucial role in the upsurge of rebellious activities during the 1960s, the question of youth has also received theoretical attention.

This chapter examines these three categories: women, blacks, and youth. By exploring the traditional marxist orientation toward each, a basis is created for the development of more recent theories concerning their revolutionary potential.

The examples are intended to demonstrate three important points in the most recent development of revolutionary theory: first, revolutionary potential should not be seen as limited to the working class or peasantry; second, revolutionary theory must respond to the emergence of new social forces; and third, revolutionary potential is not limited to the examples provided here. Indeed, as shall be seen in chapter 5, the very term "proletariat" has been undergoing a broadening redefinition in an attempt to incoporate these new forces and provide an analysis of capitalism that takes into account the vast changes that have occurred since the time of Marx.

Women

THE TRADITIONAL LEFT AND WOMEN

The Socialist Party before 1919 devoted considerable attention to women's oppression. This was due to the rise, before World War I, of a feminist movement in the United States concerned largely with women's suffrage and to the growth of a socialist feminist tendency within the socialist movement itself.

Unique among political parties of the time, the Socialist Party admitted women to membership and elected them to leadership positions. Through autonomous women's socialist organizations and women's groups within the party structure, socialist women took an active role in popular movements for women's suffrage, the spread of information about birth control, temperance, social services, and toward improving the condition of women and child laborers. The party's greatest successes contributed to obtaining for women the right to vote; particularly in their efforts in working-class communities, the socialists played a crucial role in suffrage victories in California (1911) and New York (1917).

Many socialist women viewed the capitalist system as the root of women's oppression. They saw capitalism as the destroyer of the nuclear family since it forced women and children to work in unhealthy factories and kept young people too poor to marry, thus encouraging immorality. This critique, which placed the Socialist Party as the true defender of women against the ravages of capitalism, coexisted uneasily with a nascent socialist feminist critique of the oppression of women *within* the nuclear family. In many ways, socialist-feminist thinking in this era presaged contemporary views with regard to the nature and importance of housework in the social division of labor, the sexual rights and freedom of women, and the more general issue of the equality of men and women.

Women were never completely accepted by all of the men in the Socialist Party, and women never comprised more than 15 percent of party membership. Consciousness of women's oppression was often fragmentary and contradictory, as a wide gulf existed between different activists on the subject. While the SP seldom gave the fight for women's rights organizational priority, the sheer amount of theoretical and organizational work on behalf of the rights and needs of women was considerable and represented a significant advance for the socialist movement.

The Communist Party in the 1930s also recognized the particular oppression of women, specifically working women. For the most part, the CP attempted to organize working-class women to stand "shoulder to shoulder" with male workers in the fight against capitalism. Consequently, they emphasized economic issues such as equal pay and protective legislation for women laborers.

However, in the absence of a broader-based feminist movement such as existed prior to World War I, there were few outside pressures on the CP to seriously address broader questions relevant to the oppression of women. An isolated socialist-feminist in the CP, California's Mary Inman, explored wider topics concerning the exploitation of women in the home, but she received little support from the party leadership.

While an atmosphere was created within the Communist Party in which women and other party members could raise issues of male supremicist attitudes internally, sexism within the party was never dealt with adequately and the struggle against women's oppression never received major attention.

SEXISM AND THE SIXTIES

Modern feminism sprang from within the New Left and civil rights movements, as well as drawing upon earlier feminist movements. Yet when women began to note the parallels between the oppression of racial minorities and their own subservient condition as women, both in society at large and within radical organizations, they encountered hostility from many New Left activists (not exclusively, but predominantly males). One reason for the negative reaction to feminism in the New Left was that these radicals saw women's struggles as reformist, perceiving them as being unrelated to the class system and concerned exclusively with the achievement of equal opportunity for women regardless of the overall oppressive nature of the capitalist system.

Women's struggles were also opposed by some New Leftists on the grounds that politics could not be based on an issue as narrow as the oppression of relatively privileged groups such as college students and middle-income women. One of the earliest forms of women's organizing in the 1960s, the consciousness-raising group, was seen by antagonistic leftists as a purely personal release mechanism having no political consequences. Little credit was given to it as an organizing tool having political *and* personal liberation potential.

By the early 1970s analyses of feminist issues and the activities of feminists had progressed to a point where most radical groups acknowledged the growing strength of revolutionary women and the feminist argument. Despite this, inclusion of feminist issues into left political agendas lagged. As a result, a number of leftist feminist organizations separated themselves from the organized left on the grounds that insufficient attention had been given to the struggle against sexism.

The rationale for the formation of autonomous groups was spelled out in the manifesto of the Berkeley Women's Union:

> Our experience in the left has been that when we struggle as individual women within mixed (male-dominated) organizations, our energies are constantly diverted to fighting sexism within those organizations. We have had enough of women's caucuses where we attempt to patch together the tattered "social relations" of an organization while the men discuss "politics." We do not eliminate all oppressive social relations by forming a women's organization, but we do make the struggle against them a central part of the development of our political perspective, rather than a peripheral activity.

THE REVOLUTIONARY POTENTIAL OF FEMINISM

Modern feminism is a response to an oppression which is not only economic but also based on what recent feminist theorists refer to as a *sex-gender system.*

Women constitute over half the world's population. They are exploited in the productive sphere, on the basis of their gender, by being confined to what Marx called "the industrial reserve army" and what capitalism terms the surplus labor force. Despite the rapidly increasing numbers of women who have entered the labor force on a full-time rather than part-time basis, the relegation of women to the surplus category has continued. Beyond economic rationales for such categorization is the social reality that women are continually viewed first as wives and mothers, the unpaid family caretakers, with any paid economic work seen as auxiliary. In addition to being "surplus" to the labor market, once they enter it sexism continues to operate.

By sexism or gender discrimination, feminist marxist theorists mean the distribution of tasks (and compensation) based on "ascribed" female characteristics. Similar to the case of race, sexism results in women being poorly paid, underemployed, and since they lack job seniority, among the first fired. In the 1960s emergent analyses began grappling with the systemic oppression unique to women and with the revolutionary potential of feminism.

Central to these analyses in feminist thought is a basic understanding about the relationship of women's work and the social division of labor, that is, work which is conducted outside the work place but is essential for social reproduction. In what some theorists have termed the "domestic" or "private sphere," women engage in activities which reproduce and socialize the labor force. These activities involve consumption, maintenance, and actual reproduction (birthing and raising children). Although there is widespread agreement among feminist theorists that women are oppressed both in production and consumption activities and that this unique juncture is the probable locus for a revolutionary driving force, how production and consumption fit together, how they are mediated by other influences, and how they can be organized to realize revolutionary potential are subjects of continuing debate among feminist theorists.

Irrespective of the continuing discussion, what is clear is that much of the recent change in women's economic and social roles is traceable to the feminist politics of the 1960s and beyond. Equally clear is the significance of the interaction between production and consumption for the development of a revolutionary driving force.

The analysis of a number of feminist issues continues to feed political theory and action. Such issues include:

1. Since the 1960s, reform views that focused primarily on workplace sexism — such as the demand for equal pay for equal work — have broadened to incorporate other issues related to both individual and institutional sexist practices.

2. The analysis locating women's oppression in both production and consumption spheres has been refined and expanded. Such work includes the exposition of arguments about the value of paid labor as opposed to the value of unpaid labor and the allocation of these to men and women, respectively.

3. Development of a theory of the state from a feminist perspective which stresses issues such as child care, health care, welfare rights, and the character of service-sector employment.

At least within some currents of the modern left in advanced capitalist countries, feminist concerns and feminist issues occupy a more substantial place than ever before.

Blacks

BLACKS AND THE OLD LEFT

Blacks in the United States were considered in different ways by the various segments of the American labor movement and the Old Left. The labor movement has a long history, with few exceptions in the period from 1870–1930, of discriminating against black workers. Existing racism was encouraged by the use of blacks (and immigrants) as strikebreakers by employers, often the only way for racial minorities to secure work. Still, there were examples of racial solidarity among workers, even in the Deep South.*

*Oscar Ameringer (1940) graphically illustrates this process in describing how black and white longshoremen in New Orleans forced white employers to negotiate with them, only to find themselves under attack from a Louisiana senator for "White men conspiring with niggas against the honoah and prosper'ty of the great po't of N'yo'l'ns . . ." Dan Scully, a white longshoreman, responded with ". . . white trash, are we? But you can't run your goddamn port without us . . . I guess before long you'll call us nigger lovers, too. Maybe you want to know next how I would like it if my sister married a nigger? Well, go ahead, ask me. But take it from me, I wasn't always a nigger lover. I fought in every strike to keep the niggers off the dock. I fought until in the white-supremacy strike your white-supremacy governor sent his white-supremacy militia down here and shot us white-supremacy strikers full of holes. . . . There was a time I wouldn't even work beside a nigger. You got 'em on the loose. You made me work with niggers, eat with niggers, sleep with niggers, drink out of the same water bucket with niggers, and finally got me to the place where if one of them comes to me and blubbers something about more pay, I say, 'Come on, nigger, let's go after the white bastards.' " (pp. 218–219)

The Socialist Party of the United States was largely indifferent to blacks before the great migration of rural southern blacks to northern cities during World War I. Although the party adopted a resolution opposing black exploitation, many members succumbed to the virulent race prejudice of the times. Generally, the SP viewed blacks as being exploited more by their class position than by their race. Party locals displayed widely varying attitudes toward blacks. In the south, some locals refused to admit blacks and set up segregated black locals. On the other hand, some locals courageously attempted to unite blacks and whites in the same unit. In the north, the party built a substantial black membership based loosely around *The Messenger*, a black socialist periodical published by A. Phillip Randolph. Individual party members also played a significant role in the formation of the National Association for the Advancement of Colored People (NAACP).

The Industrial Workers of the World attempted to organize black workers and fight discrimination in the period 1905-18. Particularly important were their efforts among timber workers in Louisiana and Texas. However, since there were then relatively few blacks in the areas where the IWW had strength, they had few black members.

With the formation of the Communist Party of the United States after the First World War, the major efforts to organize blacks within a revolutionary movement began. In the 1920s the communists worked with blacks in the south to create organizations of agricultural laborers. By 1928 CP interest in blacks became embodied in the concept of the "Black Nation." This consisted of a number of Deep South states in which blacks constituted a majority in many counties. At different times during the 1930s, however, the CP orientation toward blacks changed in response to the general line of the Communist International, and the black-nation concept was later dropped. While the communists attempted rural and urban organizing in the south, greater success was made in the north. Here, at various times, the communists organized blacks in their capacities as workers, as unemployed, and through local organizations struggling for "Negro rights."

The most consistent emphasis by most Old Left organizations was placed on organizing black workers. Socialists and communists, for example, sought to organize black sharecroppers; these efforts were unsuccessful because of the oppressive character of southern institutions as well as the long-range effects of mechanization in agriculture that produced a massive exodus of agrarian blacks to the northern cities.

Organization of blacks was carried out largely by white radicals. While small numbers of blacks were recruited into the Old Left parties and then often concentrated their energies on further black recruitment, their small numbers, inexperience, and turnover required continual dependence on whites for organizing the blacks. The use of blacks and whites for black recruitment was also intended to demonstrate to blacks that the primarily white radical organizations did not practice discrimination.

This approach was successful in some ways but in the long run proved to be fruitless. It is likely that tens of thousands of blacks were recruited into various parties of the Old Left between the 1920s and 1950s; it is also true that almost all of them dropped away after a relatively short time. This was due, in all likelihood, to a variety of reasons:

- Although there were some units of the Old Left with strong proletarian constituencies, the social-class composition and style of many groups was uncomfortably middle class. Despite concern for creating an undiscriminatory atmosphere for them, most blacks felt socially uncomfortable within the Old Left organizations.
- While attention was given to practical problems of everyday life, the prevailing tendency in most Old Left organizations was to focus on "bigger" theoretical issues involved in revolution, thereby giving less importance to everyday problems of discrimination.
- During the presidency of Franklin D. Roosevelt, most blacks viewed their best chance of gaining equality was from an alliance with Roosevelt and the New Deal. Although Roosevelt's programs did little tangibly for blacks, FDR did hold out the promise of federal concern.
- The Communist Party, while the most effective organization in recruiting blacks, also tended to be manipulative of them. Orientations toward blacks were determined, as with other political issues, on the basis of the central requirement of defending the interests of the Soviet Union. An example of this can be seen in the CP attacks on the March on Washington movement organized by A. Phillip Randolph prior to and during World War II, which "had the misfortune of straddling two periods of CP history; thus, it was attacked by the party for reasons which were diametric opposites from one year to the next! Before the 1941 Nazi attack on the Soviet Union, Randolph's movement was vilified because it did not vigorously oppose the 'imperialist' foreign policy of the Roosevelt administration. After 1941 the party, now prowar and loudly patriotic, accused Randolph and his movement of 'sabotaging' the war effort."

Old Left organizations competed for black participation up to the 1950s not only with each other but also with black nationalist groups. The most significant of these was the movement begun by Marcus Garvey, the Universal Negro Improvement Association. Garveyism, like many of the other movements that were purely black in ideology and membership, did not contemplate a structural transformation of American society; instead, Garvey saw the black American solution in a return to Africa. Following the collapse of the Garvey movement under persecution by the U.S. government and from internal disorganization after 1925, black organization fragmented and remained small until the 1950s.

THE CIVIL RIGHTS AND BLACK SEPARATIST MOVEMENTS

A black civil rights movement grew independently of the Old Left that was in disarray by the 1950s. This movement concentrated its attack on blatant forms of discrimination such as access to public services, accommodations, voting, education, and other political rights. Because these explicit forms of social and political discrimination were most vividly present in the postreconstruction South, most civil rights activities were centered in the southern states during this period.

This new tendency began out of black initiatives and leadership, but initially accepted full white participation. In the early 1960s it was made up of such organizations as the Southern Christian Leadership Conference (SCLC), led by Dr. Martin Luther King, Jr.; the Student Nonviolent Coordinating Committee (SNCC); and the

Congress of Racial Equality (CORE). Around these formal organizations were a large number of smaller, locally based groups that maintained a profusion of attacks on the segregationist and discriminatory practices of American society.

For the most part, these organizations and the civil rights movement as a whole had a nonrevolutionary perspective. Dedicated as they were to major changes in American society, their basic orientation was to integrate blacks into the American mainstream from which they had been so clearly excluded. Throughout the 1950s and early 1960s, the civil rights movement was less interested in transforming institutions than in gaining access to them.

By the middle and late 1960s, the civil rights movement began significant shifts in perspective and organization. Concerns about the racism internal to the movement itself, both in terms of black self-denigration and white insensitivity and domination, led to the exclusion of whites from many of the most militant and significant civil rights organizations.

The dramatic decision of the Student Nonviolent Coordinating Committee in 1966 to expel whites who had once been active members and leaders was symbolic of the shift of consciousness in the civil rights movement and the black population as a whole. In the North, black separatist groups such as the Black Muslims grew tremendously in membership and even the most staunchly "integrationist" of civil rights organizations focused their programs on activities designed to foster "black pride" and other forms of cultural and social autonomy. No longer was the civil rights movement comfortable with the idea of simply becoming part of white America. "Black Power" became the significant slogan expressing a new understanding of the depth of transformations necessary to "liberate" blacks from racial oppression.

Coupled with the new separatism of the black movement came an increasing concentration of blacks in northern urban centers and a growing appreciation of the centrality of economic inequality as an aspect of racial oppression as the black movement moved north. The upsurge of massive black urban rebellions and riots in the middle and late 1960s paralleled the development of a more revolutionary perspective among many black activists and organizations.

Organizationally and ideologically this new revolutionary perspective within the black movement was most clearly articulated within the Black Panther Party, founded in 1966 as the first marxist revolutionary black party in the United States. The significance of the Panthers rested not only on their self-delineation as a black organization but through their defining themselves as a marxist-leninist vanguard group. More important, the Panthers represented the coalescence of a variety of organizational and ideological trends within the black movement begun by Malcolm X. Before his death, Malcolm X was moving ideologically in the direction of what was to become the Black Panther Party in seeking a secularization of Black Muslim ideology. One of his major contributions to the Panthers, taken from his own experience and that of the Black Muslims, was to focus organizational activities on black convicts.

It was through Malcolm X's experience that the crucial idea of conducting organizational work among unemployed blacks, black youth, and black prisoners emerged. This marked a significant departure in organizing among blacks. Whereas earlier attempts had concentrated on black workers and black college students or, in some cases, on black women who were organized into ghetto churches, the new concentration was on the black *lumpenproletariat*, the underclass of unemployed blacks on the streets and in the prisons. This was a social category that had been carefully avoided by the Old Left and the civil rights organizers. The underclass emerged as significant during the great urban rebellions; in fact, they had been recognized earlier by the Muslims as a vital group to organize.*

The Black Panther Party made organization among the street people, the unemployed, the very young, and the tough street gangs a major goal. Persecution by the government, as well as many of the problems of working with the *lumpen*, created difficulties for the Panthers; early in the 1970s, they turned more toward the "entire" black community as the focus for organizational effort.

The Black Panther Party provided the clearest statement of the theory concerning the structural conditions creating revolutionary potential among blacks. The party argued that black people suffered a lack of access to employment, housing, medical care, education, political institutions, and other resources. This lack of access was attributed to the status of the black community as an *internal colony* of the United States.

As in the case of any colony, there was understood to be a need for self-determination; the common exploitation and oppression of blacks, on the one hand, and their close proximity in ghettos, on the other, was understood to give them a capacity for rebellion. The Panthers saw their position within the United States as identical to that of Third World nations that fight wars of national liberation against imperialism. The model that emerged is similar in many respects to the mobilizational model that has been utilized by Mao Zedong and the Chinese communists. Adhering to the ultimate goal of proletarian revolution, the Panthers held that all elements within the colony, including the black bourgeoisie, must first be involved in the struggle for black liberation.

> We now see the black capitalist as having a similar relationship to the black community as the national bourgeoisie have to the people in national wars of decolonization. In wars of decolonization the national bourgeoisie supports the freedom struggles of the people because they recognize that it is in their own selfish interest.

The Panthers believed that, in time, black workers, *lumpenproletariat*, women, and youth would have to fight against black capitalists to win full freedom. The *first* order of business, however, was seen as the need for blacks to gain control over their own community: "the people see black capitalism in the community as black control of local institutions." By uniting all of the black community, the conflict between blacks and the corporate capitalist empire would increase and thereby bring liberation closer. Once the "foreign exploiter" has been wiped out, the black proletariat would be able to defeat the black capitalists because the black bourgeoisie is weaker than the colonial exploiters.

Panther analysis of the 1960s was very close to that used by revolutionaries in most

---

*The role of the black lumpen in the rebellions has also probably been overstated; some analysis indicates, for example, that much of the rioting was done by black workers.

Third World countries. But there were differences that originated in the fact that blacks in the United States constituted an internal rather than an external colony. This peculiar circumstance created two sets of political dynamics that occurred simultaneously: revolution in the mother country *and* liberation in the colony. The Panthers therefore argued that it would be essential for the revolutionary potential of the blacks to be harnessed with that of other groups; all progressive forces must join together because, as a party leader said in 1969,

> . . . there is not going to be any revolution or black liberation in the United States as long as revolutionary blacks, whites, Mexicans, Puerto Ricans, Indians, Chinese, and Eskimos are unwilling or unable to unite into some functional machinery that can cope with the situation.

According to the Panthers, the double nature of the oppression of blacks (and other ethnic minorities) in the United States requires social and national minorities to become the vanguard of the American revolution. "Those who are oppressed the most will fight first and will fight the hardest."

The decade of the 1970s saw some limited but largely unsuccessful attempts to reintegrate black organizations with the largely white organizations of the left. During this period, the "white" left became more aware of other racially oppressed minorities in the United States such as Chicanos, Native Americans, Asians, and Puerto Ricans.* With the exception of a few noble attempts, however, the racial integration of the American left did not move beyond the state of temporary coalitions during the 1970s.

THE REVOLUTIONARY POTENTIAL OF OPPRESSED RACIAL MINORITIES

From the perspective of revolutionary theorists, the revolutionary potential of oppressed racial and ethnic minorities grows out of the systematic and institutional nature of their oppression. The discrimination that exists in wages, employment, housing, educational opportunity, health care, and the political process generally is embodied in virtually every institution of daily life.

Although many theorists in the past focused on the possibility of a revolutionary black national movement capable of cutting across economic lines, the proletarianization and urbanization of blacks and other racial minorities in the United States has forced even revolutionary nationalist groups to adopt a class analysis in relation to racial oppression. On the other hand, the existence of tangible discrimination between whites and racial minorities *within* the working class and the segregated patterns of life that have often resulted have made the special needs of minority workers, often in opposition to white workers, painfully clear.

Tomás Almaguer, a Chicano theorist, points out that, while racism and other forms of ethnocentrism existed prior to capitalism, it was only with the rise of a European-dominated world capitalist market that the oppression of the peoples of

---

*It was only in the 1970s that European socialists also began to develop significant theories about the racism growing out of the use of immigrant labor from southern Europe, Africa, and Asia.

Africa, Asia, and the Americas developed into a systematic and self-perpetuating ideology of white racial superiority.

From its earliest stages as a world system, capitalism depended on the regularized plunder of Africa, Asia, and the Americas and the enslavement or destruction of peoples of color. The history of oppression of each particular racial minority has varied, of course, and the distinct set of institutional arrangements that has perpetuated their systematic oppression has undergone significant transformations. Although there have been some improvements since the Second World War, the reality of oppression has been a constant experience of racial minorities in the United States ever since the "discovery" of the "New World" by Europeans.

Throughout U.S. history, the capitalist class has used racism in all of its aspects to keep the working class divided and thereby weaken the possibilities of ending both racial and class oppression. At the same time, the direct, short-term advantages gained by white workers at the expense of minority workers has meant that the white working class and many of its institutions (such as union seniority rules and apprenticeship programs) have contributed to the oppression of racial minorities in the United States.

Racial minorities are understood by revolutionary theorists as being driven toward revolution by a number of factors. First, the nature of their oppression as a special group and its continuance make it increasingly clear that nothing short of major social transformation will begin to address the problems confronting minority communities. Even major reforms of educational institutions, voting rights, housing programs, job training programs, and the like have failed to address the severity of the economic and social crisis facing oppressed minorities in the United States or Western Europe's urban centers.

Secondly, although it would be a mistake to see revolutionary activity emerging automatically out of oppression, theorists have argued that revolutionary *potential* does grow out of the kinds of oppressive social conditions experienced by minority communities. Minority workers are central to several key industries and have been concentrated in geographical ghettos in the heart of most American cities. Theorists have pointed out, for example, that black workers tend to be the most militant in industrial struggles and that all polls and voting patterns indicate that blacks are the most progressive social category in the United States on a wide variety of issues.

Thirdly, beyond the fight against inequality, minority activists and theorists have contended that activity jointly organized with white working-class groups is necessary for even modest success in obtaining their own goals. It is understood, of course, that such unity can only be built upon a prior commitment to the struggle for equality among the racial groups involved. In a very real way, therefore, oppressed racial minorities can be understood to play a leading role in building working-class unity as well as in achieving racial equality.

Finally, in struggling against white supremacy, racial minorities play a major role in challenging what is perhaps the largest obstacle to white workers developing revolutionary consciousness for themselves.

There is, at this time, no single, generally accepted, or even clearly dominant theory of how revolutionary potential of racial minorities can unfold in the United States or other advanced capitalist countries. It is generally accepted that the existence of real inequality between whites and other racial minorities requires the independent, autonomous organization of the minorities. Such organization is seen as particularly important to ensuring that the struggle for working-class unity does not become an excuse for the postponement or subordination of minority demands. Moreover, the actions of racial minorities for equal rights, decent housing, pay, and expanded government services have often served as a catalyst for other forms of class struggle. The development of a positive sense of cultural identity among racial groups also challenges dominant capitalist values, particularly among young people.

The urbanization of blacks and other racial minorities in the United States and their integration into the mainstream of capitalist industrial economy, although on the basis of second-class economic status, has undercut the basis for secessionist movements. As a result, growing numbers of minority theorists and activists make an important distinction between the need for organizational autonomy and the ultimate need for coalitions in the work place and in large urban centers. However, present developments do not foreclose the possibility of separatist, nationalist, or secessionist movements in the future and no adequate theory or practice has arisen to resolve this question in a compelling fashion.

Over the past twenty years, a significant body of theory has developed which details the institutionalized nature of racism in the United States and the particular forms of oppression experienced by racial minorities. Virtually all revolutionary thinkers now see the struggle against racism as a question *central* to the success of any working-class struggle. In the absence of significant improvements in the conditions of life experienced by the vast majority of blacks, Chicanos, Puerto Ricans, Native Americans, and other racial minorities, these social groups will continue to constitute a significant base for revolutionary transformation.

Youth

THE TRADITIONAL LEFT AND YOUTH

Just as blacks were recognized by the Old Left as an important group to organize, radicals have long realized the special affinities of young people for revolutionary ideas. In all wings and parties of the left, in the United States, Europe, and elsewhere, there have always been youth movements. These were considered in most places as training grounds for the future mature revolutionaries; in all cases, these youth movements provided organizational devices for the recruitment of the young and the development of their organizational skills.

Older revolutionaries saw the revolutionary potential of youth deriving less from any oppressive structural features and more from their higher energy levels, enthusiasm, and the fewer social ties they have to family responsibilities and to the social structure. In addition, especially since almost every revolution of the 20th century has involved some degree of military action, successful revolutionary movements have required a solid youth base.

Older revolutionaries have been ambivalent about youth. Many have viewed young radicals as individuals "in transition" from university status to middle-class occupations in which they soon lose their radical perspectives. Others have seen young people not as a specific social category exploited in themselves but as younger elements of existing social classes such as workers, peasants, the middle class, or the bourgeoisie. The movements organized by young radicals were seen, therefore, as simply youthful *adjuncts* of older proletarian or peasant organizations. Mao Zedong exemplifies this older point of view that the only criterion for judging whether a youth is a revolutionary is

> . . . whether or not he is willing to integrate himself with the broad masses of workers and peasants and does so in practice. If he is willing to do so, he is a revolutionary; otherwise he is a nonrevolutionary or a counterrevolutionary.

Young people born into middle-class or bourgeois families, in this view, can renounce their class privileges, "de-class" themselves, and throw their support to revolutionary elements. These, and other similar traditional views of youth as revolutionary, lasted into the 1960s when a new conceptualization of youth as a revolutionary category developed.

THE REVOLUTIONARY POTENTIAL OF YOUTH

> Come mothers and fathers throughout the land
> And don't criticise what you can't understand.
> Your sons and your daughters are beyond your command,
> Your old road is rapidly aging.
> Please get out of the new one if you can't lend your hand
> For the times they are a-changing.
> --Bob Dylan

> We are all outlaws in the eyes of America.
> In order to survive we steal cheat lie forge fuck hide and deal.
> We are obscene lawless hideous dangerous dirty violent and young.
> --The Jefferson Airplane

Youth activism in the pursuit of major social change in the United States has followed an up-and-down trajectory. After the considerable activism of the 1930s, the Second World War, the cold war, and the McCarthy period saw the emergence of the "silent generation" of the 1950s. Early in the 1960s, as noted above in this chapter, black college students through their activism contributed to the development of the civil rights movement. With the acceleration of the Vietnam war, a student movement got underway which helped to crystallize the antiwar movement. By the middle of the decade, an additional manifestation of youth rejection of mainstream society took shape in the form of the hippie phenomenon. With the end of the Vietnam war, youth activism became almost completely moribund, a tendency that was encouraged by the economic depressions of the late 1970s that made jobs and employment more of a priority for young people than social activism.

Many observers of the American situation, noting similar developments in Great Britain, France, and Germany and other advanced capitalist countries during the decade of activism — the mid-1960s to the mid-1970s — began analyzing developments to generate theories to explain the acceleration of youth activism. In the main, what distinguished the new analysis from that of the Old Left was the focus on the oppression and exploitation that young people were seen as experiencing as *a distinct social category*. New terms such as *"lumpenbourgeoisie,"* "white niggers," and "new minority" began to be used to describe what was seen as a revolutionary development autonomous of the old working class. This new view held that youth were exploited specifically because of their youngness.

Most analysts were impressed by the profound rejection of existing social relationships found among youth:

> A basic far-reaching disrespect and a profound disloyalty is developing toward the values, the forms, the aspirations, and above all, the institutions of the established order. On a scale unprecedented in the New Left's short history, thousands of youth are shedding their commitment to the society in which they live.

Students for a Democratic Society, in a 1968 resolution, "Toward a Revolutionary Youth Movement," saw that

> . . . institutions like the schools, the military, the courts and the police all act to oppress youth in specific ways, as does the work place. The propaganda and socialization processes focused at youth act to channel young people into desired areas of the labor market as well as to socialize them to accept without rebellion the miserable quality of life in America both on and off the job.

Two basic analyses emerged during this period to explain the widespread political activism of young people. The first considered young people to constitute a social class; the second argued that, even though they do not constitute a distinct economic group, young people shared distinct cultural, social, and political conditions.

Youth as a social class. The basic notion underlying this argument is that drastic changes in the organization of the economies of advanced capitalist countries have altered the use of human beings as members of the labor force. While the material conditions of many workers has improved, "class-shifting" has created a new proletariat consisting of the young.

One analysis that exemplifies this approach was undertaken by John and Margaret Rowntree in 1968. They advanced three propositions about the structural position of the young:

1. The American economy is increasingly dominated by two industries that are large, public, and growing: defense and education.

2. The defense and education industries serve crucially as successful absorbers of surplus labor, particularly of young persons.

3. Economic exploitation in the United States is increasingly directed at the young; although the data are scanty and their meaning often obscured by the way they are collected and classified, something like classical economic immiseration has been imposed upon the young.

The proof of the first proposition is found in the importance of these two industries to youth. The "total employment *directly* related to the defense industry was estimated by the Department of Labor to be 7 million jobs in 1962; one in ten employed workers in 1962 were directly employed by the defense industry."

The growth of the education industry has also been significant.* In 1965 about 5.5 percent of all civilian employment in the United States was accounted for by state and local educational systems. The *growth* of employment was even greater; over the past fifteen years, public educational employment had accounted for one out of every six new jobs created in the U.S. economy. In the last twenty-five years

> . . . the character of the American economy has changed from a largely goods-producing private economy to a government-supported economy producing war and knowledge. The defense and education industries . . . now account for more than one-sixth of the actual GNP.

The Rowntrees noted that young people experience a similarity of life experience by virtue of the structure of modern capitalist economy. This can be seen in a variety of statistical facts:

- 52.1 percent of all men between 18 and 24 years of age in 1965 were in school, the military, or were unemployed.
- 37.7 percent of all women aged 18–19 were in school in 1965.
- In 1965, 54 percent of armed forces members were under 25 years of age.
- Unemployment rates for the young were much higher than among older workers. In 1965, 14–24-year-olds made up 20 percent of the civilian labor force but constituted 44 percent of the total unemployed.

Although the Rowntrees examined data from earlier in the 1960s, the consistency of the data can be seen in more recent tendencies of employment and unemployment. This is shown in Table 4.1.

In the Rowntrees' analysis the changes in employment in the defense and knowledge industries create youth as a social class. "It is the 'know-how' and force that keep the capitalist system together; and the exploited workers in these critical industries are, overwhelmingly, young." Because most of their work is wasteful, young people become increasingly alienated from their work and society and were seen by the Rowntrees as being thrown together into a common struggle.

The shared condition of youth. The view that young people share a distinct cultural, social, and political condition rather than a similar location in the economic system represents a somewhat different analysis. This approach explained the militancy of youth, and in particular of students, as based on similarity of occupation and the life-styles deriving from occupations.

> They share an occupation — education — economic dependency, forms of housing, styles of speech, dress, music, and other symbolic identifications. They also have negative identification, such as personal alienation, lack of property, political-legal status, high frequency of interaction within the group, and large numbers in close physical proximity.

As the view developed that universities were very much like corporations and "knowledge factories," students, in this analysis, began to react against the idea that

---

*Additional discussion of the education sector of the economy will be found in Chapter Five which uses similar data to argue the more complex thesis about the development of the new working class.

Table 4.1. Employment and Unemployment, Age 16–24 as a Percentage of the Labor Force

	Employed as a Percentage of the Labor Force	*Unemployed as a Percentage of the Labor Force*
1970	23.2	48.1
1971	23.6	47.7
1972	24.2	50.0
1973	24.7	51.4

Sources: U.S. Bureau of the Census, *Statistical Abstract of the United States, 1974*. Table No. 544, p. 337 for percentage employed; Table No. 555, p. 342 for percentage unemployed.

the university's major purpose was to "prepare" them for life in the occupational structure of the system. Accelerating this tendency was the growing recognition of the complicity of the university as an institutional source of knowledge for the American power structure. The relationship between the universities and the power structure became especially apparent in much of the federally funded research conducted by the universities during the Vietnam war.

Most analysts agreed — whether they agreed that youth constituted a distinct social class — that the special position of young people in society drove them to struggle against the system. One special aspect of the youth struggle of the period took the form of cultural rebellion, being bound together by cultural symbols that distinguished youth from the adult society: music, drugs, clothing, and hair.

Some revolutionaries saw the struggle of the young as one defending a distinctive culture against adults: the generation gap became, in effect, a form of class struggle. Nor did the privilege of middle-income youth link them to maintaining the system. Tom Hayden, an SDS founder, said in 1968:

> Young white people today, whether working class or middle class, are the first privileged generation with no real interest in inheriting the capitalist system. We have experienced its affluence and know that life involves far more than suburban comfort.

Much of the analysis of the revolutionary character of youth and students became less compelling as young people turned more conservative during the 1970s. Once American troops were removed from Vietnam, much of the vehemence of the antiwar feeling and political activism, largely led and driven by young people, declined.

The transiency of youth clearly creates a structural condition in which young people, at any point in time, demonstrate little historical continuity. Most college students remain students only for four-year periods. The necessity of organizing a new generation every four years poses considerable difficulties for revolutionary organizers, even in the "best" of political times. As students stop being students and confront the dilemmas of employment and family, they lose much of their ability to be politically and socially active. And the generation that replaces them is subject to greatly variant external conditions and will be concerned about very different kinds of issues.

Youth as a social category, in summary, demonstrate distinctive capacities for revolutionary activities but these abilities are not consistently present.

Conclusion

The experience of the decades of the 1960s and the 1970s established two intellectual dilemmas for revolutionary theorists. In most of the advanced capitalist countries, this period was one of great political activism in which militancy was expressed by social categories that, in the past, had been seen, at best, as adjuncts of the working class. And, in contrast, the older industrial working class, in particular the manual workers, became relatively quiescent.

Theorists seeking to explain these new developments had to leave behind most of the explanations that had been accepted in the revolutionary movement for over a hundred years. The theoretical explanations that began to emerge, while perhaps not fully satisfactory, represent a major breakthrough in revolutionary analysis. Some theorists emerged with cultural nationalist explanations: that blacks, for example, became active in the defense of their unique sociocultural condition; or that women struggle for liberation from masculine domination by developing separatist organizations, etc. Some neomarxist theorists, in contrast, acknowledge the power of the new activism but have sought to consider the ways in which capitalism operates on distinctive social categories, not simply as a class phenomenon.

The new theoretical approach is still in the process of emerging. Many aspects of this approach remain unsatisfactory, and it is probable that it will require some time, and considerable activism on the part of distinct social categories within capitalist societies, before a satisfactory, integrated theory crystallizes.

CHAPTER FIVE

Expanding the Proletariat: New Working-Class Theories

The worldwide upsurge of student activism in the 1960s and a prior decline of industrial working-class militancy during the cold war sparked the development of new revolutionary theories capable of understanding the changing conditions of modern capitalism. Generally labeled "new working-class theories," these have concentrated on three basic areas: (1) the flexibility of capitalism in meeting the economic demands of the industrial working class; (2) the changing composition and structure of the labor force; and (3) the increased integration of the state and the educational system with the giant corporations. New working-class theory has also focused attention on the centrality of alienation as an experience in modern capitalism.

The Co-optation of the Industrial Proletariat

The marxist movements of the advanced capitalist countries have been predicting the collapse of capitalism for about one hundred years. Although Marx himself, in various writings, evidenced a complex notion of the character of class struggle under capitalism, most marxian analyses of the contradictions of capitalism rested upon Marx's ideas about immiseration. Immiseration explanations for capitalism's demise carried weight because it was the main theory developed by Marx in *The Communist Manifesto*, his single most popular work. Other more complex arguments used by Marx tended to be less emphasized by marxists.

Although the increased polarization of the class structure into a tiny bourgeoisie and a swollen proletariat did not occur at the expected rate, the immiseration theory continued to be accepted by most marxists until after the Great Depression. Indeed, many saw in the major political and economic developments of 1900–40 a vindication of marxist theory. The First World War was fought over colonies necessary for capitalist growth; depressions affected greater numbers of people in deeper ways and over longer periods of time.

During and after World War II, however, capitalism appeared to have found ways to solve the most glaring of its difficulties — especially around the issue of wages and economic conditions. This became true particularly with respect to the industrial proletariat — the working class in mines, mills, factories, and workshops. In the United States, following the organization of the CIO in the 1930s, industrial workers moved steadily up the ladder of economic gains: continual increase in wages, a steady expansion of "fringe benefits" in the form of insurance coverage, longer vacations, pensions, etc. The misery that had characterized industrial cities, the grim life that had been so much a part of the industrial workers' existence, began to change. Workers began to be drawn into the homeowner-refrigerator-second-car syndrome, and this was reflected in a loss of open and overt militancy that had characterized industrial workers during the 1930s. The postwar period was one in which major antilabor legislation, embodied in the Taft-Hartley Act and state right-to-work laws, and a purge of left-wing activists, put organized labor on the defensive. This was an era in which *Fortune* magazine was congratulating itself on the steady decline of the industrial working class, predicting the end of the class struggle in America. Similar trends, though less dramatic, took place in other advanced capitalist countries.

For revolutionaries whose political analysis sprang from a belief that capitalism would self-destruct, the period was one of confusion and disarray. They saw the working class being "bought off" as the system showed greater flexibility than had originally been expected. Capitalism's frequent overproduction crises were eased by two devices: first, improved planning in the area of production, and second, expanded control over consumption.

Planning was impossible in the system of competitive free-market capitalism that existed when Marx wrote *Capital*. The state did not interfere in questions of production, and no single firm's production was large enough to determine overall price or output in an industry. The most important kind of competition between businesses occurred over prices — and this meant continual pressure to cut costs by reducing the wages of workers.

As the tendencies in competitive capitalism toward concentration described by Marx in *Capital* came to dominate the economy, this monopolization had profound effects upon planning and wages. For many years most large corporations have had tacit agreements not to compete over prices, while limiting competition to sales and advertising. Free of the necessity to reduce prices in order to undersell their competitors, large corporations have been able to pass on wage increases for workers to consumers in the form of higher prices. In addition, the intervention of the state through the agency of the federal government — in defense expenditures and in the management of the supply of money, and through other fiscal controls — leveled the worst extremes of the business cycle although it has not eliminated periodic recessions. Where large-scale capitalist enterprises have confronted serious financial difficulties, direct government intervention on their behalf has increased.

Other changes in capitalism that have helped to mask the contradiction of underconsumption include planned obsolescence (making products that fall apart sooner) and commodity fetishism (keeping up with the Joneses). When all of these ameliorative measures are combined with the control of the media by the centers of power in society, a substantial barrier to the development of class consciousness has been created.

Under monopoly capitalism, wage and employment problems represent less of an intractable problem than they did under competitive capitalism. Yet the fundamental contradiction in capitalism between labor and capital still exists and is manifested in different forms. Analyses of these new developments are embodied in recent theories concerning the changing of the working class.

The Emergence of New Working-Class Theory

MARX AND THE NEW WORKING CLASS

Although Marx discussed the dynamic changes in the structure of the labor force in *Capital*, this was not done in the same detail as in his notes to that work, the *Grundrisse*. Here he was more explicit in describing the creation of a new stratum of high technology workers to the "nonproductive" white-collar sectors of service, sales, clerical, and professional workers. Marx explained the process in which fewer people produce more while greater numbers of people become unnecessary to the productive processes.

> Capital is itself contradiction in action, since it makes an effort to reduce labor time to the minimum, while at the same time establishing labor time as the sole measurement and source of wealth. Thus it diminishes labor time in its *necessary* form, in order to increase its *superfluous* form; therefore it increasingly establishes superfluous labor time as a condition (a question of life and death) for necessary labor time. On the one hand, it calls into life all the forces of science and nature, as well as those of social cooperation and commerce, in order to create wealth which is relatively independent of the labor time utilized. On the other hand, it attempts to measure, in terms of labor time, the vast social forces thus created and imprisons them within the narrow limits that are required in order to retain the value already created *as* value. Productive forces and social relationships—the two different sides of the development of the social individual—appear to be, and are, only a *means* for capital, to enable it to produce from its own cramped base. But in fact they are the material conditions that will shatter this foundation.

Marx was suggesting here that the manifestation of the contradiction in capitalism leading to its overthrow was to be found less in the reduction of the material conditions of the workers—their immiseration—than through their realization that they are being forced to produce superfluous goods. These superfluities include meaningless consumer items and objects of destruction embodied in military production. This type of production is necessary solely for the maintenance of capitalism.

These notions were only sketchily developed by Marx. It is necessary, therefore, to look at capitalism during the past fifty years to understand the basis of new working-class theory.

THE EXPANDING NATURE OF THE PROLETARIAT

The major trends in the development of the working class under capitalism are demonstrated in Tables 5.1 and 5.2. The first table shows how the labor force in the United States has become increasingly proletarianized. The second table demonstrates more recent changes in the structure of the labor force. Where the first shows the growth in size of the proletariat, the second illustrates the growing significance of categories of workers other than blue-collar laborers.

The shift of the labor force away from industrial jobs to white-collar, sales, service, and professional work represents one of the major structural changes in modern capitalist economies. It is a fact of history that this transition was defined by both supporters and critics of capitalism as a shift *from the proletariat to the middle class.* Theorists of varied ideological inclinations saw in this the coming of the "end of ideology," in which a new homogeneity of American society would produce a new consensus. This new consensus was ostensibly demonstrated by the decline of militancy by industrial workers and the disinterest of white-collar workers in organization. And indeed, initial attempts by unions to organize the new technological and service workers proved largely unsuccessful. Even a major radical critic, C. Wright Mills, saw the shift as one toward the middle class and discussed it largely in despairing terms.

The delineation of these categories as a new middle class de-emphasized the continuity of the relationship of these workers to production. The growing number of white-collar workers has been forced to sell its labor power in the same way as the blue-collar workers. They share the same lack of control over the end product of

Table 5.1. The Proletarianization of the U.S. Labor Force

Year	Percent Wage and Salaried Employees	Percent Self-Employed	Percent Salaried Managers and Officials	Total
1780	20.0	80.0	---	100.0
1880	62.0	36.9	1.1	100.0
1890	65.0	33.9	1.2	100.0
1900	67.9	30.8	1.3	100.0
1910	71.9	26.3	1.8	100.0
1920	72.9	23.5	2.6	100.0
1930	76.8	20.3	2.9	100.0
1939	78.2	18.8	3.0	100.0
1950	77.7	17.9	4.4	100.0
1960	80.6	14.1	5.3	100.0
1969	83.6	9.2	7.2	100.0
1974	83.0	8.2	8.8	100.0

Source: Reich 1972 in Edwards, Reich, Weisskopf, 1978, p. 180.

Table 5.2. Percentage of Changes in Occupational Groups United States, 1950–1979

	1950	1979
White Collar	37.5	50.9
Professional & Technical	7.5	15.5
Managers and Administrators	10.8	10.8
Sales Workers	6.4	6.4
Clerical	12.8	18.2
Blue Collar	39.1	33.1
Craftsmen	12.9	13.3
Operatives	20.4	15.0
Laborers, Non-farm	5.9	4.8
Service Workers	11.0	13.3
Farm Workers	12.4	2.8

Source: U.S. Bureau of the Census, *Statistical Abstract of the United States.* For 1950 see 95th edition (1974), Table 568, p. 350; for 1979 see 101st edition (1980), Table 696, p. 418.

their labor and over their conditions of employment. Using this analysis, new working-class theorists argue that the new stratum of white-collar workers are *objectively* a part of the proletariat — indeed, a new sector that has expanded the size of the total proletariat. It has only been during the past decade that there has developed some *subjective* indications of the proletarian character of this stratum. This has occurred with the increased emphasis by professional organizations on dealing with economic conditions and with the growth of associations of government employees, technical workers, and others. These associations, while ostensibly not unions, have been engaging in traditional "union" battles involving wages, hours, and working conditions.

The use of the concept of the "new working class," while valuable, has also created new conceptual problems.* Although it is essential to recognize the inclusion of technological, scientific, and highly educated and trained employees within the working class, it is also necessary to include service workers such as sales personnel, clerks, and other white-collar employees. The new working class, therefore, includes

*At the same time, it should be noted that significant numbers of marxist theorists have developed various formulations about the "new middle class" or "new middle strata." These theories, while rejecting the new middle-class theories of the *Fortune* magazine variety, argue that the differences between mental and manual labor create significant *class* antagonisms between white- and blue-collar workers. See, for example, Poulantzas, 1975, or Ehrenreich, 1977, as examples of these views. We have found these arguments less compelling than the expanded proletariat theories described in the text.

a wide variety of different types of workers; it is heterogeneous in background, skills, training, and orientations. Subjectively, many workers in these categories have defined themselves as "middle class" rather than working class because they have experienced some social mobility, particularly with respect to their parents. In the view of the new theorists, as such workers recognize their lack of control over the work process and are treated in the same way as blue-collar workers, they will begin the development of a subjective class consciousness.

THE NEW WORKING CLASS AND ITS CONTRADICTIONS

The new working class arose out of the dynamics of capitalism, operating in advanced capitalist countries. As automation of the productive process increased, as part of the attempt to cut costs under competitive capitalism, there was a corresponding decrease in the need for skilled and semiskilled assembly-line workers and an increase in the need for more highly educated technical workers and workers to distribute, sell, and keep records on the increased amount of goods being produced and circulated. The increasing role of the state in planning and creating new consumer demand through defense and other forms of "welfare" spending called for the rapid growth of federal, state, and local bureaucracies. The technological complexities of modern capitalist production also necessitated a working class with increased educational and technical skills. As a result, education took on an increasingly important training and socializing role.

The ways in which capitalism's new contradictions operate have been described by a number of leftist theoreticians. André Gorz outlined three general contradictions in advanced capitalism.

1. The basic contradiction between the expanded productive forces of capitalism and the narrow capitalist social and political relations that control these forces.

2. The contradiction between the kind and amount of training necessary for production and the incompatibility of such training with the existing hierarchical structures of industry and government.

3. The growing cost of producing the necessary labor force through education and training and the tendency for capitalist society to avoid responsibility for this social cost.

The first of these contradictions is endemic in capitalism in all of its aspects.

The modern working class has an immediate interest in uninterrupted technical advance, with all its consequences: a substantial fall in working hours, new professional status, changes in employment. Capitalism, on the contrary, has a tendency to hold back the development of the productive forces, because their development tends to bring a fall in the rate of profit and implies more and more reliance on economic instruments of a socialist character, whose effects capitalism cannot fully master.

What modern capitalism has accomplished is a diversion of workers' interests from production to consumption. Workers are "satisfied" with consumer goods while the work situation does not change in any significant way. If anything, the work situation worsens in that work becomes less meaningful as a legitimate form of activity for workers. They are uninterested and uninvolved in the work itself and in its end product. The alienating process of capitalism continues despite the capability of capitalism to produce large volumes of consumer goods.

According to these new marxist theorists, the system becomes increasingly irrational as more and more energy is devoted by workers to the waste production necessary to keep the system going. Workers become aware not only of the discrepancy between what they produce and what they receive but of the even larger difference between what they could produce for themselves were it not for waste and war production. As a result of their alienation from the forms of production, they gain an understanding of the gap between what the system actually does and what it could do. This awareness potentially creates the dynamic driving force for revolution.

The second contradiction has to do with the levels of education necessary to sustain the increasingly complex industrial system and its incompatibility with the hierarchical forms of capitalism. One of the best ways of understanding the changes that have occurred in advanced capitalist societies is to compare the semiskilled lathe or machine operators of the old industrial working class with the new semiskilled operators of a battery of automated lathes or related equipment. The semiskilled workers were trained for work on particular machines and had a higher level of personal skill than the new machine operators. The new workers, however, have a higher general level of education since their jobs require broader areas of knowledge. Because the new workers are likely to have a broader understanding of the entire productive process, they may be able to be more critical about the utilization of resources in production and on the extent and meaning of waste production. They can see when supervision becomes unproductive and when organizational demands produce irrationalities in production. Theorists of the new working class believe that the new workers are better able to get beyond their own immediate situations to understand the more general features of the production in which they are involved because their education emphasizes broad knowledge over specific occupational skills. This gives them an ability to generalize about the limitations of capitalism and its system of production. The militancy of professional and technical workers in France in May 1968 and Italy in 1969–70 provided some confirmation of this analysis.

THE UNIVERSITY: SOCIALIZING AGENT OF THE NEW WORKING CLASS

The vital importance of the university as a socializing agency for modern capitalist society is embodied in the fact that between 1960 and 1970 professional and technical workers increased in the United States by about 40 percent. This technologized end product is produced in the "knowledge factories" that we call universities. The knowledge industry, which includes universities, computer firms, and research and development "think tanks," currently accounts for almost one-third of the United States' GNP. Schoolteachers currently make up the largest single occupation in the labor force, some three million workers. The university, said Clark Kerr, former president of the University of California, "has become a prime instrument of national purpose. This is new. This is the essence of the transformation now engulfing our universities." Despite the economic difficulties of the late 1970s, universities continue to be a major institution for producing the labor forces of complex capitalist societies.

The universities currently perform two distinct functions in the production of a labor force: training and socialization. The training function is carried out, to a large extent, in special colleges such as professional schools, junior colleges, and in the nonelite state colleges. Here the focus is on training for specific skills.

The emphasis in training is on fragmentation. Knowledge is broken up into small parts and crammed into the students. There is the hope that somehow all of this will be put together, but the inadquacies of the system and the unwillingness to bear the social costs for an educational process that will create a coherent whole preclude synthesis on the part of the student.

The educational system of modern society has substituted considerably for the institutions of socialization that were important at an earlier period, in particular, the family and the church. Modern capitalist societies require socialized individuals who will work primarily for external rewards in the form of commodities—rather than those who seek to make work itself intrinsically more satisfying. Members of the modern capitalist productive order must, in other words, learn to ignore what they are producing, how they produce it, how it gets used; they must concern themselves simply with the wages they get for doing what they are told to do.

In this respect the educational system trains people for work in capitalist society. The university provides a good socialization process by offering students programs in which they are expected neither to enjoy the process of learning nor to concern themselves with gaining any significant knowledge. They are expected to be satisfied with external rewards such as grades—or some other authoritarian and external evaluation. The educational process is itself authoritarian—treating students as passive consumers of information that may be completely irrelevant to their needs or desires for knowledge. Whether the process is planned this way or not, it serves as a perfect socialization device for the new members of the expanded working class. Its output consists of people who will be alienated and passive consumers.

Like the broader society, the university has dialectically related "negative" and "positive" aspects. To the extent, limited though it may be, that the university educates students for modern technology, it also gives them the intellectual tools for understanding capitalism's shortcomings. Although they experience the contradictions of the new working class in more abstract form than workers, students have better opportunities to act on their understanding of capitalism's failures because of their youth and relative detachment from job, family, and co-opting social structures. Their experience in the university and their learning by struggling against its socializing influence may be ultimately translated into action on the part of the new working class they will join.

THE EXPANDED PROLETARIAT

The new working-class theories originally came out of an attempt to explain the decline in revolutionary activity among the old industrial working class (point-of-production workers) and the rise in activism among students and white-collar and service workers. Consequently, there was an initial tendency by some theorists to look to the new working class as the only potentially revolutionary group in society. Serge Mallet expressed this viewpoint when he pointed to the greater number of strikes among petrochemical workers than other workers in less automated industries in Europe. More recently, especially following the breakdown of the distinction in terms of level of struggle between the old and the new working class in France—in May 1968—the tendency has been toward a more integrated theory in which the new working class is seen as part of a generally expanded proletariat. Some marxist theorists, notably Ernest Mandel, argue that the working-class struggle over narrow wage issues will be revived and take on a renewed revolutionary character when imperialist profits are cut off by successful wars of liberation in the Third World—and with the resulting rise of sharper competition between the advanced countries for markets. Most of the new working-class theorists, however, focus their attention on contradictions other than wages, since modern capitalism has already proven its considerable flexibility in this area.

To the extent that contradictions in the economic sphere are important to the new working-class theorists, they see revolutionary struggles breaking out around the issues of control of both the work process and the end product. More broadly, there is a growing concern with superstructural—cultural, aesthetic, and ecological—issues that go beyond the economic base of capitalism and concern themselves with questions like individuality, the environment, community, and the meaningfulness of social and political life. As one of the theorists of the expanded proletariat writes:

> The fundamental institutions of capitalism, particularly control of the productive process, free markets in land and labor, and their supporting legal relations of property ownership, conflict with the interests of workers as creative producers. This natural opposition of interests provides the basis for the development of a revolutionary consciousness on the part of workers; a consciousness directed toward the abolition of capitalist institutions, toward the development of a society in which the social, spiritual, and aesthetic integrity of the community are placed above the need of an alien "economic rationality;" a society where we will subordinate the needs of maximal output to the creation of a work-environment conducive to the human development of the worker. Such an environment will serve to foster individuality, creativity, solidarity with fellow workers, and a society where production is subordinated to social need and individual development.

New working-class theorists hold that these superstructural issues are bound up with the capitalist mode of production. The problem for them is to discover which issues are capable of rousing the expanded proletariat to revolutionary class consciousness and struggle. This is a problem not only for mobilization (see Chapter 13 on workers' control) but also for obtaining a better understanding of the way in which capitalist social relations create revolutionary potential. To develop this understanding, theorists must determine the role that institutions play in supporting the cultural hegemony (domination) of capitalism by providing it with "legitimacy."

The search for means to shatter the cultural hegemony of capitalism was at the center of the work of Antonio Gramsci, one of the founders of the Italian Communist Party, and probably the first theorist of the new working class (with the notable exception of references in Marx). Gramsci devoted considerable analysis to noneconomic institutions, particularly those involving intellectual activity, education, and the state. Gramsci's main contribution has been his attack on mechanistic determinism and his emphasis on the important role intellectuals play in helping the working classes attain a socialist perspective. Intellectuals do not operate in a social vacuum, but Gramsci wanted to rescue from the marxian determinists the leninist notion of the professional revolutionary as a political actor who "makes history." As shall be seen in Chapter 7, Lenin saw intellectuals as playing the key role in bringing consciousness to the working class; Gramsci saw the same role for the intellectuals as being primarily responsible for the formulation of proposals for change. Because of his belief in the importance of leadership for revolution, he saw the party as having a crucial role in creating an alternative to capitalist hegemony. Gramsci is a major source of study for many new working-class theorists who have gone back to the work he left at his death in 1936.

Other theorists are attempting to understand how the new working class will relate to other groups in the expanded proletariat: women, youth, racial minorities, and the industrial proletariat. They are beginning to see the connections that exist between the common position of these groups as *exploited consumers* who have no control over what is produced, how it is produced, or for whom it is produced. Here there are interesting connections with respect to ecology. The need of capitalism to produce military waste and conspicuous consumption for profit creates an ecological danger for the planet. Consumers are taught to want automobiles rather than mass transit systems, just as they are pushed to crave more appliances that consume ever-increasing quantities of electricity. This produces continual destruction of lakes, rivers, oceans, land, and air. How ecology groups and other segments of the population will relate to each other is obviously a question that will have to be answered before a better understanding is gained of how socialism can begin to solve the contradictions of capitalism.

The one certainty is that the technological developments of capitalism have not resolved its own contradictions. Capitalism may have become stronger and learned to meet, at least partially and temporarily, the economic demands of its workers. But as noted in an American New Left pamphlet written in the mid-1960s,

> . . . modern capitalism and its policy of imperialism has aroused political responses which have the potential to destroy it. The response to America's attempts to secure markets abroad is, increasingly, the emergence of national liberation movements. Similarly, waste production and the management of demand, domestic imperialism, seems to be leading to the development of a large-scale domestic movement (a new left) reacting against meaningless jobs and manipulative consumption. In fact, the development of some of the industries key to the survival of modern capitalism (e.g., mass media, mass education) themselves contain the roots of its potential destruction. For people — especially the young and the blacks — are becoming more and more aware of the gap between potential social wealth and the reality of their own lives, whether in the ghetto, in the classroom, or on the job.

The Advantages and Limits of New Working-Class Theory

Two general problems with the "old" working class—the blue-collar, manual, industrial workers—contributed to the evolution of the new working-class theories. First, there was the structural change taking place in the working class in which blue-collar work declined in importance and white-collar employment grew. Second, industrial workers in the advanced capitalist countries failed to manifest the revolutionary potential originally attributed to them by marxian analysis. This led to an increasing disenchantment with industrial workers by some revolutionary theoreticians.

The tendencies of professional and technical workers to organize unions to protect themselves economically, initially posed the possibility of the existence of the new working class. When European technical workers began to organize militantly, and especially after these workers became extremely active in France and Italy in the late 1960s, new working-class theory became more acceptable in many revolutionary circles.

The concept of the new working class, however, sets important conceptual and organizational problems for revolutionaries. All too frequently revolutionaries still operate in a mode of marxian analysis that sees the working class as becoming larger, more homogeneous, and more exploited. Yet it was recognized a long time ago that, under certain conditions, the bourgeoisie was able to make concessions to some elements within the working class—the so-called "aristocracy of labor"—and buy off their militancy. Not only was the old working class heterogeneous but the new working class represents an even more heterogeneous social category. Consisting as it does of such disparate occupations as sales clerks, janitors, engineers, and scientists, the failure to recognize the important distinctions that exist within the new working class can lead to important defects in organizing.

The new working class as a revolutionary category has yet to "prove" itself in revolutionary practice (though the same could be said about the "old" working class in most advanced capitalist countries). While some organization and consciousness have been manifested in the United States, the levels of consciousness achieved are distinctly lower than those that have developed in such countries as France or Italy. Even in Europe, however, there have been considerable inconsistencies in the levels of activism of members of the new working class.

A distinctive problem that remains in all countries is the integration of the actions of the old and the new working classes. There have been some tendencies on the part of old working-class organizations to look upon the new working class as ephemeral or effete; in turn, occasional orientations of "superiority" are manifested by professional workers. The need to overcome these distinctions and to join the forces of both against the common enemy of capitalism remains a major problem for revolutionary activists.

Over and above the problems of uniting various segments of the wage labor force, much theoretical and practical work remains to incorporate existing class analysis with the ever more complex theories and movements related to other contradictions of advanced capitalist societies. It is not clear, for example, that racial/ethnic and gender-based divisions of labor may simply be *subsumed* under even the most sophisticated class analysis. Although significant theoretical progress has been made in integrating class analysis with other aspects of the division of labor under capitalism, a compelling and generally accepted theory has yet to be achieved. Perhaps even more important, concrete practical activity, producing significant organization for revolutionary change based on either expanded working class theory or integrating these new theories with race/gender theories, also waits to be successfully accomplished.

PART TWO

Revolutionary Organization Theory

In what relation do the communists stand to the proletarians as a whole?

The communists do not form a separate party opposed to other working class parties. . . .

The communists are distinguished from the other working-class parties by this only: (1) In the national struggles of the proletarians of the different countries, they point out and bring to the front the common interests of the entire proletariat, independently of all nationality. (2) In the various stages of development which the struggle of the working class against the bourgeoisie has to pass through, they always and everywhere represent the interests of the movement as a whole.

The communists, therefore, are on the one hand, practically, the most advanced and resolute section of the working-class parties of every country, that section which pushes forward all others; on the other hand, theoretically, they have over the great mass of the proletariat the advantage of clearly understanding the line of march, the conditions, and the ultimate general results of the proletarian movement.

—Karl Marx and Friedrich Engels,
The Communist Manifesto

Whether one believes that dissatisfaction with the operations of the system is most prevalent in the working class, the peasantry, youth, blacks, or somewhere else, some people become more involved in seeking revolutionary change than others. How shall these revolutionaries organize themselves? This question poses what will be called the *organization* problem. It originates in the dilemma of relating conscious revolutionaries to those people or groups within which revolutionary energies are being generated.

The advice from *The Communist Manifesto* that opened this section provides only the barest outline of an answer. And indeed, the advice of Marx and Engels on the organization question was rather fragmentary. One format, clear by implication and Marx's actual practice, is the emphasis on international organization. Marx's main organizational effort, the International Workingmen's Association (more commonly called the First International) was an international body seeking to guide the national and local organizations that had developed in various parts of Europe.

Beyond this model, Marx and Engels provided few answers to organizational questions, although there were implicit relationships in the way they sought to establish the ideological hegemony of the International over its constituent elements. In conflicts over ideological issues between Marx and anarchists, the issue of centralization versus decentralization was initially posed. For various reasons concerned with their beliefs about releasing revolutionary energies, the anarchists favored decentralized and autonomous organization.

The lineal inheritors of marxian thinking shifted their emphasis, after the demise of the First International, to the development of *mass parties* at the national level. These took root in Britain, France, and Germany in the late 19th century. These mass parties are generally referred to as social-democratic parties. Mass parties consist of hundreds of thousands of members and hold themselves open to the entire working class as well as other sympathetic classes. The party and its auxiliary organizations, such as unions, cooperatives, and associations, intended to encompass much of the day-to-day work, thought, and energy of its members.

Rather than developing as a result of any formally delineated organizational theory, the mass parties simply grew organically. They were the product of day-to-day adaptations of the working-class movement in Europe. As a form of organization, despite the rapid growth of the movement, the mass party received less theoretical attention than an opposing concept—the theory of the vanguard party developed by Lenin. The main discussion in this book of mass-party organization has had to be drawn, therefore, from actual practice rather than from theoretical writings. The major exception is the work of Rosa Luxemburg, who wrote on the mass party while attacking leninist-organization theory.

Vladimir Ilyitch Lenin opened the discussion on organization *as a theoretical matter* when he set out the concept of vanguard organization in 1902 in *What Is to Be Done?* In this book, Lenin was not concerned with an explicit attack on the social-democratic form of mass-party organization. He believed that such a form might be desirable but was impossible in the authoritarian society of czarist Russia. In arguing for a centralized party of professional revolutionaries dedicated to leading the working class toward revolution, however, Lenin presented the case of a new and different form of organization. *What Is to Be Done?* kindled a major controversy within Russia and later in the entire revolutionary movement as to forms of organization and their consequences. That controversy not only has continued but is manifest in the varying organizational practices found in the contemporary revolutionary left. It is worth noting that most successful revolutionary transitions in the 20th century have been under the direction of a vanguard party.

These two organizational solutions—the mass party and the vanguard party—constitute the two major organizational alternatives of the socialist movement. The anarchist theory of organization represents a third distinctively different approach. It stresses, in contrast to the socialist approaches, principles of localism and spontaneity. While anarchist forms of organization were relatively insignificant for many decades, the resuscitation of the approach during the 1960s, particularly in the student movement, requires a reexamination of the original anarchist organizational ideas.

We turn first in Chapter 6 to a comparative discussion of the three basic organizational approaches. This abstracts the basic structural features of vanguard, mass party, and anarchist theory from the specific historical contexts in which each approach developed. We turn then to a more detailed consideration of each of the three organizational forms, first in their classical manifestations, and secondly, in the modern American left. We begin, in Chapter 7, with Lenin on the vanguard organization by summarizing the basic ideas of *What Is to Be Done?* and incorporate into his argument relevant elements of his pamphlet *One Step Forward, Two Steps Back*. While coming chronologically after the mass party, Lenin's theoretical statement provides the clearest idea of revolutionary organizational theory. Chapter 8 follows with an examination of the mass parties of social-democracy, paying special attention to Germany and to the Socialist Party of the United States, and closing with a criticism of the vanguard notion by Rosa Luxemburg. Chapter 9 considers anarchist organization theory. Focusing on the modern American left, Chapter 10 examines some of the manifestations of revolutionary organization of the past decade, relating these organizations to the three classical models.

CHAPTER SIX

Organization Theories: Basic Models

At issue in the debate on organizational theory are conflicts over several basic assumptions.

The first assumption distinguishes the revolutionary approach from the *putsch* or *coup d'état*. Whereas marxists and anarchists generally agree that the workings of the social system produce revolutionary energies in various social categories such as the proletariat, putschists have no confidence in the likelihood of action by the people and therefore see a need to organize a conspiracy. Conspiracies are often organized against existing injustice in the name of someone, e.g., the proletariat, if that someone is believed unable to make a revolution for itself. This view, espoused by an early socialist group led by Louis August Blanqui, was strongly rejected by marxists and anarchists because of their belief that putsches do not produce *social* revolutions. Conspiracies that seize power generally replace one set of rulers by another and effect little change in existing social relationships. The putschist model is exemplified in the classical Latin American revolution where the government changes but social, economic, and political relationships remain unchanged.

The second assumption is embodied in the question: If revolutionary energies are generated in different social classes, will these energies produce organizational forms by themselves or is some conscious direction necessary? The answer to this question separates the marxist from the anarchist approach. The marxists argue that organization does not develop automatically; it is necessary for conscious revolutionaries to organize themselves and the working class into distinctive organizations to fight for power. In contrast, the anarchists believe that organization will develop spontaneously within the revolutionary class; the revolutionary class will go through various experiences and eventually learn to make itself sufficiently efficient to overthrow the exploitative system.

The anarchist theory of organization, which is the simplest, is indicated diagramatically in Figure 6.1.

The diagram is intended to illustrate the existence of localized, small-scale, autonomous groups, each setting its own orientation but all functioning to produce revolutionary action. Membership is open to anyone subscribing to general programmatic views and who is willing to join. Discipline is personal rather than organizational. Each unit is relatively autonomous of the next. There is an exchange of information and coordination but no hierarchy nor discipline. It should be noted that the model discussed represents an ideal type, a theoretical view of organization, rather than a representation of past reality. In practice, the anarchist Bakunin, in his controversy with Marx against centralization, organized a clandestine vanguard group.

Figure 6.1 The Anarchist Theory of Organization

Toward Revolution

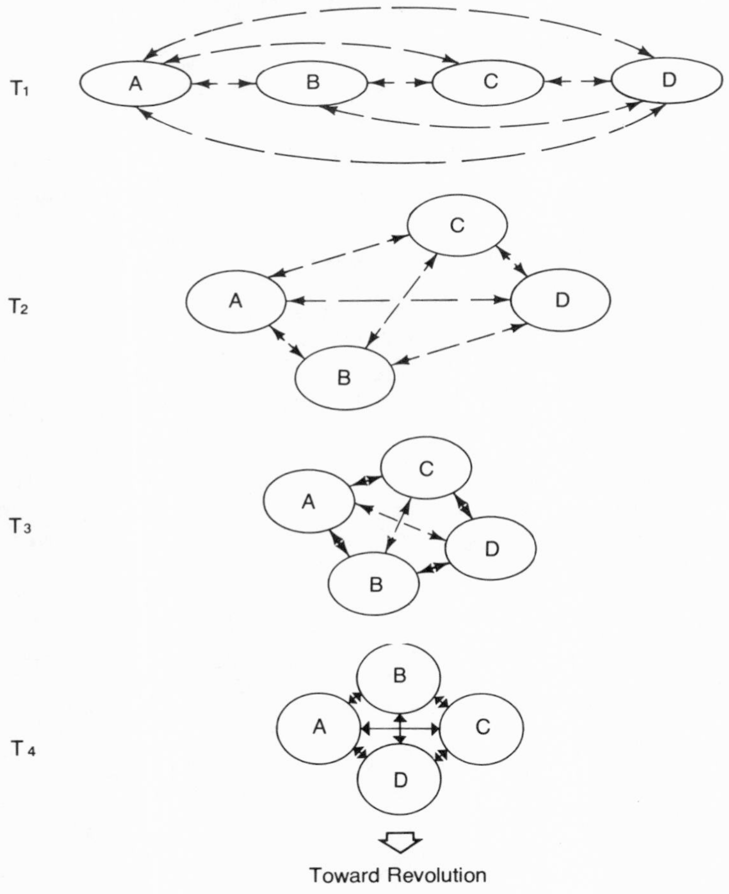

The diagram is intended to illustrate the relationship *between* organized units and not within them.

Differences between marxists on organizational forms are based on other implicit assumptions. These are subsumed in the problem of how conscious revolutionaries can organize themselves to best amplify, encourage, and focus the revolutionary energies of the proletariat.

Marxist assumptions are based on beliefs that contrast a series of alternatives:

- the need for professionals *versus* amateurs in developing revolutionary action
- central *versus* local orientations
- clandestine *versus* open organization
- the need for ideological clarity *versus* the need for organizational unity

The vanguard approach characterized those that chose the first in each of these alternatives; mass-party adherents have by and large chosen the second alternative.

The argument for professionalism is based largely on the belief in the need for efficiency in making revolutions. This approach holds that revolutionary upsurges do not occur with great frequency and that, as a result, revolutionaries must be prepared to take advantage of them as they arise. This not only implies conscious and deliberate preparation, but also the need to develop a core of people who know how to function adaptively and effectively on a minute-to-minute basis during revolutionary crises. This issue takes concrete form on the question of membership in the revolutionary organization. Should the organization take in anyone who agrees with its general ideological program? Or should membership be more restricted and encompass only those willing to subscribe to a detailed program *and* to dedicate themselves to implementing this program on a full-time basis? The first approach is embodied in the mass party, the second in the vanguard party.

The argument for centralism against localism is based on the belief that it is only through the development of a general struggle against systemic exploitation that a social class such as the proletariat learns that it is being exploited as a class—as a social category—rather than as individuals. As long as the focus remains on local problems, workers cannot develop the broader consciousness necessary to make them effective revolutionaries and they can only deal with problems as trade unionists.

The argument for clandestine activity versus openness is not as vitally involved with the vanguard approach as the previous two issues. Yet it is an important part of vanguard theory in autocratic or totalitarian contexts where revolutionary organization must remain secret to avoid being destroyed by the police. Even in more "open" situations, however, most vanguardists hold to some degree of semisecret organization in the belief that there is little point in exposing to the ruling class what one is doing to overturn the system.

The argument for ideological clarity is not simply one that contrasts clarity *against* unity. Unity, like apple pie, is favored by every revolutionary. The issue arises on the question as to whether the revolutionary organization should present a single view in mobilizing the population or can handle a variety of views. Since vanguardists believe that the infrequency of revolutionary crises requires the ability to move rapidly when they develop, they also hold the idea of developing experts who can present a single, correct set of tactics. This creates the need for an internal process of decision-making that will be swift, efficient, and purposeful. In theory, vanguard organizations resolve the problem of efficiency and democracy through the process known as *democratic centralism*. In this process, when a decision is to be made, the issue is debated internally during a formal disscussion period. At the end of this period, there is a vote, generally by some representative body. The decision of the majority then becomes binding on all.

Again, a distinction must be made between organizational theory and organizational practice. While the vanguardist approach creates a conscious elite, the mass party approach produces a de facto elite even if that elite denies its own existence. This occurred historically with social-democracy. Similarly, while democratic centralism has operated successfully in various vanguard organizations, the prevailing reality—particularly in Russia following the revolution—emphasized centralism at the cost of democracy. As the Bolsheviks consolidated their rule, after 1920 the democratic aspects of democratic centralism became increasingly mythical.

Diagramatically the vanguard theory of organization is represented in Figure 6.2.

The diagram illustrates the small vanguard party (A) which has created (solid-line arrows) intermediate organizations (B) and/or entered (dotted-line arrows) existing mass organizations (C) such as unions. The intermediate organizations may be "front groups" created for specific purposes, such as a defense committee, or they may be existing organizations with views akin to that of the vanguard organization. The peripheral mass organizations are groups that encompass large numbers of people whose activities, vanguard theorists contend, will move the membership toward a more radical critique of society. Members of the vanguard, in addition to being active within the party, will be active in peripheral mass organizations and intermediate organizations. Potential recruits in the mass organizations may be encouraged to participate in higher levels of activity involving greater commitment in the intermediate organizations. In the intermediate units people can be tested further and in closer relationships. The vanguard organization may create study groups as intermediate organizations to which potential recruits from the peripheral area may be recruited. The diagram also shows the internal organization within the vanguard party: this is hierarchical, with a top organization (generally a "central committee") elected by a national convention, directing the efforts of all subordinate local groups.

Figure 6.3 illustrates the mass-party form of organization.

The mass party (A), especially as reflected in the social-democratic reality of pre-World War I Europe, was viewed as the central political organization of the working class. The political organization is surrounded by a vast, complex, and interlocking set of organizations, some of whose members are also members of the political organization and may also hold membership in other associated organizations. The associated organizations include unions, cooperatives, and a complex host of voluntary and professional organizations. The relationship to the unions, one of the largest of the associated organizations, poses special problems since the dynamics of political organization and those of unions can be quite different. While not all members of an associated group belong to the central political organization, the leadership almost invariably does.

The associated organizations are viewed as devices that engage the energies of the

Figure 6.2 The Vanguard Theory of Organization

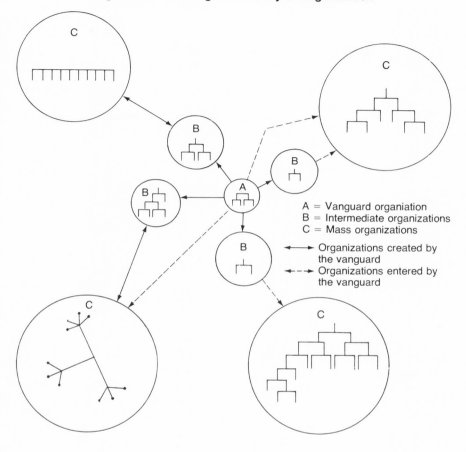

A = Vanguard organiation
B = Intermediate organizations
C = Mass organizations

←——→ Organizations created by the vanguard
←--→ Organizations entered by the vanguard

rank and file and continually gear them toward political action. The mass-party concept, therefore, is oriented to the idea of involving a great many people on a part-time basis according to their interests and inclinations, all the time drawing them toward political action and the political party.

Within the party and the associated organizations, hierarchy exists. This is the formal organizational hierarchy that actually dominates day-to-day life. In German social-democracy, the best example of the mass-party approach, important internal distinctions existed between the rank and file members, volunteer core activists (*vertrauensmänner*), and functionaries (full-time paid officials). The latter group was also divided between local, regional, and national officials with parliamentary representatives constituting a special group with unusually important influence.

* * *

Figure 6.3 The Mass-Party Theory of Organization

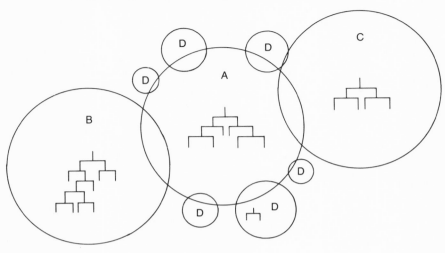

A = Mass party
B = Unions
C = Co-operatives
D = Adjunct, supportive, sympathetic organizations

The three basic organizational solutions that developed between 1860 and 1920 have undergone modifications in recent times. The upsurge of student activism in the 1960s saw a revival of anarchist forms; these were brought to dramatic attention during the student uprising in France in 1968. Forms of organization combining elements of mass-party and anarchist structures, although with significant variations, were represented in the 1960s in the Students for a Democratic Society (SDS) in the United States. The variations in these cases have been largely due to the relatively short life of these organizations; to develop the mature mass-party organization characterized by German social-democracy in the years before Hitler took power required decades.

Vanguard organization represents an important form of organization. Most modern leftist organizations emphasize their leadership role with respect to some mass of people; that is, they define themselves to some degree as vanguardist.

CHAPTER SEVEN

The Vanguard Theory
of Organization

Vanguard organization emerged in the context of Europe's most autocratic regime. With a police force that constituted 40 percent of state employees, Russia's social system, dominated by the czars, was highly undemocratic. Critics were liable to find themselves exiled for even moderate criticism of the regime. Parallel to this backwardness was the undeveloped state of the working class, still tiny and made up of people fresh from centuries of peasant experience. The bulk of the population consisted of peasants whose physical existence was brutal, still being close to their recent emancipation as serfs in 1861.

The vanguard theory of organization was formulated by Lenin as a result of intensive debates in the anticzarist movements of Russia at the turn of the century. During the last half of the 19th century, the earliest of the nonmarxist Russian revolutionaries went through two phases in seeking to overthrow czarism. Initially "going to the peasants" to convince them of the need for change, revolutionaries found themselves imprisoned or exiled to Siberia. In frustration they turned to terrorism. Despite many successful assassinations (and some important failures), terrorism failed to overthrow the despotic system.

A new phase of marxist revolutionary activism got underway just prior to the new century. Inspired by George Plekhanov, the new movement discovered the urban working class when strikes and other protests developed in Russia's industrial centers. This provided revolutionaries with a new social focus toward the proletariat and directed them away from the peasantry. Much of Lenin's work was addressed to the various approaches of radicals in dealing with the working class and its reaction to exploitation.

The major intellectual tendency against which Lenin hurled his considerable polemical talents was known as Economism. The Economists were characterized by two distinct orientations:

1. The basis of revolutionary struggle emerges from the *experience* of the working class, not only from the general experience of working in a factory but also from the conditions encountered and from the desires of workers for specific solutions to specific grievances confronted daily in the work place. The Economists encouraged the development of trade unionism on the grounds that such organizations were best understood by workers and that workers would best be activated by them. By bringing workers into action against their employers, the Economists believed their level of consciousness would be raised and, at the same time, czarism would be undermined.

2. Rather than revolutionary forces organizing and propagating a program for the destruction of the czarist system, the Economists believed that protest must begin spontaneously among the workers and that they must develop their own organizations in their own way. Such organization is appropriate to the level of working-class understanding and development.

Lenin directed his polemic in *What Is to Be Done?* against both of these views. From his attack flows the theory of the organization of revolutionaries into a vanguard organization. This was to be a political organization of sophisticated revolutionary thinkers and activists capable of formulating criticism not only at the factory level but at all levels of czarist society.

Lenin began his attack on the Economists by identifying them with various Western European ideological streams oriented toward reform rather than revolution. These reformist ideas had been germinating in Western socialist thinking as capitalist social institutions had undergone change. Because suffrage as well as other concessions were extended to workers in Great Britain, France, and Germany, some prominent socialists such as Alexandre Millerand in France and Eduard Bernstein in Germany believed that capitalism could gradually be reformed into a socialist society. Lenin saw Economism as a Russian manifestation of reformism; he argued that reformism was not only inappropriate to the more democratic Western European situation but was impossible in the despotic circumstances of czarism.

Because many revolutionaries were working in independent and fragmented local groups, each seeking to encourage workers to develop their own organizations, much of Lenin's book was directed against spontaneity and localism. He attacked the disunity of the revolutionary movement and its lack of theory. He urged all revolutionaries to combine into a single, central political organization that would turn its attention to the central issue of fighting czarism. An organized, unified party would end the predominence of isolated and individualized activities and shift the focus of revolutionary work to the national level. Instead of encouraging demands aimed at the individual factory, these should be raised to a systematic and determined struggle, and organized propaganda should be carried out. Such an organization should be ready to support every protest but would use every working-class outbreak "to build up and consolidate the fighting forces suitable for the decisive struggle."

The revolutionary organization must be composed of skilled revolutionaries. Lenin felt it was the lack of such skilled people that caused the movement to continually break down. He made a basic distinction between "professional revolutionaries" and those who engage in revolutionary activities on occasion. He viewed revolution-making as serious business, to be approached on a full-time basis. While other activists are important to a movement, they are more spontaneous and less conscious and therefore do not belong in a vanguard organization. This analysis followed not only from the autocratic character of czarism but also from the high illiteracy and lack of organizational experience of Russia's workers, most of whom were fresh from a backward peasantry.

The need for strict selection of party members stemmed from Lenin's premise that there could never be an automatic overthrow of the capitalist order. Despite his adherence to Marx's theory about the generation of a class-conscious proletariat, Lenin believed that a socialist revolution is the product of years of difficult struggle. Furthermore, he did not believe that there would be gradual disintegration of capitalism through reform and the slow, accretive growth of socialism. His thinking, therefore, represented a distinct break with the mechanistic determinism that characterized most of the international socialist movement of the time.

Proletarian revolution requires a maturity of both "objective" and "subjective" factors. Objective factors consist of phenomena such as economic crises, wars, and depressions. Subjective factors include the state of consciousness of the proletariat. The most important subjective factor is the achievement by the proletariat of *political* class consciousness, to be distinguished from *union* consciousness. Union consciousness leads the workers to deal only with their immediate employer; they learn to sell their labor on terms more favorable to themselves. But such consciousness does not make them aware that the exploitative relationship between employers and workers can be overturned.

The realization of the need for the new and nonexploitative social relationships implicit in socialism can only come from political class consciousness. This higher consciousness is not an automatic result of the proletarian class struggle. Whereas union consciousness develops from the conditions in which workers find themselves, socialist consciousness develops "only on the basis of profound scientific knowledge."

According to leninism, the highest form of proletarian class consciousness is represented by marxian socialism, a full understanding of which requires knowledge of history, philosophy, and economics. Such knowledge cannot normally be obtained while working in a factory, although Lenin stressed the importance of applying such knowledge to the specific problems of the working class. Since marxian science is not generally available to the proletariat, "socialist consciousness is something introduced into the proletarian class struggle from without, and not something that arose within it spontaneously."

Thus, one major task of the vanguard party is to provide revolutionary theory for the masses of workers. This places on members of the vanguard party the responsibility to command socialist theory, to be "theoreticians." It was for this reason that Lenin attacked proposals to open membership in the party to anyone who engaged in revolutionary work or accepted the party's program. To open membership in this way would open the party "to vagueness and vacillation." Lenin insisted that vague membership introduced a disorganizing idea into the party; it confused class and party, and "precisely because there are differences in degree of consciousness and activity, a distinction must be made in degree of proximity to the Party." Lenin feared that the party would become a "tail ender" instead of leading the working class, and lower itself to the level of mere strike making. In addition, with loose membership, party members would be more prone to form local groups on their own and redirect the emphasis from all-Russian (nationwide) activities to local work. This would weaken the authority of higher party bodies. "Now we have become an organized party, and this implies the establishment of authority . . . The subordination of lower party bodies to higher ones."

Lenin held that membership in the party must be restricted: it must require a full-time commitment to revolution-making. The party should consist of intellectuals and those whom the workers "produce from their ranks . . . who desire to protest, who are ready to render all the assistance they can in the struggle against absolutism . . ." Trained by the core of revolutionary intellectuals to understand socialist theory, the new recruits of workers and intellectuals would constitutue a cadre of revolutionaries capable of determining day-to-day tactics and of leading the proletariat on the basis of these tactics.

One important concept formulated by Lenin was that of secrecy. Because czarism did not tolerate even moderate criticism, let alone a revolutionary attack, secrecy was necessary to the functioning of the vanguard. Out of this necessity developed small clandestine organizations, "cells," each with limited knowledge of the membership and actions of other cells. Party organization was to be based on a hierarchy of cells, with each local cell represented by a member in the cell at the next level up. Each member of a higher body was to be known only within their own cell, making it difficult to discover the network of organization within the party. This basic cell organization has since served as a pattern of secretive organization in countless circumstances.

Lenin felt this organizational form had great advantages since it ensured the unity and centralization of the party. He recognized the powerful, centralizing influence that capitalism exerted on society. If such a society was to be destroyed, then strong, central organization was crucial. Hence, the Central Committee, the highest cell in the party, would be the "supreme institution," and all major decisions would flow from the top downward.

This did not mean that the party would be undemocratic in a centralized movement: this problem was resolved through the principle of *democratic centralism*. This operated, in theory, on two bases:

1. Complete internal democracy during a discussion period on any issue under review.
2. Once a decision is reached, the minority submits to the majority and all members express the view of the majority.

Lenin's orientation toward the character of the revolutionary party and other issues precipitated a split in the Russian Social-Democratic Party between Lenin's group, which took the name *Bolsheviks* (meaning "majority") and the opposition, which became known as the *Mensheviks* (meaning "minority"). The Mensheviks strongly objected to Lenin's orientations toward centralization. They accused Lenin of being authoritarian and undemocratic, of leanings toward bureaucratism, and criticized his notion of having all important decisions come from the center.

Lenin responded by charging that the Mensheviks were "perverting 'the democratic principle' into anarchism" for "Democracy does not mean the absence of authority . . . if there is any democratic principle, it is that the majority must have predominance over the minority . . ." Lenin contended: "In its struggle for power the proletariat has no other weapon but organization," and "unity of organization . . . is inconceivable without formal rules, without the subordination of the minority to the majority and of the part to the whole."

Tendencies toward centralism rather than democracy became a product of the conditions under which the Russian socialists operated. Because communication was not easy between the party's center and the members spread all over Russia, the center made most decisions. These were transmitted through an illegal press and a clandestine organizational apparatus. The effect, however, was to emphasize decision-making at the center rather than democratic debate among the members.

The centralized and secretive organization conceived by Lenin was contrasted by him to other workers' organizations such as unions. While unions must be supported by social-democrats their membership should not be restricted to revolutionaries. Every worker who understood the need to fight the employer would be able to join a union. The very objects of unionism were unattainable without a wide membership.

But in this respect of wide membership, unions were distinct from the vanguard party that bore the crucial responsibility for leadership. Lenin rejected the idea of appealing to the "crowd" for the best methods of fighting the czarist police and troops; such appeals dragged the movement backward organizationally. Arguing against the notion that "it is a bad business when the movement does not proceed from the rank and file," Lenin contended:

> . . . without the "dozen" tried and talented leaders (and talented men are not born by the hundreds), professionally trained, schooled by long experience, and working in perfect harmony, no class in modern society can wage a determined struggle.

These leaders will guide the spontaneous movements of the masses of workers. Their leadership is critical; while mass spontaneous action is capable of much, it cannot develop, in the course of the struggle, a program for socialist revolution or bring about sufficient centralization of power to overthrow the czarist state.

For Lenin, no revolutionary movement could be durable without a stable leadership to maintain continuity, gain experience, and direct the energies of the masses. The more widely the masses are brought into the movement against the czarist state, the greater the necessity for such organization, and the greater the need for stability of leadership. Lenin pointed out, for example, that it was easy for a demagogue to sidetrack the more backward elements among the people. He asserted that the existence of a stable organization would increase "the number of people from the working class . . . able to join the movement and perform active work in it."

The centralization of the secret functions of the organization did not mean that all the functions of the movement would be centralized or that the participation of the workers would decrease.

. . . there can be no talk of throwing anyone overboard in the sense of preventing them from working, from taking part in the movement. On the contrary, the stronger our Party organizations, consisting of *real* Social-Democrats, the less wavering and instability there is *within* the Party, the broader, more varied, richer, and more fruitful will be the Party's influence on the elements of the working class *masses* surrounding it and guided by it.

Through wide membership in "loose" and "public" organizations, Lenin contended that the workers would advance many from their ranks for revolutionary activities. Indeed, it was expected that, in time and with experience, the bulk of the party would come from the working class as workers developed their capabilities as revolutionary theoreticians under the tutelage of the party. But without a centralized party to organize extensive work, such people could not be utilized.

A centralized party can support full-time revolutionaries, freeing them from normal employment to engage in day-to-day political work. These revolutionaries, "boundlessly devoted" to the revolution, would enjoy the "boundless confidence of the widest masses of the workers." This would make it even more difficult for the police to destroy the movement. A strong party would give "firmness" to the movement, prevent the possibility of premature actions to overthrow czarism, and pick opportune moments for such revolutionary activities, thereby conserving revolutionary energies.

Thus, the proletariat would achieve the socialist revolution "through its ideological unification on the principles of marxism being reinforced by the material unity of organization."

*   *   *

Lenin gave flesh to the skeleton of his ideas in the years after writing *What Is to Be Done?* By the time of the March 1917 revolution, a revolution that, incidentally, was largely spontaneous, the Bolsheviks had become a tightly organized group capable of speedy decisions. Under Lenin's direction, they emerged as the preeminent political group and seized power, through the soviets (councils), in November 1917. In the years during which Bolshevik control was consolidated, the Communist Party (as it was soon renamed) went through a process in which it repressed opposition groups within and outside of the party. After Lenin's death, this process accelerated. Lenin's successor to party leadership, Joseph Stalin, used the emphasis on unity, discipline, and centralization to establish a rigid, encompassing control over the party. Eliminating all factions and opposition, Stalin superintended the physical destruction of oppositionist elements (including many of his supporters) in the 1930s. The critics of the vanguard approach argued that this was but the logical extension of the leninist vanguard idea. Its supporters countered with arguments that the historical conditions in Russia, such as the underdeveloped economy, the "backward" proletariat and the encirclement by hostile capitalism, led to the excesses of Stalin's rule.

While a heated controversy was generated by Lenin's theory of organization, this basic pattern was subsequently exported to a wide variety of countries and circumstances. Even in Lenin's lifetime, he argued for the applicability of the vanguardist approach under many different conditions — even in conditions where relative openness and democratic procedures existed. And while the pattern was adopted by vanguardists throughout the world, its next major achievement in a successful revolution occurred in China. The form has been used, however, in a great many other circumstances.

The vanguard approach laid down by Lenin has remained unchanged in these other countries and in its various applications. As we shall see, marxists such as Mao Zedong have elaborated aspects of the vanguard notion in the actual act of taking power. These extensions of the vanguard idea are more concerned, however, with the way in which the party relates to the masses in the actual process of taking power. Accordingly, Mao's developments will be discussed in Chapters 11 and 15.

CHAPTER EIGHT

Mass-Party Organization

Setting out a theory of mass-party organization is far more difficult than is the case with vanguard theory. With the exception of Rosa Luxemburg, who dealt specifically with mass-party organization in her attack on the vanguard notion, theories of the mass party took the form of attacks on specific abuses rather than positive statements as to the advantages of this form of organization.

Accordingly, the description of mass-party theory must be based primarily on abstraction from reality, particularly the reality of the German Social-Democratic Party. We may use it as a model of the mass-party idea because it was the envy of most social-democratic and socialist parties that, like the German organization, were members of the Second International formed in 1889. Even Lenin acknowledged the powerful organization of the working class that had developed in Germany. And, as a model, we can compare the degree to which other social-democratic parties failed to live up to the organizational manifestation of German social-democracy.

This chapter begins by discussing some of the major theoretical implications of the mass-party approach. It then turns to an examination of the German and American examples. Finally, it ends with the theoretical statements of Rosa Luxemburg.

The Contradictions of Mass-Party Organization

Just as vanguard organization confronts a dialectical contradiction — a pull in conflicting directions — between centralism and democracy, the mass party confronts a different but equally difficult set of contradictions. On the one hand, the strain toward *massness* imposes on the mass party the need for continual growth. On the other, growth imposes limits on the degree to which the mass party can remain revolutionary. In other words, how can an organization remain revolutionary if an attempt is made to bring everyone into the party?

For mass-party organizers, membership is as central a problem as it is for vanguard theorists. The difference lies in the open quality of membership, in contrast to the narrow definition held by the vanguardists. If a mass party is to avoid becoming a narrow political sect, it must establish a broad set of political principles. It must, in addition, accept a relatively broad range of views within the organization and practice a high degree of internal democracy. The central value that emerges is thus less concerned with ideological clarity or correctness and more with organizational unity. Unity, however, has often been obtained less through the "correctness" of a set of political views than through political horse-trading — compromising — within the party. As compromises take place, the tendency has been to dilute the revolutionary program.

A second and related problem exists with respect to the development of leadership in the mass party. Leadership is conceived as being representative of the views of the members; the general membership is seen as the sovereign body which expresses its will through majority rule. The mass party is considered to be "advanced" in relationship to the proletariat only until, at the moment it takes power, it is indistinguishable from the proletariat since it encompasses that class. Leadership, therefore, serves a representative function in which the leaders are conceived as embodying the will of the membership. This contrasts with the vanguard theory in which the leadership is seen as being more advanced and theoretically sophisticated than the membership.

The very success of mass-party organization creates a third problem, the contradiction between accomplishments obtained through reforms and the revolutionary process. A mass party that is successful in building membership has tendencies to become very protective of its gains; it prefers not to risk what it has achieved. It accumulates not only real property but extensive "social property" in the form of the positions held by officials and the influence that the party wields in day-to-day affairs. The definition of "success" tends to shift from the degree to which the party can produce revolutionary transformation to the inventorying of the change in the material circumstances of the party and its constituency. Instead of asking "Have we made our revolution?" the party says "Isn't it impressive that the transport workers have just won a 6 percent wage increase?" As the party and its constituency improve their material conditions, they may become less willing to risk everything in a single cataclysmic revolution. "What if we lose?" ask party officials, as they recommend a more prudent course. The thought of jeopardizing their hard-fought achievements in a direct clash for power has a tendency to become traumatic — indeed, after time, inconceivable. Thus, success in the form of gradual improvement can become an end in itself and can end up limited to rhetorical expressions on ritual occasions such as May Day.

For those who accept the validity and possibilities of reformism, there is little objection to the mass-party approach. Revolutionaries, however, who argue against the possibilities of reforming capitalism must come to grips with the contradictions in the same way that vanguardists must deal with the problems of centralism versus democracy.

Before turning to German Social-Democracy as the model of the mass party, we should summarize the salient characteristics of the mass party:

- Emphasis on the political party as the central focus of revolutionary organization

- Establishment of a network of auxiliary, supportive, economic and social organizations around the central political organization
- Establishment of a broad political program rather than one which narrowly directs the work of its members
- Relatively open membership with broad agreement with the party's program sufficing to fulfill membershp criteria
- Greater central control than anarchist organization; greater emphasis on local autonomy than vanguard organization
- Encouragement of broad initiatives and wide-scale involvement in action rather than in the setting of strategies by elite committees

The German Social-Democratic Party

In 1912 the German Social-Democratic Party and the auxiliary organizations of which it was the centerpiece elicited the admiration of organized socialists throughout the world. The party, with a membership slightly under one million, had just won 28 percent of the seats in the national legislature, making it the largest single party with the support of 34 percent of the electorate. The breadth of party support in Germany is indicated by the seats it held in various other legislative bodies: 220 in the state legislatures, 2,800 in city parliaments and councils, and over 9,000 in rural communities. The prowess of the German working class stood as the model, the paragon of socialist organizational virtue. Class and party were believed by many, inside and outside Germany, to stand closest to achieving socialist power. The organization, however, was to take an increasingly conservative direction rather than continuing the revolutionary traditions with which the party had begun. But the organizational power was so considerable that the party would survive its long journey through a major split occasioned by Germany's entry into World War I and its destruction for over a decade during the Nazi era. Despite this, the party was reconstructed after the Second World War and still maintains a large working-class base.

The transformation from a revolutionary to a reformist orientation occurred over several decades. When the party was formed in 1875, it was sufficiently revolutionary to have won the approval of Friedrich Engels, Marx's collaborator and the defender of Marx's legacy. Almost immediately, because of its growing strength, it had to confront the carrot-and-stick competition of the prime minister, Otto von Bismarck. The carrot took the form of social legislation providing protection for workers, intended to "steal the socialists' thunder." The stick took the form of outlawing the party. While the party was to remain illegal for twelve years, it met this challenge not through illegal organization but through evasive action. Although socialists could not have a party, they could be elected to parliament. The organizational solution was ingenious: a skeleton party was maintained in Switzerland while the supporters of social-democracy moved into a host of nonpolitical organizations. In Switzerland, the party published a newspaper that it smuggled into Germany; it also held occasional conferences. But the real day-to-day building of the movement occurred in the thousands of ostensibly nonpolitical unions, clubs, and organizations. During the period of 1878–90, despite its illegal character, German social-democracy increased its share of the total vote from 7.5 percent (1878) to 19.7 percent (1890).

The party in 1912 was the product of a long process of organization-building, ideology-formation, and the establishment of habits of compromise. Organizationally, this was manifested not only in the size of the party—its vote and its parliamentary delegation—but in a host of other regional and local political bodies. Party members were represented by the hundreds in provincial legislatures, city councils, and other governmental organizations. Outside the political arena, the party's auxiliary organizations involved the energies of millions. It operated kindergartens and experimental schools; its youth was organized in a myriad of organizations from boy-scout-type groups to nature lovers. Its hikers sang socialist songs as they tramped the mountains. Its chorale groups, singing societies, and musical organizations gave thousands of performances for movement organizations. With insurance funds for workers, death benefits, and other forms of social welfare, its unions could boast of taking care of members from cradle to grave. And there was much more. There were Esperanto associations where social-democrats could discuss socialist theory in what they believed to be the new universal language. Socialist vegetarians gathered to support each other in non-meat eating. Social-democratic teetotalers campaigned against alcohol—without the militancy of Carrie Nation but with a lot more socialism. The complexity of the network of auxiliary organizations sometimes led many—German social-democrats, their admirers, and their detractors—to think of the movement as a "state within a state."

The value of these organizations to social-democracy, once Bismarck's laws were eliminated in 1890, was incalculable. Not only did they provide a wide-ranging network, but they established the trust that develops only when people engage in long-term social relationships with each other. Moreover, they gave people the skills to operate formal bureaucratic organizations—factory workers and delivery boys could chair meetings, take minutes, or operate equipment. Such skills are a crucial feature in the development of a social movement; invariably, the earliest stage of working-class organization requires not only the development of leadership skills in a handful of people but the broad diffusion of abilities to the rank and file. A major success of Germany's mass party was that it had spread these skills to an unparalleled extent.

It is also important to realize the symbolic meaning which the party and its auxiliary organizations had for its members. The economic exploitation of developing capitalism had placed tremendous demands upon the German workers. Although workers had bettered their material conditions through their own institutions, many still found it difficult to pay party dues over and above their union dues. Whereas life before the party had been not only economically miserable, it had been socially empty as well. The German working class lived out its life in shoddy housing, with bare subsistence in food, and with no way of improving itself either economically or intellectually.

The German working-class movement changed much of this. Even if life was hardly a bowl of cherries economically, the biting edge of misery and insecurity had been broken. Despite the growing bureaucracy of the party and its size, members could find expression for their interests in almost every sphere of human life. The most ordinary person—not only the industrial worker, but housewives, maids, minor clerks in banks and offices, agricultural laborers—could not only express themselves but found appreciation of their expression from their peers.

What the movement provided, in human terms, was a sense of the ability of human beings to command their own existence rather than to be pawns of fate or to have some higher power resolve their problems for them. The movement gave those people whom society had defined as having little worth a sense of their own significance, importance, and social contribution.

The ideological development of the German movement accompanied its organizational growth. From early gropings of workers toward organization in the 1860s, Ferdinand Lassalle formed the Universal German Workingmen's Association in 1863. Lassalle's orientations, while socialist, were not marxian. At the same time, a group of marxists under the leadership of August Bebel and Wilhelm Liebknecht began to organize. After the unification of these two organizations in 1875, a clearer marxist and revolutionary perspective prevailed. The party explicitly directed its efforts toward the proletariat and conceived of its ultimate goal as a socialist revolution.

On its emergence from illegality in 1890, the party adopted both a minimal and a maximal program. The minimal program involved union and parliamentary action. The maximal goal was socialism and involved the socialist revolution. By having a dual approach, the party laid the groundwork for the emergence of reformism.

Reformism took the form of an attack on Marx's analysis of capitalism by Eduard Bernstein. Although he had worked closely with Engels and was his literary executor, Bernstein challenged the revolutionary views of Marx. His critique was based on the gradual loosening of the political situation in Germany, most notably the elimination of the antisocialist laws and the success of the movement in winning social legislation. The publication of Bernstein's *Evolutionary Socialism* in 1899 constituted the first major theoretical attack on the marxist assumptions of the party. Not only did Bernstein argue against Marx's theory of immiseration by indicating that the condition of the working class was not deteriorating, he also produced data to show that the middle class was not being proletarianized. Bernstein envisioned a gradual improvement of the conditions of the workers that would eventually lead to a socialist society.

Bernstein was answered by Rosa Luxemburg, who pointed to the continued existence of irresolvable contradictions in capitalism that blocked the gradual transition to socialism. The issue of reformism was ostensibly "settled" in a party congress in 1903 when reformism was condemned. Yet it soon became clear that the adoption of a resolution at a party meeting did not necessarily produce concomitant action: German social-democracy had moved into a situation of considerable radicalism in its rhetoric but reformism in its actual behavior. This tendency did not become clear until 1914, when the social-democratic deputies in the legislature voted for war appropriations.

The shift toward reformism in concrete behavior while adhering to revolutionary rhetoric is an interesting process. It develops out of concrete day-to-day problems. It is possible to see, in several key events in the development of German social-democracy, how the process got underway and developed its own dynamics.

- In 1880, despite having been driven underground by Bismarck, the party expelled Johann Most and Wilhelm Hasselmann for supporting terrorism. The party feared open support for terrorism would lead to even greater repression.

- Despite its skepticism about parliamentarism, with the repeal of the anti-socialist laws the party entered into serious parliamentary competition. Elections were seen as a way not only of electing representatives to the Reichstag but as a means to educate the people. But the creation of an electoral bloc enforced various compromises. The socialists felt the need at times to enter into electoral blocs with the liberals. The need to win a larger parliamentary representation therefore involved the socialists in regular relationshps with bourgeois parties.
- Terrible frustration developed in 1908 over Prussian suffrage. Under the German constitution Prussia dominated the legislature, but the system of Prussian suffrage was grossly weighted against the working-class vote. In the elections to the Prussian assembly in 1908, the social-democrats won six seats with a vote of 600,000. The conservatives continued to dominate the assembly with their 212 representatives who had been elected by 418,000 votes. This experience and the developments in the Russian revolution of 1905 led to a debate about the use of the mass or general strike to attain the political ends of equal suffrage. The union leadership opposed the mass strike idea and got the party to forgo the strike for fear that the government would seize their funds and that their reserves would be depleted in providing strike relief. This effectively surrendered an important strategic weapon.
- In 1912 the sheer electoral success of the socialists made them the largest single bloc of deputies in the Reichstag. Had they not participated in "normal" parliamentary activities but maintained an abstentionist stance, they would have paralyzed the work of parliament and thereby supported the reactionary bloc within the legislature. Socialists thus became engaged in day-to-day parliamentary business.
- In 1913 the socialists confronted a parliamentary crisis involving taxation. The socialists had always abstained in the vote on budgets on the grounds that these were instrumentalities to maintain the bourgeois government. When the government wanted an increase in the army in 1913, the socialists voted against the increase. But on the issue of how to raise the taxes to pay for the increase, the socialists were confronted by the dilemma of voting for more progressive direct taxes as against the indirect taxes that would have fallen more heavily on the working class. The socialists voted for the more progressive taxes but, in the process, found themselves supporting the increased military allocations.

These and other compromises reinforced the increasingly conservative stance of German social-democracy. By 1914 compromise had become so routine that the leadership was unable to live up to its long-standing commitment to oppose war. Under the pressures of German nationalism—just as the French and most other socialists were doing in their own countries—the overwhelming majority of parliamentary delegates voted in favor of war credits. Only fourteen out of more than one-hundred socialist members of parliament violated party discipline to maintain the principle of international working-class solidarity. The war vote of the German socialists was, in its time, as great a shock to the working-class movement as Watergate was to the United States in the 1970s. With this action, the reformist character of German social-democracy became clearly established. Subsequently, revolutionary tendencies were to move outside of the party.

*   *   *

In the pre-World War I period of growth of the mass social-democratic movements, German social-democracy constituted the strongest and most powerfully organized group. In other European countries and in the United States, the movement was weaker. In France the political party was distinctly separate from the unions, where anarchist tendencies remained powerful. The party was not so tightly organized as in Germany, having suffered a considerable number of splits. In Great Britain, the Labor Party emerged as a product of the unions, with the party membership taken essentially from the union membership. Less subject to divisiveness than the French, the British party reflected a view of the world through the perspective of unionism. The Labor Party tended to be heavily reformist and its theoretical work, of which there was not a great deal, was concerned largely with the justification of the reformist approach to change.

The Socialist Party of the United States

The American Socialist Party between 1900 and 1919 was the most successful mass socialist party in American history. At its peak in 1912, just before the First World War, Eugene Victor Debs, the socialist candidate for president, polled 897,000 votes, about 6 percent of the total vote. While small compared to the Germans, the 118,000 members of the Socialist Party in 1912 were spread throughout the country. Several socialists were elected to Congress and many to the state legislatures. In 1911 the party elected mayors in seventy-three cities and towns in twenty-four states, as well as 1,200 lesser officials in 340 cities and towns. During this period socialist mayors were elected in medium-sized cities such as Milwaukee, Minneapolis, Berkeley, Flint, and Butte, Montana.

The Socialist Party's (SP) considerable popular support during this period was possible because of the breadth of views encompassed within its peculiarly American perspective. Socialists saw the American revolutionary movement as forming a series of concentric circles. In the outer circle were people who experienced some vague kind of radicalism, a dissatisfaction with existing social, political, and economic arrangements. Closer in were the people who had consciously come to accept socialism as representing the future and who regularly voted for socialist candidates. The heart of the movement was composed of the members of the Socialist Party who worked with the many nonmarxist radicals—populists, currency and agrarian reformers, single-taxers, and others—and sought to bring them toward a more conscious socialism.

This view was not a vanguard view, however, since the SP encompassed broadly different groups. These included groups such as the "constructivist" Milwaukee socialists (whose "step-at-a-time" politics were based on their belief that by electing socialists to public office, the United States would gradually be changed from capitalist to socialist) and the Industrial Workers of the World—IWW—(who supported militant class struggle in the work place). In addition, there were various ex-populists, Christian socialists, and revolutionary marxists in the organization, as well as a sizable number of anarchists and syndicalists.

The wide divergence of views can best be seen in the various approaches that SP members had to the unions. The basis of divergence involved several distinct issues: the question of industrial unionism (as against craft unionism) and the conservatism of the only large-scale trade union confederation in America, the American Federation of Labor (AFL). Not only was the AFL conservative in its views about society but it was distinctly unenthusiastic about the development of industrial unions for semiskilled workers.

All socialists agreed on the need for industrial unionism; indeed, there were some industrial unions within the AFL and these were often led by socialists. But there was wide disagreement on how the party should relate to the AFL. The "constructivists" favored remaining in the AFL to influence developments organizationally within the mainstream of labor. To Debs and others, this was anathema: "To kowtow to [the AFL] and to join hands with its leaders to secure political favors can only result in compromising our principles and bringing disaster to our party." It would be "as useless as to spray a cesspool with attar of roses." Debs favored the establishment of industrial unionism and therefore supported the Industrial Workers of the World when that organization was formed. Another important supporter of the IWW inside the SP was "Big Bill" Haywood, an important figure in organizing western miners. After the IWW was organized in 1905, Debs continued to support it for some time. Proceding through a series of splits, Debs broke with the organization but continued to support the idea of industrial unionism. The IWW soon moved in syndicalist directions, rejecting electoral work and emphasizing the need for economic organization to overcome the exploitative capitalist system. Their syndicalism as well as their policies of organizing *against* the AFL estranged them from other socialist supporters of industrial unionism such as Debs. Haywood and the other syndicalist-oriented people eventually left the Socialist Party to focus their work in the IWW.

There had to be a very loose party constitution to keep such wide divergence of views together under a single organizational roof. This had been created at the founding conference in 1901, which gave the state organizations considerable autonomy. The constitution provided that:

> . . . the state or territorial organization shall have the sole jurisdiction of the members residing within their respective territories, and the sole control of all matters pertaining to the propaganda, organization, and financial affairs within such states or territory.

Although a National Committee had been created, it was prohibited from interfering in matters affecting a local organization without their consent. The power of the National Committee was also limited by making all their actions subject to national party referenda.

The problems with this decentralized form of organization soon became clear. Not only were different — and contradictory — positions taken by the various state units, but state leaders became excessively concerned with their own problems to the detriment of national cooperation. Under a new constitution adopted in 1904, a new National Committee was created. This committee elected a National Executive Committee of seven members to operate the national office. A National Secretary was also elected by the convention to handle national lectures and literature. This secretary could deal with local branches but the state organizations would retain power within their states.

With a constitutional amendment in 1905 that changed the National Executive Committee to a body elected by national referendum, growing bureaucratization of the party began. Though intended to be an arm of the National Committee, the National Executive Committee soon acquired the National Committee's powers to dispatch organizers around the country, allocate funds, grant charters, etc.

The functioning of socialist newspapers provides a good example of the party's diversity. There was no official paper for the entire party until 1914. Before then there were a large number of privately owned national and local newspapers and magazines. These produced a wide range of views from simple muckraking or vaguely socialist manifestos to the most biting of marxian criticism. The breadth of expression through the press contributed enormously to the widespread appeal of the party. Members and sympathizers could subscribe to whatever publication suited their political inclinations. Membership, which was locally based, called for little adherence to a single ideological viewpoint.

At the national level, there was considerable factional fighting and organization. The most influential member of the party, Eugene Victor Debs, refrained from taking part in the faction fights and refused to run for party office.

> I confess to a prejudice against officialism and a dread of bureaucracy. I am a thorough believer in the rank and file, and in *ruling* from the *bottom up* instead of *being ruled* from the *top down*. The natural tendency of officials is to become bosses. They come to imagine that they are indispensable and unconsciously shape their acts to keep themselves in office.
>
> The officials of the Socialist Party should be its servants, and all temptations to yield to the baleful influence of officialism should be removed by constitutional limitation of tenure.

Like Rosa Luxemburg, Debs placed great faith in the working class. He wanted the workers to join and run the party.

> The Socialist Party is the party of the workers, organized to express in political terms their determination to break their fetters and rise to the dignity of free men. In this party the workers must unite and develop their political power to conquer and abolish the capitalist political state and clear the way for industrial and social democracy.

The decentralization of the press and Debs's antielitism, however, had the opposite result of what they were intended to accomplish. Party elections were often won by the most well known national figures.

Despite factional struggles that racked the organization, there was, until American entry into World War I, a general unity of purpose. All groups shared a basic commitment to the need for change and the formation of a socialist society. There was considerable adaptiveness to changing circumstances and most groups were able to adapt their tactics to these changes. A split occurred in 1912–13 when Bill Haywood was recalled from the National Executive Committee for advocating sabotage. The antisabotage clause had been added to the party's constitution in 1912 because many party members feared that excessively militant rhetoric would harm the party's efforts to organize. Although membership fell off temporarily, by the start of World War I in 1914 membership had risen close to its former strength. American involvement in the war was much more harmful. The party remained large despite its opposition to the conflict which led to severe government repression during and after the war. However, the composition of the membership changed. Many native-born members left the party and were replaced by new immigrants from Europe. The party never recovered its base among nonimmigrants. It was only after large segments of the party split in 1919 in the debate on the prospects for revolution in the United States — a split that reflected the influence of the Bolshevik revolution — that the Socialist Party became a small group with little political influence outside of a handful of cities and unions in the United States.

The Mass Party as Revolutionary:
Rosa Luxemburg on Organization

Her life brutally cut short when she was assassinated in 1919 by reactionary German thugs, Rosa Luxemburg recently became influential again among revolutionary theorists, particularly because of the affinity of many of her ideas with those of the New Left. A Polish Jew by origin, she was active in the socialist movements of Russia, Poland, and Germany, making her major contributions to the German movement. This universalism was deliberate since Luxemburg sought to implement the internationalist aspects of socialist thinking through her personal involvements.

Her attack on Lenin's theory of organization was not undertaken as an "outsider," a non-Russian, but as someone who had been active in the Russian social-democratic movement for many years. Nor did her criticism represent a right-wing view since Luxemburg had already established a reputation in the ideological battle against reformism.

The basis of Luxemberg's critique of Lenin's theory of organization is the same as the criticism she made of most of the major parties of European social-democracy. She criticized the "mechanical-bureaucratic" tendencies of the German party as strongly as she criticized Lenin's "ultracentralism." Her critique of both rested on her profound belief in the ability of the working class to think and act for themselves. Luxemburg saw the tasks of leadership as limited. They were:

> . . . to give the cue for and the direction to the fight; to so regulate the tactics of the political struggle in its every phase and at its every moment that the entire sum of the available power of the proletariat which is already released and active will find expression in the battle array of the party; to see that the tactics of the Social-Democrats are decided according to their resoluteness and acuteness, and that they never fall below the level demanded by the actual relations of forces, but rather rise above it.

Luxemburg's major analysis of leninist organization was contained in an article written in 1904, "Organizational Questions of Russian Social-Democracy." She agreed with Lenin that the existing organizational setup in Russia was "unbearable and politically out of date" and that a "unitary, compact labor party for the entire empire" must be built. Yet she felt that the degree of centralism proposed by Lenin would have a disastrous effect on the emerging socialist movement in Russia.

Far from requiring centralism in Russian conditions, Luxemburg believed that such conditions required greater flexibility and experimentation. Because the movement was young, the subordination of all local party organizations to a central power would destroy initiative and experimentation. Luxemburg felt that Russian social-democracy's most important and fruitful tactical developments had been the products of spontaneous actions by the movement rather than the inventions of leaders or central committees.

While Luxemburg shared Lenin's opposition to the revisionists, she felt his organizational plan would have effects opposite to what he wanted: centralism would increase the power of "bourgeois intellectuals" since the working class had yet to learn through experimentation.

> Nothing will deliver a still young labor movement to the intellectuals' thirst for power more easily than confining it in the straitjacket of a bureaucratic centralism which degrades the worker to a pliant tool of a "committee." And, on the other hand, nothing so surely protects the labor movement from an ambitious intelligentsia as the independent revolutionary action of the working class, as the increasing of their feeling of political responsibility.

Far from such dependence upon intellectuals, Luxemburg argued that the working class had the "right to make its own mistakes."

> We must frankly admit to ourselves that errors made by a truly revolutionary labor movement are historically infinitely more fruitful and more valuable than the infallibility of the best of all possible "central committees."

The difference between Luxemburg and Lenin can be seen in the orientations of the two to the idea of discipline. Lenin had argued in *What Is to Be Done?* about the beneficial effects of factory life on the working class, contending that factory discipline made the proletariat ripe for party discipline. Luxemburg responded in withering terms:

> The "discipline" which Lenin has in mind is implanted in the proletariat not only by the factory but also by the barracks, by modern bureaucratism — in short, by the whole mechanism of the centralized bourgeois state. It is nothing but an incorrect use of the word when at one time one designates as "discipline" two so opposed concepts as the absence of thought and will in a mass of flesh with many arms and legs moving mechanically, and the voluntary coordination of conscious political acts by a social stratum. There is nothing common to the corpselike obedience of a dominated class and the organized rebellion of a class struggling for its liberation. [It is only by breaking up and] uprooting this slavish spirit of discipline that the proletarian can be educated for the new discipline, for the voluntary self-discipline of Social-Democracy.

Luxemburg's scorn was not reserved solely for Lenin's centralized party; she saw much of the same process taking place with German social-democracy. She felt that the German Social-Democratic Party and the unions had grown increasingly stodgy as a result of their emphasis on parliamentarianism and unionism, rather than on direct mass action. They overestimated the importance of the organization, viewing it as an end in itself.

Luxemburg saw that this bureaucratization had the tendency to put union and party affairs increasingly in the hands of professional specialists. In addition, the relation between the leadership and the rank and file was becoming one where initiative and the power of making decisions was reserved for the party elite while the more passive virtue of discipline was kept for the masses.

Luxemburg's fears concerning centralization applied to the leninist conception of organization as well as the German mass party. Luxemburg believed that the determination of tactics could not be "invented" by a social-democratic leadership because tactical policy was "the product of a progressive series of great creative acts in the often rudimentary experiments of the class struggle."

This implicit belief in the spontaneity of the masses became explicit as the Russian revolution of 1905 unfolded. In her pamphlet "The Mass Strike, The Political Party, and The Trade Unions," Luxemburg analyzed these unprecedented events in which backward Russia — expected by socialists everywhere to be the last country in Europe to develop a revolutionary movement — surprised the western world. Luxemburg realized that the mass strike represented an entire period of class struggles, not just a single act. The workers in Russia had reacted spontaneously to a series of events. Spontaneity was important because in each individual act such a wide variety of elements was involved that "no single act [could] be arranged and resolved as if it were a mathematical problem." While attempts by the leadership to get the workers to strike at particular times proved ineffective, the workers often surprised the leadership by calling strikes when they were not expected.

Luxemburg consequently felt that if an era of great political struggle began in Germany, the proletariat might have to carry the load by itself. It would not matter what the party or union leadership did:

> Whether they stand aside or endeavor to resist the movement, the result of their attitude will only be that the trade union leaders, like the party leaders in an analogous case, will simply be swept aside by the rush of events, and the economic and the political struggles of the masses will be fought out without them.

Contrasting the movements in Russia with those in Western Europe, Luxemburg saw that "the class instinct of the youngest, least trained, badly educated and still worse organized Russian proletariat is immeasurably stronger than that of the organized, trained, and enlightened working class of Germany or of any other Western European country." She concluded that "a year of revolution has therefore given the Russian proletariat that 'training' which thirty years of parliamentary and trade union struggle cannot artificially give to the German proletariat."

Despite her sharp criticism of the increasing bureaucratization of the German Social-Democratic Party, Luxemburg remained a believer in the mass party. She felt that the German party was the "model organization of the proletariat" for the entire international socialist movement. She tried to use the party program and structure to expel revisionists like Bernstein. In fact, she favored "a more rigorous application of the idea of centralism in the constitution and a stricter application of party discipline" as a means of struggling against opportunism within the German party.

Only after the German Social-Democratic Party voted in favor of war credits in 1914 did Luxemburg split from the party. She was one of the leaders of the Spartacus

League (the forerunner of the German Communist Party) when it was formed in 1916. Her organizational principles were made clear in this description of the League in late 1918, less than three weeks before she was assassinated:

> The Spartacus League is not a party that wants to rise to power over the mass of workers or through them. The Spartacus League is only the most conscious, purposeful part of the proletariat, which points the entire broad mass of the working class toward its historical tasks at every step, which represents in each particular stage of the Revolution the ultimate socialist goal, and in all national questions the interests of the proletarian world revolution . . . The Spartacus League will never take over governmental power except in response to the clear, unambiguous will of the great majority of the proletarian mass of all of Germany, never except by the proletariat's conscious affirmation of the views, aims, and methods of struggle of the Spartacus League . . .

> The victory of the Spartacus League comes not at the beginning, but at the end of the Revolution: it is identical with the victory of the great million-strong masses of the socialist proletariat.

CHAPTER NINE

The Anarchist Theory of Organization

It seems almost an anomaly to speak of anarchism in a section treating revolutionary forms of organization, since anarchism's reputation is antiorganizational. This is testimony to the extent to which anarchy must be rescued from the slanders of its opponents, left and right. No doubt anarchy has its strict individualists to whom *any* form of social organization or even coordination is anathema,* but the largest segment of the various anarchist movements and thinkers have been outspoken in their support for active organization among revolutionaries and the proletariat. Anarchists are not opposed to organization, per se, but against compulsory, hierarchical, or authoritarian forms of organization.

The anarchist theory of organization is based on a belief that organization must develop from the bottom up, not from the top down. Anarchists argue that such organization is not only feasible but has been accomplished in many large-scale social forms, pointing to the international postal system and the Swiss Confederation as examples. For anarchists, successful organization must be:

- *Voluntarily* accepted by participants; not imposed by some authority
- *Functional*; it must perform some definite and specific activity
- *Temporary*; it exists only to the extent that it performs functions, otherwise it should disappear
- *Small*; preferably on a face-to-face basis, at which level most problems can reasonably and intelligently be worked out

*Irving Louis Horowitz (1964) in his introduction to *The Anarchists* sets forth a useful typology of anarchist strategies and beliefs. Our treatment of anarchist theories of organization is not concerned with those forms of anarchism *self-consciously* calling for return to the feudal order or basing themselves upon notions of the individual who is "above" social being. The former is reactionary; the latter bourgeois. We are, instead, concerned with revolutionary anarchists who base their programs on an understanding of the class divisions within the capitalist order, however they plan to overthrow that order.

93

- *Locally autonomous*; each organizational unit should be independent of others. Necessary coordination and integration should take place without the surrender of local control

Anarchists proceed from assumptions about human nature shared with marxists and most other revolutionaries. People are seen as having a variable nature determined in large part by environmental factors. Like marxists, most anarchists are hesitant to describe human nature as "good." They agree with the marxists that human nature is seen in its worst light under an authoritarian system directed by a small minority for its own narrow interest. Anarchists, from the late 18th century to the present, all agree on one basic principle: authority, in any form, is the enemy. Destroy it and a more rational and just society will be the result.

The utopian aim of voluntary cooperation as a basis for society is shared by most revolutionaries. Fundamental differences between anarchists and other revolutionaries arise not over ultimate goals but on the immediate questions of the organizational structure of revolutionary groups, how power shall be taken from the bourgeoisie, and the kind of organization to be instituted during and directly after the ousting of the bourgeoisie from power. For anarchists all these questions are intimately bound to each other and to the final vision of a noncompulsive cooperative society.

The integral connection between means and ends is an important assumption of most anarchist theory. In one form, pacifist anarchism, the argument is made that power achieved through the means of violence must lead *only* to an end of more violence. Most anarchists, however, are concerned only that nonauthoritarian means be used to organize the people in winning a nonauthoritarian social future. Violence against antirevolutionary forces is acceptable for most; for a smaller number of groups at various times, it is obligatory.*

One of the great issues dividing the European labor movement in the 19th century was the question that the anarchists posed as libertarian socialism versus authoritarian socialism. Both sides agreed that the working class would be the vanguard of the revolution against the bourgeoisie, although the anarchists tended to be somewhat more interested than the marxists in the peasants. In the First International, the "libertarian" and "authoritarian" socialist trends were reflected in Michael Bakunin, the anarchist, and Karl Marx, the socialist, and their respective followers. Bakunin believed that Marx wanted to "turn the International into a sort of monstrously colossal state, subject to a single official opinion represented by a strong central authority." The Bakuninists expressed their feelings about the authoritarianism of the marxist socialists in a document known as the *Sonvillier Circular*:

> We do not wish to charge the General Council with bad intentions. The persons who compose it are the victims of a fatal necessity. They wanted, in all good faith, and in order that their particular doctrines might triumph, to introduce the authoritarian spirit into the International; circumstances have seemed to favor

---

*Another well-perpetrated myth is that anarchists are bomb throwers, terrorists, and lovers of chaos. Although the description fits some anarchists, many others based their strategies solely on mass action and strongly opposed individual acts of terrorism. A good example of the bomb-throwing myth is displayed pictorially in Kedward (1971).

such a tendency, and we regard it as perfectly natural that this school . . . should believe that the International . . . must change its erstwhile organization and be transformed into a hierarchical organization guided and governed by an executive . . . We must nevertheless fight against [such tendencies] in the name of the social revolution for which we are working, and whose program is expressed in the words, "Emancipation of the workers by the workers themselves," independently of all guiding authority, even though such authority should have been consented to and appointed by the workers themselves. We demand that the principle of the autonomy of the sections should be upheld in the International, just as it has been heretofore recognized as the basis of our Association; we demand that the General Council . . . should return to its normal function, which is to act as a correspondence and statistical bureau. . . . The International, that germ of the human society of the future, must be . . . a faithful representation of our principles of freedom and of federation; it must reject any principle which may tend toward authoritarianism and dictatorship.

After the demise of the First International, caused by the split between Marx and Bakunin, the anarchists made several attempts to form their own international organizations. These met with little success primarily because of the anarchist emphasis on localism. From the first, anarchists took the view that the struggle should be focused on economic and social questions rather than political ones. The revolution was to be fought for economic and social transformation, and political power as authority was to be abolished and not simply transferred to a new group. This meant that the struggle was to take place in a decentralized manner and through decentralized groups.

The revolutions of 1848 were, for most revolutionaries, a crucial intellectual watershed. Revolutionaries had been content, until 1848, to follow the lead of bourgeois forces and to associate themselves with demands for representative institutions and the end of feudal privilege. After 1848 the orientation to a complete transformation of the social system and to becoming geared to that new social force, the proletariat, became clear. Marxists and anarchists agreed on this reorientation. The anarchists, however, went further in proposing the abolition of all centralized control and the development of voluntary federation.

The early anarchists found confirmation of their vision of federated autonomous communes in Rousseau's prehistoric golden age. Both Bakunin and Kropotkin looked to the Russian peasant system of communal land tenure and 19th century communes in Andalusia in southern Spain for justification of their belief in the practicality of the anarchist vision. Marxists and other socialists, of course, saw this as evidence of the reactionary nature of anarchism and its lack of relevance to expanding industrial economies.

The importance of local organization in accomplishing both the revolutionary overthrow of capitalism and the development of the new collective means of production was promulgated in the 1880s by Peter Kropotkin. A Russian prince, Kropotkin devoted his life to the development of anarchist theory. He argued for a form of social organization that would be manageable by human beings.

. . . our conception of the coming social revolution is quite different from that of a Jacobin dictatorship, or the transformation of social institutions affected by a convention, a parliament, or a dictator. . . .

We believe that if a revolution begins, it must take the form of a widely spread popular movement, during which . . . in every town and village invaded by the insurrectionary spirit, the masses set themselves to the work of reconstructing society on new lines. The people—both the peasants and the town workers—must themselves begin the constructive work, on more or less communist principles, without waiting for schemes and orders from above. From the very beginning of the movement, they must contrive to house and to feed everyone, and then set to work to produce what is necessary to feed, house, and clothe all of them.

They may not be—they are sure not to be—the *majority* of the nation. But if they are a respectably numerous minority of cities and villages scattered over the country, starting life on their own new socialist lines, they will be able to win the right to pursue their own course.

As to the government, whether it be constituted by force only or by elections, . . . we put no faith in it. We know beforehand that it will be able to do nothing to accomplish the change by working out *on the spot* the necessary new institutions. . . . The whole of history shows us that men thrown into a government by a revolutionary wave have never been able to accomplish what was expected from them. And this is *unavoidable*. Because in the task of reconstructing society on new principles, separate men, however intelligent and devoted they may be, are sure to fail. The collective spirit of the masses is necessary for this purpose. Isolated men can sometimes find the legal expression to sum up the destruction of old social forms—when the destruction is already proceeding. At the utmost, they may widen, perhaps, the sphere of the reconstructive work, extending what is being done in a part of the country, over a larger part of the territory. But to impose the reconstruction by law is absolutely impossible, as was proved among other examples, by the whole history of the French Revolution. Many thousands of the *laws* passed by the Revolutionary Convention had not even been put into force when reaction came and flung those laws into the wastebasket.

While anarchists produced considerable individualized actions through the "propaganda of the deed" (assassinations and bomb-throwing), revolutionary syndicalism has been the most significant organizational embodiment of anarchism. Revolutionary syndicalism is essentially revolutionary unionism; it argues that the proletariat should organize in unions which engage in class struggles with employers not simply for wages and working conditions but for the right to control production and its consequences. It projects a strategy of destroying capitalism through the general strike, after which the workers, through their revolutionary unions, return to the factories, begin production, and utilize the products to establish an egalitarian system of exchange.

Revolutionary syndicalism developed wide support in France, Spain, and Italy, and to a lesser extent, in the United States. In France, revolutionary syndicalism grew dominant in both the General Confederation of Labor and the Labor Exchanges (*Bourses de Travail*). In Spain and Italy, major union federations were dominated by anarchists. The American manifestation, the Industrial Workers of the World, was organized as an industrial union alternative to the conservative, craft-dominated American Federation of Labor.

Despite considerable strength, the revolutionary syndicalist organizations suffered either catastrophic defeats or the gradual undermining of their doctrines. In France the syndicalists became less revolutionary with time and, by the First World War, had become bread-and-butter unionists with anarchist ideological overtones. In the United States the IWW was persecuted incessantly and survived only as an organizational fragment after World War I. A catastrophic general strike in Italy in 1920 shattered the illusion of the general strike as an almost-automatic transition to proletarian power. There were also unviable transitory anarchist organizations based on peasant communes (in Spain) and military bands (in Russia). None of these forms showed significant strength over time.

Marxists and anarchists have continued to debate the virtues and defects of various forms of organization. Socialists argued that decentralized anarchist organization would be unable to meet the challenge of repression by the highly organized and centralized bourgeoisie; anarchists, in other words, could start a revolution but not win or complete it. The anarchist reply was that the socialist victory — which would only establish another repressive government — would not be a revolution. As leninism developed, anarchists argued further that highly organized groups such as vanguard parties actually destroyed spontaneity and undermined the revolutionary potential of the working class.

The experiences of the 1960s which saw the emergence of a New Left embracing both organized and spontaneous tendencies, represented, at least in part, an uneasy reconciliation of the two tendencies. In particular, the reemergence of spontaneity and small-scale organization revitalized interest in anarchist organization theory. This will be discussed in greater detail in the next chapter.

CHAPTER TEN

Organizational Forms of the Modern American Left

The 1960s saw the emergence in the United States of widespread activism and the generation of important organizational experiments. Although these experiments did not survive through the 1970s, they left an enduring set of ideas that continue to be present in the modern left. These ideas stress control from below and a de-emphasis on hierarchy.

Older organizational forms and approaches continued to be significant in the United States until the cold war began in 1947. There were two distinct approaches:

1. Mass party organization in the Socialist Party, which traced its lineage back to the beginning of the century, though lacking the size of its pre-World War I model.

2. Vanguardist organizations, of which the largest was the American Communist Party, but also including several trotskyist organizations.

The opening of the cold war in 1947 saw the resuscitation of long-standing repressive policies by the U.S. government with respect to the left. Radical groups were extensively infiltrated by the FBI. By the mid-1950s, infiltration was so widespread that many Old Left groups broke down; others became moribund.

At the beginning of the 1960s, *no* effective radical or socialist groups remained in the United States. The revival of political radicalism came with the stirrings of the civil rights movement. Within several years a host of new organizations began to develop. Some, like the Student Nonviolent Coordinating Committee (SNCC) were part of the early 1960s civil rights movement in the south, while northern groups, such as the Black Panther Party, emerged somewhat later. Students for a Democratic Society (SDS) also had its antecedents in civil rights, where a number of its key figures were originally trained. Late in the decade, as the volatile civil rights, antiwar, and student movements evolved, many different experiments, particularly aimed at generating local collectives, got underway. Most of the formal organizational manifestations that developed during the 1960s died just after the turn of the decade.

During the 1970s a period of relative quiescence descended on the American left, especially when compared to the hectic actions of the 1960s. Although single-issue environmental and social-action groups continued to proliferate, the existence of anything approaching a mass movement, much less a mass *organization*, seemed less and less a reality. Numerous miniscule vanguardist sects having little impact on the broader society continued to rise and fall throughout this period. Several attempts at reviving mass-party organizations, in the form of the New American Movement and the Democratic Socialist Organizing Committee, took place. None of these attempts developed into significant mass movements.

The period between 1962 and 1972, however, was one of enormous experimentation on the part of the New Left in the United States. The New Left was characterized by several distinctive features:

- Organizational emphasis on spontaneity rather than hierarchy.
- Emphasis on individuals finding their own level of political activity rather than the organization requiring certain levels of participation.
- Relatively vague concepts of membership; many people considered themselves "members" who were only adhering to the organization's ideology.

This chapter examines several organizations of the New Left: the Student Nonviolent Coordinating Committee, Students for a Democratic Society, the Black Panthers, and several additional organizational forms including Weatherman and the more amorphous and spontaneous collectives that developed in the aftermath of SDS during the 1970s.

Student Nonviolent Coordinating Committee (SNCC)

The ferment that originated on black southern college campuses in the early 1960s was unusual; it represented a sharp departure from the kinds of behavior manifested by black college students in the decades before. Not only did students reject the old forms of "Uncle Tomism" in their own personal relations, they moved off the campus into surrounding communities to challenge the racial segregation on which the southern social structure was based. This movement was unplanned and undirected; it was as if the idea had lain dormant in the heads of thousands of students and all it required was one group to try it and bring it to the attention of all the other individuals so that they would organize themselves and do the same. In the terms of the analysis done earlier, it was a largely spontaneous movement, locally based, with no central direction.

As hundreds of such groups formed, the need for some kind of integration of ideas and activities became plain. SNCC emerged out of this demand for coordination among local groups. At its outset, a group of fifteen students with a number of observers from sympathetic older civil rights organizations met and formed a "temporary" SNCC. They established an office, hired a secretary, and published a newsletter, *The Student Voice*, whose first issue appeared in June 1960. SNCC became a permanent organization after a conference of several hundred delegates in October of that year.

SNCC never was a membership organization. It involved organizers and students (and later ex-students) who were actively engaged in full-time struggle against segregation. As one SNCC person said, "I'm going head-on into this stuff. I don't care who the heck it is—if he's willing to come down on the front lines and bring his body along with me to die—then he's welcome." Most SNCC members explicitly rejected the idea of being "leaders" of the struggle in the south. Instead, SNCC participants viewed themselves as catalytic agents, releasing the energies of oppressed southern blacks by showing them that they could assert their rights as American citizens.

Nor did SNCC have anything that resembled a platform or a program. Its organizers were not concerned with the formation of a revolutionary organization to seize political power. SNCC's program, to the extent that it was coherent, was intended to move black people in the south to break with the fears with which they had lived for so long.

Of necessity, through the way in which SNCC organizers worked, they were often required to take leadership positions in the communities in which they organized. The organizers were deeply committed to the notion that the strength and power of the movement must come from the people themselves. Catalysts may be necessary to show people how to control their lives, but the explicit role of the leader must be avoided. The point was "to show Negroes in Hattiesburg that it is possible to speak loudly and firmly to a white sheriff as an equal—something they're not accustomed to doing."

This required that SNCC organizers speak to sheriffs as equals as well as to lead the way to registrars to get voting registration underway. In the living memory of the south, such behavior by blacks was unknown. In the southern context, this kind of action was regarded as revolutionary: to involve southern blacks in the conduct of public affairs as American citizens was conceived as literally undermining the roots of society. The response, formal and informal, by the southern power structure was drastic; beatings, electric cattle-proddings, midnight raids, shootings, and killings visited on SNCC organizers soon became standard fare.

While it was crucial to SNCC organizers that they lay their lives on the line, it was equally important that southern blacks begin to participate in the process of deciding things for themselves. This idea was enshrined in the notion of "participatory democracy" of which SNCC became, with SDS, an early implementer. SNCC organizers might play an important role in bringing people together and standing in the front line of any action, but once people coalesced, they needed to learn to express their opinions, talk with others, and participate in deciding what to do and how to do it. Meetings were structured deliberately to enhance participation; this required organizers to learn to be quiet and let other people speak.

By 1964 SNCC maintained 150 full-time workers—who constituted the entire "membership"—and had a budget of $250,000. Annual conventions of the organizers were very much like local meetings. People came to exchange ideas, compare experiences, and meet and sing together—rather than work out their ideology or platforms. The individual organizers returned to work at whatever projects were felt to be needed—a food co-op, a voter-registration drive, etc. While these actions might be reported to the headquarters in Atlanta, official approval was not needed to carry on activity. In addition to an executive committee, there were two chief officers—the chairman and the executive secretary. A field secretary in each major geographical area was known as a project director.

SNCC's success in spurring local activity led to modifications in its organizational structure in 1965. Whereas SNCC had begun as a coordinator of students groups, it was changed to consist of the full-time organizers, by now increased to two hundred. This entire group became the basic decision-making body. Although an executive committee with considerable powers was established, as well as a three-member secretariat, the emphasis on loose organization and the development of local initiatives continued. Local people chose their own programs and selected personnel for their areas.

The anticentralization spirit and belief in spontaneity produced its own set of difficulties. Letters and phone calls might not be answered; meetings started late or haphazardly; agendas had to be formulated when the meetings convened; actions were often undertaken without adequate planning, although with experience some of these problems were worked out; long-range strategies were rarely given serious attention; anyone willing to work was accepted, thereby leading to situations in which people were thrown into crises requiring great experience after receiving only some quick training in nonviolence and other organizational techniques.

Largely black in its membership, the role of the white activists in SNCC became increasingly unclear. While whites were unequivocally welcome at the beginning, by 1966 SNCC moved to become an all-black organization. This represented a traumatic break for both white and black organizers, but the blacks believed it was necessary for black organizers to demonstrate to black southerners that blacks could organize for themselves. This break, along with the shift to a northern strategy, governmental repression, and an ideological crisis, was responsible in considerable part for the demise of SNCC.

Despite its short life and its failure to develop a consciously revolutionary ideology, SNCC introduced several new ideas that became part of the revived American radicalism:

- It demonstrated that it was possible to work with one of the most oppressed groups in American society.
- SNCC showed that even the most oppressed people could be brought to high levels of activism and involvement thereby countering the established belief that southern Blacks were incapable of organization.
- SNCC demonstrated that it was possible to avoid the development of a leadership group despite many consequent organizational deficiencies.

SNCC also served as a training ground for a host of organizers. These included Stokely Carmichael, John Lewis, Bob Moses, James Forman, Abbie Hoffman, Gloria Richardson, Julian Bond, and many others. This group was to disperse into many different organizational aspects of the movement in the late 1960s.

Students for a Democratic Society (SDS)

SDS was formed in 1960 out of the ashes of an Old Left group, the Student League for Industrial Democracy. Founded by 60 members, SDS grew into a national organization with nearly 100,000 members in 400 chapters throughout the country by the end of 1968. Its influence was even larger than its membership, however, since SDS, at times of crisis on individual college campuses, garnered the support of far greater numbers of students than their affiliated membership represented.

While oriented initially toward traditional party politics in attempting to reform the Democratic Party, SDS took a turn to the left in 1962 when the Port Huron Statement was issued. The Statement called for a massive infusion of peace groups, students, blacks, and other groups of liberals and leftists to produce a radical realignment of the Democratic Party.

By 1965, as the Vietnam war accelerated, SDS became the major antiwar organization on the American campus and soon was regarded as the most important leftist group in the United States. Within a few years, SDS had become a household word, associated indissolubly in the public mind with student protest. Its success was so considerable that SDS was invaded by youth wings of the Old Left organizations. SDS became the progenitor of Weatherman, the Revolutionary Union, and several other groups after a split in 1969 destroyed the organization.

Politically, the major reason for the growth of SDS was the burgeoning war in Vietnam. Organizationally, SDS's commitment to participatory democracy as a societal goal and an organizational form also proved to be vital to its rapid development. SDS's founding document, the Port Huron Statement, called for individuals to be able to "share in those social decisions determining the quality and direction of [their lives]." This belief in "letting the people decide" and decentralized decision-making stemmed from

> . . . the need to create a personal and group identity that can survive both the temptations and the crippling effects of this society. Power in America is abdicated by individuals to top-down organizational units, and it is in the recovery of this power that the movement becomes distinct from the rest of the country and a new kind of man emerges.

SDS therefore began its organizational life apprehensive of bureaucratic and hierarchical forms of organization and sought to create an organization where power flowed from the bottom up. Leadership (or the common concept of it) was viewed as being harmful; SDS members often spoke about how they "had no leaders."

The heart of SDS, typical of the anarchist approach to organization, was in the local chapters, organized predominantly on college campuses. Chapters had almost complete autonomy in deciding on their activities, except that they were "expected to operate within the broad terms of policy set by the national convention and the national council." Chapters could be formed by any five people holding membership in the national organization. Although chapters were formally chartered by the National Council or the Regional Council, chapter formation usually depended on local self-starting by an SDS enthusiast.

The local and autonomous thrust of SDS became part of its organizational approach through its decision to leave the implementation of programs adopted on the national or regional level to the local chapter. Sometimes many chapters worked on a national project, as with the antidraft actions taken against colleges sponsoring the Selective Service College Qualification Examinations in May 1966. Other national programs, such as the "Vote with Your Feet, Vote in the Streets" protest against the 1968 presidential elections (because all the major candidates were defined as terrible) fizzled because of local inaction.

For most of its existence, the national officers of SDS were the president, vice-president, national secretary and fourteen other members forming a National Interim Committee. The president was the "spokesman for SDS," the vice-president was the president's assistant and director of internal education, and the national secretary was the chief administrative officer. The National Interim Committee was to take care of emergency business arising between the quarterly National Council meetings.

In 1967, because of concern with the existence of a hierarchy in the national office and a wish to produce greater equalization of the national leadership, the structure was changed. Three equal secretaries became the main national officers. The national secretary was responsible for the functioning of the national office. The interorganizational secretary was responsible for liaison both within the organization and with other national and international groups. The education secretary was in charge of internal education. A smaller National Interim Committee was formed, consisting of the three national officers and eight other members elected at the convention.

Regions were organized along geographic lines, such as Ohio-Michigan and Southern California. They functioned similarly to the national organization, except that they elected a regional coordinator or "traveler" and sometimes adopted regional programs.

There was a national SDS newspaper, *New Left Notes*, whose editor was appointed by the national secretary. It printed news of activities in regions and chapters, National Council resolutions, and articles written by members. Some regions and chapters also put out their own newspapers, magazines, and newsletters.

This detailing of national and regional organization creates an unfortunate emphasis on the upper levels of the organization since these levels were far less important in SDS than the chapters. Considerable variations existed in the chapters depending on size and the amount of factional warfare in each. To get some notion of the organization of the chapter, let us consider the Cornell University chapter of SDS as an example.

Before 1968, when the chapter was small—with only forty dues-paying members—there were only two officers—a president and a treasurer. The president's job was to call meetings, set agendas, and maintain contact with the national office. The treasurer's function was to collect dues and pay bills. The chairing of meetings revolved among members. The object of rotation was twofold: to disperse the skills among a broader group than the officers and to diminish the likelihood that leadership would "crystallize"—that some individuals would become perpetually prominent in representing SDS to the campus. Business was transacted at weekly meetings in which projects were discussed and reports given. Sometimes there were weekend parties or discussion sessions where members could get to know each other informally.

As the chapter grew, the need for organizational evolution became apparent. Membership rose to the hundreds and the weekly meetings usually attracted several hundred people; during campus confrontations, attendance at SDS meetings went into the thousands. The changes involved replacing the president and treasurer with seven co-chairpersons. Each headed a standing committee: campus affairs, national affairs, community affairs, research, cultural affairs, draft resistance (reflecting the chapter's close ties with *The Resistance*, a national draft-resistance organization), and education. Weekly business meetings were held, but it was hoped that members would also participate in the activities of at least one of the standing committees. Temporary committees were also organized to work on particular projects. The co-chairpersons made up the steering committee, whose job it was to prepare the agenda for the weekly meetings and to select a chairperson for the forthcoming meeting. Steering committee meetings were open to all members and all those in attendance could vote. The steering committee had no other power, as all major decisions were made by the entire membership. Elections were held at least three times a year to assure membership control over the co-chairpersons.

Despite the democratic form and mass base, several organizational problems were never resolved. A few people, because of popularity and articulateness, were continually reelected co-chairpersons and did a disproportionate amount of the public speaking. This tended to produce some leadership crystallization since a broader leadership was not effectively produced.

Leadership was also disproportionately male, despite active participation by many women. While women headed some committees, they held a distinctly secondary place to the men. This occurred in a period in which the kinds of questioning about sexism now current had not yet been formulated – but dissatisfaction with male dominance was becoming more conscious. Within the Cornell SDS, female leadership failed to develop.

The very size of the Cornell chapter created organizational problems that were never satisfactorily resolved. Increased size precluded the kind of intimate discussion and knowledge of other members as persons that had characterized the earlier period. The structural change creating committees represented, in part, an attempt to retain a smaller organizational environment to accompany the larger structure of the weekly meetings. The "affinity group" idea was also briefly discussed – the creation of small groups working together on a particular project – but did not take hold.

The chapter broke up around the same time that the national SDS organization was shattered in a massive split during the summer of 1969. Factionalism had existed in the chapter up to the split but had been contained. When national SDS split, the effects on the chapter were drastic and led to its effective demise.

The Black Panthers

The Black Panther Party was formed in 1966 by Bobby Seale and Huey P. Newton in Oakland, California. The party developed a program calling for "land, bread, housing, education, clothing, justice and peace," and organized itself as a vanguard party. The vanguard form of organization was seen as essential by the leaders of the Black Panther Party because of the weakness of blacks despite their enormous potential strength. Referring to blacks in the United States, party leader Eldridge Cleaver said: "That is a lot of strength. But it is a lot of weakness if it is disorganized, and the overriding need is for unity and organization . . . the need for one organization that will give one voice to the black man's common interest. . . ."

The Panthers saw a need for tested revolutionaries to minimize the danger of "Uncle Tom informers and opportunists" (although they were to be heavily infiltrated by the police). Like Lenin, they believed "the Vanguard Party must provide leadership for the people. It must teach the correct strategic methods of prolonged resistance through literature and activities."

The Panthers saw a vanguard party as especially necessary because of the peculiarities of their situation in America. Without such an organization, the *lumpenproletariat* could not be effectively mobilized and, because of reactionary tendencies of the *lumpenproletariat*, they could be organized to fight against the revolution:

> This is the genius of Huey Newton, of being able to TAP this VAST RESERVOIR of revolutionary potential. I mean street niggers, you dig it? . . . But I mean to really TAP it, to really TAP IT, to ORGANIZE it, and to direct it into an onslaught. . . . Huey Newton was able to go down, and to take the nigger on the street, and relate to him, understand what was going on inside of him, what he was thinking, and then implement that into an organization, into a PROGRAM and a PLATFORM, you dig it? . . . This is the genius of Huey Newton, the engendering, the establishing of the first vanguard party in the liberation struggle in the Western Hemisphere.

In formulating an approach to the work of the party, the Panthers defined themselves in terms of the group with which they sought to work. This involved educating the black population by example:

> There are basically three ways one can learn: through study, through observation, and through actual experience. The black community is basically composed of activists . . . the black community is basically not a reading community. Therefore it is very significant that the vanguard group first be activists.

Throughout the early 1970s, the Black Panther Party became a major focus of police repression that, coupled with internal factionalism, reduced their effectiveness significantly.

Despite attempts to develop a national organization, by the mid-1970s the Panthers had become a black political organization centered in Oakland, California, concentrating on local issues. Their emphasis was placed on community programs such as child-care centers and electoral campaigns within the Democratic Party. They remained essentially a vanguardist organization but functioned within black and liberal Democratic circles.

The 1970s: Variations in Organizational Forms

Perhaps the most dramatic organization to emerge from the shambles of the internally split SDS in 1969 was the Weatherman. One of three factions, Weatherman is interesting because it defined itself initially as a vanguard organization and subsequently decided to go underground. A second organizational development that took shape even before SDS collapsed was the widespread collectives movement, a large number of locally based organizations emphasizing more of an anarchist than a marxist orientation. Although the collectives movement went into decline after several years, some aspects of its experience have been incorporated in the antinuclear movement.

In its short but active life, Weatherman went through various internal changes in quick succession. From its beginning, however, Weatherman stressed the importance of appropriate internal organization in fighting a revolutionary war inside the United States. Weatherman believed "a cadre organization, effective secrecy, self-reliance among the cadres, and an integrated relationship with the active mass-based movement" was essential for success. What was needed was "a centralized organization of revolutionaries," one which "combined at some point with discipline under one centralized leadership."

When Weatherman was formed, its adherents did not believe that this kind of marxist-leninist party could be built because three vital things were missing: a tested leadership, a common revolutionary theory, and a mass revolutionary base. Weatherman therefore sought to create the conditions for a revolutionary party.

One way to create these conditions was through the formation of revolutionary collectives:

> The development of revolutionary Marxist-Leninist-Maoist collective formations . . . is not just the task of specialists or leaders, but the responsibility of every revolutionary. Just as a collective is necessary to sum up experiences and apply them locally . . . the collective interrelationship of groups all over the country is necessary to get an accurate view of the whole movement and to apply that in the whole country. Over time, those collectives which prove themselves in practice to have the correct understanding (by the results they get) will contribute toward the creation of a unified revolutionary party.

The way in which Weatherman operated would create the conditions for a revolutionary party. The collectives would:

> . . . demand total, wholehearted commitment of the individual to struggle against everything that interferes with the revolutionary struggle, and to transform oneself into a revolutionary and a communist: collectives through which we can forge ourselves into effective "tools of necessity" and through which we can realize, concretely, in our day-to-day lives, such well-known Maoist principles as "Politics in command," "Everything for the revolution," "Criticism-self-criticism-transformation."

Weatherman collectives were to have both external and internal functions. Internally, changing one's self meant rejecting and struggling against the values of American society: male chauvinism, individualism, and competition. For example, Weatherman decided that, to fight male chauvinism within the organization, all monogamous relationships would have to be broken up—"People who live together and fight together, fuck together." After some brief experiments in this direction, it was decided that there was "great possibilities for love between two people struggling to be revolutionaries" and the earlier policies were scrapped.

The Weather Bureau was the central policy-making group within the organization, the Weather Machine. In addition to setting the national political line, the Bureau controlled the newspaper, *New Left Notes* (later named *Fire!*). As in other democratic-centralist organizations, there was widespread debate within the collectives and between the collectives and the Weather Bureau.

The Weather Bureau had the authority to choose the leaders of the collectives. It is reported that they picked members whom they felt had the most courage, fought the hardest, and were the most articulate politically. The Bureau also made the important decisions on secrecy, that is, who to inform about certain illegal activities.

After 1970 the Weatherman organization went underground and expelled a large part of its membership in the process. It suffered some deaths through explosions and a number of arrests. Despite the fact that little is known about the organization, it is reasonable to believe that the Weather underground had its roots in the vanguardist and cell structure formed at the time Weatherman was created. Although successful in creating a public front group, Prairie Fire, in 1974, the influence of Weatherman politics on the left declined shortly after it went underground.

COLLECTIVES

This popular organizational form began to emerge around 1968. The term "collective" represents the meshing of a broad variety of organizational approaches, mostly experimental. Alternative terms such as "gangs," "families," and "affinity groups"* were sometimes used instead of "collective."

The popularity of collectives as an organizational form originated in the success of large-scale organizations such as SDS and the antiwar movement. Many activists were concerned about the loss of personal contact caused by increased size, and moved into collectives to reduce the scale of personal interaction in the larger political battle. Many activists were also fed up with that concomitant of large size: bureaucracy. Activists wanted organizational forms which precluded the emergence of specialized and hierarchical roles. Still others were opposed to large organizations because of their beliefs that size, bureaucracy, and hierarchy inhibited the participation and involvement of people and that growth would be choked. By developing more manageable and smaller-scale organizations, they believed the movement would continue to grow and spread its influence.

At the same time, many radicals wanted to develop relationships with political cothinkers that were not only political but "human." That is, some radicals wanted to construct organizational forms that would deal not only with the long-range problems of revolutionary social change but with day-to-day satisfactions in the daily

---

*The term "affinity groups" was also applied to temporary and special-purpose teams formed for a special event, e.g., to march together in a demonstration or to be prepared to defend each other.

process of living. The need to begin leading socialist lives now, even while living under the hegemony of capitalism and battling it, became important.

Others argued that, while large-scale organization may be necessary, it invariably has a tendency to become elitist. One particular form of elitism is always present in the tendency toward male-domination and the underrepresentation of women in leadership roles. Many women's groups in the early 1970s believed that women could function better in smaller-sized groups and that such groups would be less likely to give rise to elitism.

While not all of the problems for which they were created were solved, collectives emerged with several distinct tendencies:

- Most collectives agreed on the need for working toward a common political outlook. There could be a range of tolerance as to what is "common," with some collectives having narrow political interests while others were broader.
- Most collectives agreed on the need to *end the existing social order* and the establishment of some kind of egalitarian—socialist, communist, anarchist—society.
- Most collectives agreed on the need to engage in *active political work*—"external work" as it was called. In some collectives this could consist of a single project conducted by all members (e.g., operating a free school, making revolutionary films), while in others, members might engage in individual tasks. In the latter case, individual work was considered a part of the action of the collective and examined and agreed upon by the collective group. Some work, in other words, was considered unacceptable because it was politically insignificant or incorrect.
- Most collectives agreed on the need for *internal democratic practices*. Some practiced centralism while others de-emphasized it, but few collectives had an authoritarian internal system.
- Most collectives practiced *criticism, self-criticism, and transformation* in internal affairs. These terms refer to the frequent and intensive discussions in which members evaluated their own and each other's work and attempted to reinforce each individual's strong points and help them correct their shortcomings.

Beyond these common areas there was less agreement on several ideas.

- Some collectives believed that, in addition to working together, it would be necessary to experience the development of more intensive social relationships through *living together*. This was sought through developing a common residential basis, more commonly called a commune. In residentially based collectives, different forms of internal sharing could be found. Some communes totally rejected all private ownership, including clothing, while others maintained some elements of personal property. All residential collectives strove to reorganize the division of labor so that work did not get divided into traditional sex roles with the women doing the housework.
- Some collectives not only believed in common tasks but in the need to *do the job together* at the same time. This approach was based on the idea that common experience provides the best basis for criticism and self-criticism and therefore for transformation.
- Many collectives regarded themselves as *temporary* organizational forms that would be *transitional* to mass organization or vanguardist forms. Other collec-

tives believed that, with enough collectives functioning, the collectives could themselves become an organizational form appropriate to make a revolution.

Collectives spread widely through the United States in the early 1970s although they were rarely found in purely rural areas.* They were almost invariably local; they avoided publicity — not only because of their revolutionary quality but because publicity tends to produce public leadership. Whenever a "straight" newspaper ran a story on a collective, journalistic dynamics required that such stories be personalized. Journalists therefore selected the "leadership" in terms of what they thought would create a good story. At the same time, public exposure set up internal strains about publicity. As a result, collectives generally sought to avoid public exposure; little has therefore entered the records on this interesting form of leftist organization.

Conclusion

The emergence of the New Left in the United States constituted a sharp organizational break with the experiences of previous revolutionaries. Paradoxically, the development of this widespread organizational innovation derived considerably from the annihilation of the Old Left through FBI infiltration. Of crucial significance, however, was the formation of a civil rights movement in the south by black students. Developing without the organizational trappings of the past, either from the Old Left or from black movements such as garveyism, the new student movement rapidly drew to it many volunteer workers from the north.

Each new organizational form found the need to begin its experience literally from scratch. The lack of experience was converted into virtue when the New Left contended that spontaneity was more important than organization, that mass popular participation was more important than the development of a coherent leadership, that history was itself a drag on organizational development.

Fueled by the urban rebellions of blacks and the antiwar and student movements, New Left experiments developed widely between 1965 and 1972. After 1972 the movement declined rapidly, but important organizational residues remained. Most important of these was an emphasis on participating in popular manifestations, while giving little credence to formal participation in organized electoral groupings. Although political groups such as the New American Movement and the Democratic Socialist Organizing Committee were formed, most of the new and younger leftists avoided political attachments. Instead, there was more participation in specific, single-purpose groups such as the Clamshell Alliance and the Abalone Alliance, i.e., specific groups formed to fight against the spread of nuclear power.

While the New Left passed from the scene, its organizational influences continue, to the extent that a left continues in the United States, with the emphasis on localism, spontaneity, and antihierarchy in internal organization.

---

*A considerable number of countercultural communes were also formed during the early 1970s in rural areas. These communes were often dedicated to subsistent self-renewal. While some revolutionary elements found their way into these communes, most were not revolutionary in character because of their avoidance of political and social transformation. Instead they were largely concerned with creating self-enclosed private solutions to the problems of survival in capitalist society. Most revolutionaries regarded these communes as "cop-outs" in the battle against capitalism.

PART THREE

The Theory and Practice of Revolutionary Mobilization

Contradictions in social systems such as capitalism create unrest among various subordinate groups and open possibilities for revolution, but they do not guarantee either the collapse of the system or its inevitable replacement with socialism. At best, the contradictions of the system limit its capability to cure itself and produce possibilities for the development of revolutionary consciousness and action in the bulk of the population. At the same time, while social groups are capable of providing the human base for a revolutionary transformation (Part I) and models for organizing conscious revolutionaries (Part II), revolutionaries must face the problem of developing revolutionary consciousness and action in the people while translating action into strategies to effect the transformation of state power.

Revolutionary mobilization differs from other forms of mobilization in the sense that it is integrally linked to the concepts of taking power and making a socialist transformation. Populations have been mobilized by political leaders for many centuries and for many reasons; unless such mobilization is directed at socialist transformation, however, it remains largely a cynical exercise intended by particular interest groups to take political control on their own behalf. The aim of socialist transformation is vital to the concept of mobilization as it is being utilized here.

In analyzing mobilizational theory a major problem originates over the question of the relationship of theory to practice. While the mobilizational theory to be outlined is relatively simple, its implementation is complex and intricate. Much of the problem in understanding mobilization is that one must examine actual practices and seek to extricate from them the elements of theory they incorporate. What makes this problem especially complicated is that most mobilization techniques are *situationally specific*; they are developed to resolve a specific problem at a particular place and time and under existing local conditions. Many mobilizational techniques, therefore, make sense only in a specific context and are often not transferable.

The problem of *context* is therefore vital to understanding mobilizational practices. Many mobilizational approaches which have had important revolutionary potential when introduced would draw no interest in a different situation. Industrial organization, discussed in Chapter 13, was once considered a revolutionary approach in the United States. It would hardly be so regarded today when many workers are organized into industrial unions which support the status quo.

Mobilizational theory is also difficult to treat systematically because no program is inherently revolutionary unless it is connected to the goal of achieving socialism. Industrial organization may seem less than inherently revolutionary because of changes in historical context; it could only have been revolutionary within the context of the existence of a revolutionary movement committed to socialism. Since industrial organization took the form of industrial unionism *without* a relationship to a revolutionary movement and socialist orientation, it is not surprising that it took the reformist forms that developed in the United States. In Europe, in contrast, industrial organization never had revolutionary implications and the forms of unionism varied considerably from the U.S. experience.

Resolving the problem of revolutionary context is not all that simple, however. For example, engaging in armed battles with the police might constitute an important revolutionary tactic for mobilization in the context of taking state power; in other contexts, however, it might be irrelevant, negative, or even suicidal, particularly in the early stages of struggle. It is therefore not possible to build a typology or ranking of mobilizational practices in terms of their inherent revolutionary qualities. As an alternative, Part III turns to an examination of various mobilizational strategies, programs, and tactics which have played a significant role in the revolutionary tradition and contain elements which may still be significant in the current world context. We also include some discussion of reformist mobilizational practice (community organizing) and mobilizational practice which was at best ambiguous in terms of its revolutionary intent (campus confrontations). We include this material because we believe that this practice embodies mobilizational elements that may be incorporated into revolutionary practice in the future.

Because of the importance of historical context in mobilizational theory, Part III begins with a chapter setting out some historical contexts in which mobilizational theory developed. Chapter 11 examines the background within which Marx turned to the issue of mobilization and looks at his organizational approach to developing a relationship with the proletariat. The chapter then examines the evolution of this approach through the Russian experience, and in particular that of Lenin, before turning to specific theoretical contributions by Trotsky and Mao. Chapter 12 sets out the four main elements involved in revolutionary mobilization and examines the locations for applying different approaches, at the point of production and elsewhere, although as shall be seen this differentiation is not as clear-cut in practice as it is in theory. Chapter 13 turns to mobilizational forms based at the point of production and examines industrial organization, the insurrection, nationalization, soviets and workers' control, and the general strike. In Chapter 14, after considering the issue of reformist forms of mobilization, we examine campaigns, including electoral strategies, community organizing, and confrontations. The final chapter of this Part, Chapter 15, considers a gamut of mobilizational approaches implicit in revolutionary warfare.

CHAPTER ELEVEN

Mobilization Theory in Historical Context

How revolutionaries should relate to the people expected to make a revolution did not become central to the thinking of theoreticians until it became clear that the proletariat would not make any automatic movement toward revolutionary insurrection.

First, while Marx and Engels (and others) saw significant proletarian movements developing between 1830 and 1848, there were no proletarian successes during this period. In 1830 the working class played an important but subsidiary role in revolutionary events in France; by 1848, in France and elsewhere, the proletariat was beginning to play an independent role. The events of 1848 demonstrated that, *if* revolutions were to be successful, the participation of revolutionaries themselves (what has been discussed in Part II as the theory of organization) was vital. At the same time, it was becoming clear that, just because conscious revolutionaries were involved in events, the proletariat did not necessarily follow the revolutionaries or acknowledge their wisdom. The issue of how to relate to revolutionary populations began to emerge as an intellectual problem of enormous consequence.

A second development also became clear: the working class, while becoming revolutionary in different periods, was not in constant "motion" toward revolution. There were periods of quiescence when workers became "tired" or indifferent; while the driving force may have been operating, it did not act as a *constant energizer* of the working class. There were to be periods of ups and downs in revolutionary energies. This discovery meant that conscious revolutionaries had to relate to the working class in different ways under different conditions. A corollary element was that not all workers came from the same experience: there were differences in experience, background, and national origin. It was also learned that some workers

113

became more revolutionary than others. Over a period of time these facts gave rise to increased awareness about the relationship of revolutionaries to the people.

As the size and power of the working class increased during the latter part of the 19th century, questions about how to *move* toward revolutionary action became important. On the one hand, there was a general anticipation in revolutionary circles that continued growth of the proletariat would culminate in a socialist insurrection that would usher in the new era. On the other hand, reformist elements within the socialist movement argued that a peaceful, evolutionary, and gradual transition to socialism would occur. Questions about mobilization were posed sharply during the Russian revolution of 1905 when workers in Petrograd, Moscow, and elsewhere shook the foundations of czarism with only peripheral involvement by conscious revolutionary elements. The Russian events placed questions of organization and mobilization at the center of theoretical work on the part of many theorists, although the focus of most thinking tended to concentrate on organizational issues.

The success of the Russian Revolution of 1917 sharpened the issue of mobilization. It was believed that unless socialist revolutions developed in industrialized Europe, the revolution in Russia would ultimately collapse or degenerate. How communists could and should stand with respect to the working class therefore became the subject of intense debate. As the revolution degenerated in Russia, these theoretical issues became enmeshed in the conflict for control within the Russian Communist Party. Over the next two decades, mobilization for purposes of generating revolutionary energies became subordinated to concerns to mobilize the working classes to defend the Soviet Union. Despite this historical decay, the central theoretical questions involving mobilization have remained.

Marx On Mobilization

Although Karl Marx is least remembered for his contributions to mobilization theory, he was, with Friedrich Engels, responsible for the elaboration of a number of principles of revolutionary organization that influenced revolutionaries that followed him. Marx contributed a great deal to developing a method of social analysis to aid in the formulation of mobilization programs, strategies, and tactics, but he wrote and did little with direct reference to these subjects himself. To a great extent, this was because he believed that working-class organizations like unions would inherently bring workers to revolutionary consciousness and action. The role of the international communist party that he played a major part in establishing was, like his lecturing and pamphleteering, primarily informational and intended to give direction and ideological coherence to the spontaneous revolts against capitalism. Ultimately, Marx's lack of attention to mobilizational issues rested on his expectation that the socialist revolution would be quickly forthcoming, essentially spontaneous, and in an insurrectionary form that would, like the Paris Commune of 1871, elaborate its own leadership, organization, and goals.

Marx lived in revolutionary times in which political ferment occurred continually. There was a proliferation of political groups, tendencies, and movements, particularly among elements of the bourgeoisie. The period after the French Revolution was one in which the bourgeois groups sought to consolidate their power against the dying remnants of feudal regimes. But feudal tendencies were far from dead in Europe and the entire post-Napoleonic period was one in which a great many localized struggles continued to take place. At the same time that bourgeois elements were involved in political and economic struggles with feudal and monarchical groups, the working class was developing an active political and economic existence.

It was within this context that Marx delineated his first organizational principle: the need for *separate, distinct organization* by the proletariat. In the battle between bourgeois and feudal elements, both made appeals, from time to time, for working-class support. One of the forms of phony socialism that Marx and Engels inveighed against in *The Communist Manifesto* was "feudal socialism," in which some reactionary feudal elements sought to win working-class support because they, like the working class, were opposed to capitalist domination of society. Marx saw the need to support more progressive forces such as the bourgeoisie against more reactionary defenders of feudalism. But such support could not and should not take place within the organizational context of the bourgeois parties since, once the capitalist class had established itself, the working class would have to take up its own battle. Independent and autonomous organization was therefore necessary.

Marx's second organizational principle was to emphasize the *primacy of international organization*. By the time he and Engels began their work, local organizations of workers were fairly widespread in Europe, but these organizations tended to be isolated from each other. International organization made sense not only to break down this isolation but because workers were going through similar experiences in Great Britain, France, Germany, the United States, and elsewhere. This common experience should produce a common consciousness, Marx believed, and this could only be obtained by creating an organization that cut across national lines.

Marx also recognized the divisive quality of nationalism. While he considered national development to be progressive in contrast to the feudal organization of Europe that had prevented a bourgeoisie from emerging, Marx knew that parochial national distinctions could separate one group of workers from another. He gave organizational meaning to these views through his contributions to the First International.

In approaching the problem of mobilizing the workers, Marx defined the importance of revolutionaries addressing themselves to workers at *the point of production*, the work place, since it was here that exploitation was given daily meaning and where the contradictions of capitalism would be most apparent. Marx was less enthusiastic about organizing workers at their place of residence or, for example, in their capacity as consumers.

Most workers were still, at the time, only newly arrived migrants from the rural areas. As residents, they still turned for help to kinsmen and neighbors from their places of origin; indeed, they had less in common with other workers as residents than as workers. The common feature of work, however, obliterated the importance of origin or place of residence. Further, the spontaneous development of unionism emphasized the importance of the point of production as the locus toward which conscious revolutionary elements should gravitate if they wanted to mobilize the working class.

Marx recognized a third element of mobilization when he showed an understanding of the tension between the need to *generalize experiences* of the workers, while dealing with the localized differences between one factory (or employer) and another, one region and another, and between differences in national origins and backgrounds. Marx saw capitalism as a worldwide phenomenon that would subject all workers to the same exploitative experiences. Accordingly, it was necessary for revolutionaries to emphasize the *general* features of capitalism so that broad-ranging consciousness could develop. At the same time, to simply talk about the general features of exploitation would have little meaning to most workers. The work of conscious revolutionaries required the utilization of the concrete but limited experiences of workers in individual workshops to relate them to general features of the system. As early as 1844 Marx recognized the *differences* in the national situations of France and Germany, not only of the different tempo of capitalist development in the two countries, but also the differences in national history, character, and experience. For Marx, therefore, the general features of revolutionary development always had to be placed into the context of local circumstances. This had to be manifested by *programmatic flexibility while emphasizing the general features* of workers' experiences.

For Marx, the most concrete manner in which revolutionaries should address the working class was through a *program*. In *The Communist Manifesto*, the analysis of social relations and the development of capitalism was given specific direction in the second section by the delineation of a program. This program took the form of demands for the abolition of property in land, a progressive income tax, abolition of inheritance, centralization of credit and communications and transport in the state, extension of state ownership in factories and in land, equal liability of all to labor, the combination of agriculture and industry to break down the distinction between town and country, and free education for all children and abolition of child labor.

The demands set forth in *The Manifesto* reflected Marx's views as to the character of revolutionary programs, an approach that was further developed at a later stage by Trotsky. Marx did not see the demands as being implementable under capitalism; rather, the demands were of such a nature that each would seem commonsensical to workers. In seeking to fulfill these demands, the working class would weaken the entire system of capitalism. Indeed, Marx believed that had any or all of the demands been achieved, capitalism would have been weakened beyond repair.

Thus, the revolutionary program was intended not only to formulate proposals that would make sense to the working class but would lead them to undermine the system while struggling to obtain what appeared to be intelligent and reasonable proposals.*

---

*It is necessary to note here that *The Manifesto's* demands, while seeming somewhat ordinary today, were very revolutionary in 1848. For those who would argue that capitalism could adjust to Marx's demands, it might be worth noting that a genuinely progressive income tax system still does not exist in the United States despite over fifty years of experience with a graduated tax. Most of the other demands remain to be won.

The Russian Revolution and Its Aftermath

LENIN'S MOBILIZATIONAL ORIENTATIONS

The period following the active theoretical leadership of Marx and Engels was given over to the organizational development of working-class movements and parties. These developments have been detailed in Part II. Mobilizational issues began to emerge as the subject for serious debate in Russia, where a small but highly concentrated working class was becoming increasingly revolutionary. The primary theoretician about these events, Lenin, turned to organizational matters in thinking about the prospects for mobilizing the working class. As was pointed out in Chapter 7, Lenin saw the working class capable of great energies but unable to get beyond simple union consciousness without the existence of a revolutionary party. The function of the party, therefore, became to translate the ordinary energies of the working class into revolutionary directions by, first, generalizing the character of working-class exploitation, and second, by delineating the system rather than individual employers as the exploiter.

The first test came during the 1905 revolution when workers began a national general strike and the concept of soviets (workers' councils) spread throughout Russia. These events confirmed Lenin's view that the revolutionary party was central to effecting the transition from capitalism to socialism. When the March 1917 revolution overthrew the czar and created a bourgeois provisional government in its place, Lenin became even more convinced of the need for a revolutionary party with a program for taking power. The party had to translate this program into a series of immediate demands and slogans that would mobilize the working class. One such slogan, "All power to the soviets," argued for the taking of state power by the institutions created by workers, soldiers, and peasants, rather than leaving it in the hands of the bourgeois provisional government. Another slogan, "Land, Bread, Peace," embodied the hopes and aspirations of the three major revolutionary strata: land for the peasants, bread for the workers, and peace for the soldiers.

The need to draw the bulk of revolutionary elements into their orbit forced the Bolsheviks to develop a continuingly changing set of tactics to undermine the government and give greater power to the soviets. At the same time, the Bolshevik mobilization tactics brought thousands of workers and others into their party.

The experience of the Russian Revolution was one which demonstrated the need to grasp the feelings of the revolutionary segments and develop programs that would enhance their energies and focus them against the existing governmental machinery. With this experience, mobilization became a central issue to the work of many revolutionary groups.

TROTSKY AND THE TRANSITIONAL PROGRAM

Second in importance only to Lenin in the Russian Revolution, Leon Trotsky brought an unusual intelligence to mobilization theory. Trotsky's main contributions are twofold. First, as a practicing revolutionary during the 1905 and 1917 revolutions, he demonstrated acute sensitivity in grasping the moods of revolutionary populations and articulating them within a program aimed at the taking of power. Whether through his work with that unique Russian invention—the soviets—or in building an army literally from nothing, Trotsky demonstrated capabilities for crystallizing the acute unhappiness of workers, soldiers, and peasants, and focusing them for the overthrow of czarism.

But Trotsky as *actor* was, like all historical personages, unique. Much of his approach was personal, idiosyncratic, unreproducible by others. His main contribution *theoretically* to mobilization theory rests in a second area to which he turned after his exile, when he was forced to engage in purely intellectual work.

In developing a series of programs in the 1930s for a world marked by movement toward fascism in Europe, Trotsky sought to deal concretely with immediate events in a manner that was reasonable and "made sense" to large numbers of people. At the same time, he focused on approaches—slogans, analyses, arguments—that would move people toward a more revolutionary position.

Trotsky made a major contribution to mobilization theory in his concept of the transitional program. He first formulated this idea while preparing a document for the founding conference of the Fourth International in 1938. Unable to attend the conference because of his exile in Mexico, Trotsky drafted a document, *The Death Agony of Capitalism and the Tasks of the Fourth International*, to serve as the basis for discussion at the meeting. He argued:

> The strategic task of the next period . . . consists in overcoming the contradiction between the maturity of the objective revolutionary conditions (e.g., the advanced state of capitalism) and the immaturity of the proletariat and its vanguard. . . .
> It is necessary to help the masses in the process of daily struggle to find a bridge between present demands and the socialist program of the revolution. This bridge should include a system of *transitional demands*, stemming from today's conditions and from today's consciousness of wide layers of the working class and unalterably leading to one final conclusion: the conquest of power by the proletariat.

Trotsky then set out a broad worldwide program of transitional demands that included demands for a sliding scale of wages and hours (to protect workers against inflation and unemployment), strengthening of unionism, development of factory committees (particularly to implement the sit-down strikes that had recently become a widespread phenomenon in the United States and in Europe), workers' control of industry and an end to secrecy in business enterprises, and alliance of workers and farmers against their common exploiters.

This program was directed at the liberal-capitalist countries. But Trotsky also formulated briefer programs for underdeveloped countries, fascist countries, and for the Soviet Union. Trotsky's approach sought to deal with three levels of concern:

1. Democratic rights and liberties. In a period of spreading fascism and totalitarianism, Trotsky tied the working-class movement to defending democracy, not

only because it was necessary for its survival but because he believed that democratic rights would engage the working class and other social groups.

2. Immediate demands for economic improvements. Recognizing that workers were often dissatisfied with long-range promises about socialism, Trotsky called for improvements in economic conditions and social welfare, and an end to speed-ups.

3. Transitional demands. These would serve as the transition into the socialist phase of existence. The heart of the program, these demands called for goals that seemed reasonable and understandable to workers such as a sliding scale of wages and hours. At the same time, the attainment of these demands would challenge the fundamental power of the bourgeoisie. The demand "Open the books" would not only end business secrecy but would expose how the bourgeoisie exploited its workers. Crowning this section of the program were demands calling for the formation of factory committees that would implement the program at the factory level. These committees (the equivalent of Russian soviets) would ultimately challenge the capitalists and make the transition to a socialist society.

Trotsky conceived of his program as transitional in two senses. First, it bridged the gap between the consciousness of the proletariat and the urgency for a revolutionary program in the face of fascism. Second, the demands constituted an approach to the development of institutions that would make the transition from capitalism to socialism. Thus, demands for a sliding scale fitted the consciousness of the workers but would, at the same time, direct them against their employers more intensively. The demand for factory committees was also geared at providing an organizational device which would not only increase participation and heighten consciousness of the workers but would, in time, take over the responsibilities for running factories *and* the society.

Trotsky did not believe that the demands of the transitional program were capable of being achieved within capitalism. In response to a question as to whether one of the demands could be realized, he responded:

It is easier to overthrow capitalism than to realize this demand under capitalism. Not one of our demands will be realized under capitalism. That is why we are calling them transitional demands. It creates a bridge to the mentality of the workers and then a material bridge to the socialist revolution.

The concept of the transitional program does not make the work of mobilization simple; mobilization remains a vital but difficult part of the work of all revolutionaries. Had the transitional program the magical power attributed to it by some of Trotsky's followers, there would have been far greater (and more successful) revolutionary events in the world after he formulated the program in 1938.

The capability of capitalism to absorb some of the elements of the transitional program can be seen in the adoption, after considerable conflict, of the concept of the "sliding scale of wages" in the escalator clauses found in many union contracts in the United States. These clauses protect workers against inflation by adjusting wages to the cost of living. Though the escalator clause was adopted, capitalists resisted with great firmness the demand to "open the books." This became an issue when auto employers contended that they could not afford to pay higher wages; the demand that they prove it by opening the books was successfully resisted during a long and bitter strike.

If somewhat complex and difficult to implement, Trotsky's concept of the transitional program provides an approach to the mobilizational dilemma of revolutionaries. It argues:

- Programs of immediate demands must be appropriate to local situations and not drawn up to encompass the world.
- Programs must be geared not only at implementing the revolution directly but at maintaining a democratic environment within which revolutionary movements can function, and an economic environment that improve the conditions of the mass of the people.
- Programs must be transitional in the sense that they fit the moods and psychology of the groups to which they are addressed. Unless demands can be formulated in a meaningful way for workers, farmers, youth, minorities, and others, they will be meaningless. It is therefore the responsibility of revolutionaries to formulate demands as slogans, testing them, and discarding those that are meaningless.
- Programs should be transitional in the sense that they construct organizational forms to make the transition from capitalism to socialism. Demands should not only be meaningful to the masses but should *move* them. If a demand is attainable within capitalism, this should not be sneezed at; but it also represents a weakness in the way the demand was formulated that permits its cooperation by the bourgeoisie.

Mao on Mobilization

Just as Marx's approach to mobilization flows from his analysis of the driving force, Mao Zedong's concerns with mobilization are integrally tied to his organization theories and to his beliefs that mobilizations must be part of the development of future arrangements. Unlike many other revolutionaries who believed that the detailed unfolding of a socialist society could only take place *after* a revolutionary seizure of power, Mao developed an approach to mobilization that argued for its organic relationship to the future organization of a communist China.

Few revolutionary thinkers have had as many opportunities to develop so broad a range of theoretical approaches — and to implement them — as Mao. Because of the economically backward character of China, with a tiny but highly concentrated proletariat and an enormous peasantry that suffered misery and exploitation to a degree unparalleled in human history, the Chinese communist struggle for power lasted more than two decades. Unlike other revolutionaries, Mao had to conduct his battles for power while being responsible for actually running a sizable segment of Chinese society. Even though that segment was small and surrounded by military enemies, this situation forced Mao to organize and mobilize simultaneously.

It was this experience that gives Mao's writing its distinctive style. Reading Mao in the context of advanced capitalist societies often leads readers to view him as repetitious and simplistic. This is because he was concerned with explaining ideas to peasants who, while they might have enormous experience, were not used to generalizing or seeing the possibility of change. Mao also had to elaborate a theory that located driving force in the peasantry, to formulate a multiplicity of organizational approaches that were geared to protracted revolutionary warfare, and to be concerned with creating social arrangements that represented the future shape of society and that would generate revolutionary ardor in the peasantry. He therefore formulated an organization theory based on communicating with the peasants and relating conduct to action.

ORGANIZATION AND COMMUNICATION

Mao recognized that a major hindrance to the involvement of peasants was their isolation from the major events that had gotten underway when the Manchu dynasty was overthrown in 1911. Although China had been shaken by the Taiping rebellion during 1850–66, most peasant uprisings were localized and isolated events. Mao recognized the need to develop organizational forms that would draw peasants into a continuous communications structure. Unless some such structure could be created, it would be impossible to formulate programs that would be meaningful to the peasants.

The movement of communist cadres into the villages was facilitated by the gradual breakdown of the tight kinship system that had tied peasant exploitation to the land-ownership patterns and the religious organization of society. As the traditional social system weakened, the landlords became more visible to peasants simply as landlords and not as leaders of the kinship and religious systems. Mao stressed the need to identify the landlords as exploiters and landownership as their exploitative mechanism. The key to peasant mobilization was the formation of peasant associations, a form of organization that would be especially useful as the old patterns of rural organization fell into disuse.

The peasant associations served to undermine the residual powers of the clan and temple elders. Moreover, their very character placed the associations into conflict with the old authorities over the issues that were most meaningful to peasants: the ownership and operation of land and the distribution of its products. The associations also served as an important aggregating element through which the communists could address the peasants on the peasants' ground rather than in environments dominated by the old authorities.

Mao therefore defined the formation of such peasant associations as a primary element in organization wherever the communists could establish a base of operations. It should be emphasized here that Mao was not simply satisfied with taking physical control of an area through the power of the Red Army; unless such control could be accompanied by the development of peasant organizations which would interact with the communists and ultimately give them support, the communists would be little better than the bandit warlords that dominated local Chinese politics during this period.

At a later stage, once the Chinese Revolution was successful in the rural areas and the communists swept into the urban centers along the coast, similar forms of urban organization became necessary. The urban proletariat in China's cities, especially in the coastal areas, had been a major source of support for the young Chinese Communist Party. The isolation of the cities from the mass of rural, peasant China and the folly of a political line set out by Stalin that required the communists to unite with the Kuomintang, permitted the destruction of the urban proletarian base in the Shanghai general strike of 1927. Although Mao had already begun a reorientation toward the peasantry, the 1927 events pushed him further toward the development of a peasant base.

Patterns in urban organization followed those already established in the rural areas. People were organized both at their place of work and their residence (for those people who did not work). The creation of block and neighborhood organizations also drew in the other elements of the population. Neighborhood organizations also provided an additional communication system to reach urban factory workers where they lived.

The purpose of this was to draw people into taking action on their own behalf. This was extremely important in rural and urban areas, where the suppressive character of the older system had created strong orientations toward noninvolvement in political life. Local urban committees made residents aware of government policies, carried out public security activities and recreation, undertook public sanitation responsibilities, public works and relief, and began to arbitrate local disputes.

Throughout the period of transition—that is, before the communists took power in all of China—these forms of organization were utilized to maintain support, to involve people in direct and immediate political actions against the landlords, and to recruit new members. After 1949, when communist control of mainland China was consolidated, these same instrumentalities were used to involve rural and urban populations in political mobilization. In various subsequent campaigns, such as the Great Leap Forward and the Cultural Revolution, these approaches were essential for continuous involvement of the people.

EXEMPLARY ACTION IN DAILY LIFE

A basic problem confronted the Chinese communists who were able to sustain military bases in the rural areas but who found themselves excluded from China's cities after 1927. This was the problem of not falling into the prevailing pattern of warlordism that then characterized China. Warlordism was a product of the decay of imperial central authority. All over China, political and military leaders, adventurers, robbers, and others formed small-scale armies and took control of local areas. Anyone able to command a handful of soldiers and some guns could set himself up in business as a warlord, exploiting the local population, and living off the meager surplus produced by the local peasantry.

It would have been easy for Mao and the Chinese communists to fall into this same pattern. Instead, Mao argued for the development of a human social base so that the communist forces would not only continue to survive but, indeed, grow.

For Mao it was essential that the Red Army be economically self-sufficient and not depend upon exacting tribute that peasants expected to pay to the warlords. Accordingly, a first principle was that communist troops be self-sufficient or pay for what they needed. A second principle was that troops should behave in an exemplary manner with respect to the local population.

Moreover, communist soldiers engaged in farming and production. Mao did not view such activity as impeding their work as soldiers:

> Some people say that if the army units go in for production, they will be unable to train or fight and that if the government and other organizations do so, they will be unable to do their own work. This is a false argument. In recent years our army units in the Border Region have undertaken production on a big scale to provide themselves with ample food and clothing and have simultaneously done their training and conducted their political studies and literacy and other courses much more successfully than before. . . . While there was a large-scale production campaign at the front last year, great successes were gained in the fighting. . . .

The Chinese communists mobilized the people by setting examples through behavior, through self-sufficiency, nonexploitation, teaching literacy, and similar approaches. They demonstrated that it was possible to drive away the troops of the warlords or of Chiang Kai-shek, who would have returned the peasants to the "normal" patterns of exploitation. Mao showed, therefore, that exemplary behavior could be used to mobilize people who had previously been politically inert.

In addition to the specific mobilizational techniques developed in the context of the Chinese Revolution, Mao also mastered the art of rephrasing general socialist concepts into plain language. A whole epistemology is reduced to: If you want to know the taste of a pear, you must change the pear by eating it yourself."

Mao incessantly preached strategic approaches just as he sought to simplify analysis and put it into contexts which peasants could understand. The Chinese Revolution developed an enormously broad social base as a result and the victory over the Kuomintang thus became possible.

Conclusion

Approaches to mobilization are given their most specific meaning and form in the search by revolutionaries for means to activize the people. Although the initial approach of Marx and Engels began with a tendency toward determinism, experience soon indicated that revolutionaries would not only have to develop distinct forms of organization but would also have to take an active role with respect to the proletariat. Each period of revolutionary activity brought forward new ideas about mobilization: Marx and Engels with the initial emphasis on independent and international organization; Lenin on the character of the vanguard party if the proletariat was to transcend simple activism and find a revolutionary direction; Trotsky's distinctive concept of a transitional program and its translation into slogans; Mao with his approach to organization not only to mobilize the masses but to give embodiment to the institutions of the socialist future.

Mobilizational approaches represent, at the present time, a vast collection of strategies and tactics, techniques and approaches. Many of these have proven to be very useful in moving social classes into action; under some circumstances, however, these same approaches have proven to be ineffective. The analysis of mobilization represents, therefore, one major imponderable of revolutionary theory. Why is it that people are responsive to some ideas at particular times but unresponsive at other times? Some answers will be provided in the remaining chapters, but much analysis remains for developing a fuller understanding of mobilization theory.

CHAPTER TWELVE

Mobilization:
Theory, Practice, Issues

The purpose of revolutionary action is to transform the class structure of society. Because it can be co-opted by nonrevolutionary groups, the very process of mobilization must contain two distinctive features:

1. The goals of mobilization in terms of *revolutionary intent* must be clear. Without the establishment of clear goals, mobilization degenerates into a set of limited procedures and the purpose of revolutionary action — societal transformation — is forgotten.

2. Mobilization should involve people in the determination of policy and not simply in implementation. Unless people begin to control their own lives, the goals of mobilization may be impeded by elite groups acting to further their own interests.

The advantages of involving large numbers of people in revolutionary action becomes clear through three ends which such action produces.

1. When many people experience a common activity, it provides them with a shared set of understandings. While all workers may experience the degradation of factory life and the alienation of disembodied production, this experience becomes more meaningful when they *respond* to it together. Common experience is an excellent "teacher," bringing forth better understandings by individuals that they are neither unique nor repressed because of some personal defect, but rather because of the common operations of the system.

2. Common experience provides individuals with a sense of their collective strength. When workers engage in a strike action, or peasants undertake an attack on their landlord, they simultaneously gain a sense of their own common strength and of the weakness of the enemy.

3. Common action upsets the domination of everyday life and permits people to see the possibilities of social transformation.

Throughout the 19th century, European revolutionaries shared an optimistic view that the oppression and exploitation of class society would automatically enlist vast sectors of the population in support of revolutionary organizations. The actual seizure of power was generally conceived as a relatively quick mass insurrection based on armed force. When, in the last part of the 19th century, some socialists began to argue that a peaceful electoral transition to socialism was possible, they also believed that the contradictions of the capitalist system would lead the majority to accept the socialist alternative.

It has become increasingly clear in the 20th century that there is nothing *automatic* about revolutionary transformation. Consequently many revolutionaries have learned to develop strategies and tactics which explicitly treat the *transition* from the present oppressive system to the desired goal. These transitional strategies and tactics must address themselves to the needs, understandings, and willingness of the people to act and orient themselves toward the broader goal of revolutionary transformation. In this sense every mobilizational strategy must embody an analysis of the issues that speak to immediate needs and struggles of the population but, at the same time, point to central contradictions in the system that only social revolution can resolve.

Historically, the low level of class consciousness among various working classes has often meant that revolutionaries had to devise mobilizational strategies whose daily emphasis was far from the ultimate question of state power. Often strategies initially conceived as revolutionary degenerated into reform movements directed toward ameliorating immediate problems rather than challenging and replacing the system as a whole. This represents the problem that revolutionaries often refer to as *reformism* or *opportunism*. Unionism throughout the world, but particularly in the United States, provides a striking example of this problem. On a number of occasions, the relative weakness of revolutionary parties has forced them into temporary alliances with progressive elements of other social classes. Frequently such alliances have entailed the loss of revolutionary goals; they surrender the leadership and ideological control of such alliances to the other class elements involved. At the same time, the opposite problem of *sectarianism* has occurred when revolutionaries have focused on the goal of social transformation at the expense of developing programs that speak to the daily needs of the bulk of the population. Battling with increasing exactitude over precise formulations of future goals, sectarian groups detach themselves from any real contact with a social force capable of changing anything.

The Elements of Revolutionary Mobilization

Revolutionaries differ in their assessment of the causes behind the degeneration or collapse of various mobilizational strategies. Although some of the more extreme have argued that anything less than armed struggle is co-optation, most revolutionaries since Luxemburg and Lenin have seen the roots of reformism and opportunism on the one hand, and sectarianism on the other, in the failure of revolutionaries to develop an adequate strategy for connecting day-to-day work to the ultimate goal of socialism.

Four basic elements appear consistently on the question of mobilization, explicitly addressing the connections between daily practice and the goal of a socialist society.

RAISING CONSCIOUSNESS

Unless people are aware of their exploitation and its source, they are relatively helpless and inert. Mobilization is intended to concretize the everyday experience of exploitation in such a way that individual members of an exploited class begin to generalize from their own individual experience. Once a general understanding develops so that individuals learn that their experience is not a product of their personal inadequacies ("I'm dumb," or "I don't have enough education," or "What can *I* do?"), they should become capable of acting with other people experiencing the same condition.

This process of developing a common experience is also useful for learning against whom energies should be directed. Consciousness is raised through a twofold process of learning about the similarities shared by all members of a class and learning about the general characteristics of a system so that people "know the enemy."

In addition, programs must be designed to *implicitly and explicitly* raise the question of capitalism versus socialism. Revolutionary class consciousness embodies not only a sense of solidarity among a class against a commonly perceived enemy, but a sense of the historical possibility and necessity of overcoming capitalism and replacing it with socialism before peoples' needs can be met.

INCREASING PARTICIPATION

Most political systems are built on expectations that the mass of the population will have little to do with determining their political (and therefore social and economic) futures. Ostensibly democratic systems, while permitting participation, limit it to periodic voting, at least as far as the overwhelming majority of the population is concerned.

The active mobilization of the energies of workers creates a larger quantum of "social energy" which can be utilized to undermine the exploitative system. In addition, mobilization develops experience appropriate to the transition to the new social form in which people will be seriously and continuously involved in the determination of their own lives. Mobilization is thus intended to increase levels of participation so that people better understand their own capabilities and acquire the experience necessary for the socialist transition.

A vital aspect of increasing participation is that it must not be limited simply to action or the implementation of policy. Unless there is increased participation in the determination of policy — in the analysis of events and the planning of revolutionary strategies — mobilization degenerates into simple manipulative techniques that give participants a false sense of their involvement. In this respect, the need for increasing participation is most significantly addressed within revolutionary organizations themselves. Peoples' experience within their own revolutionary institutions form the basis of their belief in their ultimate ability to run the larger institutions associated with economic and social planning and to manage work place and community institutions. The development of inaccessible bureaucracies and hierarchies within the revolutionary movement is subversive, therefore, of the intent of mobilization.

UNDERMINING THE SYSTEM

Most revolutionaries dislike the idea of activity for its own sake. Unless action can be used to develop consciousness and undermine the system, it is seen as having little value. Since Marx, the specific goal of the revolutionary process has been the seizure and transformation of *state power*. Neither Marx nor other revolutionaries developed a fully adequate theory of *the state*. It is generally understood that the state is the totality of institutions, ideology, and activity necessary to the capitalist system.

The state, from a marxist perspective, is seen as maintaining three basic functions, each of which may be given different emphasis in various stages of the development of capitalism:

1. The accumulation function. Capitalism is based on the continuous accumulation of capital by capitalists. The state must create the conditions, legal and institutional, for accumulation to continue unimpaired. If taxes on profits, for example, become confiscative, the bourgeoisie would be unable to continue to exist.

2. The legitimation function. Most social systems work best when they depend upon voluntary compliance and not on coercion. This is especially true of capitalism, which must continually legitimate itself to extract maximum energy from people. Legitimation includes the production of ideas about "success" and "failure" within the system as well as justification for the inequities that are part and parcel of capitalism.

3. Reproduction and system maintenance. Not only must the human race reproduce itself biologically but a system must reproduce the population to carry on its activities, day-by-day and over time. In capitalist society, these activities are embodied in the state. At the same time, a complex of law, law-making machinery and enforcement, administrative and judicial, is required to pressure and, if necessary, coerce compliance with the system. Enforcement involves a network of institutions: the police, the armed forces, courts and judges, prisons and detention systems.

The state performs its functions, then, at a number of different levels of abstractness ranging from ideological control to direct physical intervention against anticapitalist forces. As a result, the struggle over state power occurs on a number of different levels. The revolutionary perspective holds that the struggle is not only concerned with *what* the state does, but *how* it does it. Seizing the state is not a simple physical activity; post offices, radio stations, governmental buildings, work places, and corporate offices may be occupied, but the ideological assumptions and habitual behavior that underlie the manner in which these institutions operate are more difficult to uproot. Similarly, elections may be won by anticapitalist forces, but election in and of itself does not constitute a seizure of state power. Fundamental questions of private property and direct popular involvement in decision-making are of paramount importance here.

Therefore, unless the capture of the bourgeois state is accompanied by a *transformation* in the manner in which it functions, little of revolutionary significance will have been achieved. The contest for state power must embody activities in which large numbers of people begin to participate directly in collective decisions which affect their lives.*

In the early stages of revolutionary mobilization it may be enough for strategies to "pay off" with small victories sufficient to demonstrate that people are capable of making changes in society. At later stages, as the revolutionaries gain strength and affect the balance of class forces, it becomes necessary to develop strategies explicitly aimed at limiting or eroding capitalist prerogatives and challenging their power. In the final stages, it becomes necessary for revolutionaries to devise transitional entities that begin the takeover of state functions.

BUILDING AND SUSTAINING THE REVOLUTIONARY ORGANIZATION

A final element in the mobilization process is that it should serve as a bridge between workers who are developing consciousness and those who are already-conscious revolutionaries. All revolutionaries, no matter what form of organization they choose to join, recognize that there is a distinction between those already conscious and those developing consciousness. That distinction is generally regarded as deplorable, and in an ideal situation, becomes minimized as more of the people participate. However, ideal revolutionary situations do not exist and the distinction is one that must be reckoned with.

As people become active they not only develop self-expression but provide indications of their willingness to make greater (or lesser) commitments to revolutionary action. For those willing to make more commitments, mobilization provides the opportunity for identification and, therefore, for inclusion into the ranks of more conscious and more deliberate revolutionaries.

For socialists who believe that the connection between everyday struggles and the revolutionary goal is best embodied in the development of a revolutionary organization, the question of increasing the revolutionary ranks becomes centered on increasing the size and effectiveness of the organization. For this reason, mobilizational strategies must include the specific concern of attracting new members to the organization and sustaining or increasing the commitment of those already active.

The need to recruit and sustain membership in revolutionary organizations is, of course, reciprocally linked with the increase of revolutionary consciousness, mass participation, and victories against the system. Each of these functions plays a vital role. The ability of conscious revolutionaries to keep all four functions in mind and to maintain them in the proper perspective represents one of the major dilemmas of revolutionary action. All too frequently, mobilizational action has been geared to one or two of these functions; or a function such as recruitment has been permitted

*For further development on this theme see Part IV on Future Arrangements.

to become primary and overshadow the other functions. Unless mobilizational action fulfills all and in the correct proportions, serious failures will develop in the future, just as they have in the past.

Where to Mobilize?

The question of where to mobilize flows from the analysis revolutionary theoreticians have made about the location of driving force. But in its most fundamental way this issue has been put in terms of (1) organizing workers at the point of production — that is, the place in which people experience their exploitation most directly, or (2) other locations.

Organizing and mobilizing at the point of production was the initial and primary locus of revolutionary activity. This concentration followed from the "natural" proclivities that workers had to organize themselves in the earliest days of capitalist development. When the earliest forms of class action began as spontaneous strikes, revolutionaries soon realized the organizational and mobilizational potential of workers within their work places. Revolutionaries therefore encouraged the growth of trade unions, which were viewed not only as organizational manifestations of the proletarian drive against capitalism but as the most suitable forms to keep the working class engaged in continuing class action.

But unions, it was quickly discovered, tended to define their activities as limited to the improvement of wages, hours, and working conditions. Rather than attacking the entire system of exploitation, unions in most countries concentrated on the interests of their members in a single work place or working for a single employer, or at its broadest sense, in terms of the workers of a single industry.

Revolutionaries came to see their task as converting unions into broader organizations. From the earliest development of unionism, revolutionaries believed that the inherent contradictions of capitalism would produce a conversion of class-collaborationist organizations into those of conflict.

Early revolutionaries also discovered that there were other places within which the working class (and others) could be organized. For one thing, point of production mobilization, while reaching laborers, did not reach their families. As the socialist movements sought entry into the political arena by winning the right to vote, it became all the more important that instrumentalities be created to organize the families of workers, to bring them into action to demand their democratic rights. This fact, as well as electoral representation on the basis of geography, led to the formation of geographically based organizations that sought to mobilize people on the basis of their locational interests. More recently some revolutionaries have argued that many aspects of daily oppression, such as the lack of housing, poor education, and inadequate transportation and health care are experienced not at the point of production but in the community, i.e., at the point of consumption of goods and services. The logical consequence of this approach is to direct mobilization toward programs that confront the state in its manifestation as agencies and institutions of government.

Another basis for organization and mobilization developed with the recognition that workers (and others) were dissatisfied with their role as consumers. Workers found that they were paying high prices for food and other necessities of everyday life. The growth of a movement of cooperatives that would purchase food in bulk and sell it at reduced prices demonstrated the potential for mobilizing people as consumers.

Revolutionaries have continually debated about the most effective locations within which to mobilize and organize. Many organizations decide upon a single strategy — point of production, for example — and concentrate their energies by requiring their members to become factory workers. Sometimes this strategy may be focused even further: if a group believes that workers in particular primary industries (steelmaking, auto manufacturing, etc.) will be most revolutionary, their membership may be targeted for work in these industries. Other revolutionary groups take a more eclectic approach, contending that revolutionary energies can develop in a multiplicity of places. In such cases, mobilizational activities may occur around elections while normal everyday organizing in the work place continues.

The resolution of the question as to where to organize and mobilize follows, to a considerable degree, from the issues discussed under driving force (Part I) and theories of organization (Part II). Here we can only set out the basic manner in which the issues have been discussed.

Enduring Aspects of Mobilization

Although mobilization involves the development of strategies and tactics that are highly fluid and situationally specific, a number of continuing issues have emerged. These involve (1) the development of programs and their embodiment in slogans; (2) the use of study groups as an educational and mobilizational device; and (3) philosophical questions about legality, morality, and the relationships of ends and means. These are not the only enduring issues involved in mobilizational approaches; other issues also arise from time to time.

PROGRAMS AND SLOGANS

Protest movements have always projected political and social programs — either implicitly or explicitly. Systematic political programs, however, have their origin in the political parties formed after the development of capitalism. The embodiment of a political orientation can be found, for example, in documents such as *The Federalist Papers*. Successively, different political parties formulated varying programs that outlined their approach to the world and to politics.

This procedure was also followed by Marx and Engels in *The Communist Manifesto* where the authors, on behalf of the International Workingmen's Association, set out a program of ten points. Other socialist parties elaborated such programs over the years. The programs of socialist parties often reflected the internal schisms and conflicting views of how power should be attained, differences on specific issues (the question of peasants, for example, was one which generated considerable controversy for many years in Germany), as well as differing conceptions of the character of the state.

One conception of programs that emerged was that of *minimum* and *maximum* programs. This idea developed in Germany as a means to distinguish between a program of immediate, specific, and concrete demands, implementable within the framework of capitalism (the minimum program), from demands which were considered to be long-range and embodied the essence of socialism.

Programs, as such, were not considered to be mobilizational; they were regarded as important public statements by the party or organization. Their mobilizational aspects were embodied in slogans. The use of slogans by socialists dates from the time that Marx and Engels concluded *The Communist Manifesto* in 1848 with the words "Proletarians of all countries unite, you have nothing to lose but your chains!" Ever since, all revolutionary movements have sought to present complex programs in simple sets of ideas.

The approach to the use of slogans involves some general principles:

- Slogans should embody the essence of a program accurately. If designed improperly, they will mislead people.
- Slogans should be brief and pithy. They should be framed in such terms that they can be easily memorized and repeated so that many people can quickly learn their use. When they become too long, they will be difficult to fix in people's minds. If brief they can be chanted during marches and demonstrations, thereby educating other people while reinforcing the ideas in the minds of the demonstrators.
- Slogans should have immediate contextual meaning. Unless a slogan relates to the immediate experiences of large numbers of people, it becomes a meaningless collection of words. Before the Second World War, for example, the U.S. Communist Party's slogan "The Yanks Are NOT Coming" drew its context from the approaching war, but gained its special meaning from the play upon words from the popular song of the First World War, "Over There," in which a key phrase was "The Yanks are coming."

A sense of what revolutionaries seek to accomplish can perhaps best be understood by illustrating three slogans used at different times and explaining their social contexts.

All power to the Soviets. In the period between the March and November 1917 revolutions in Russia, councils (soviets) began to develop in factories, army units, and among peasants in the rural villages. As more aspects of life came to be dominated by these soviets, the Bolsheviks raised the slogan "All power to the Soviets" to counterpose their spontaneously democratic authority to the authority of the provisional government, an amalgam of political forces largely of bourgeois origin. The intent of the slogan was not only to legitimize a popular democratic political organ but to effect a transition in power.

Let the people vote on war. Prior to the Second World War, when there was considerable antiwar feeling in the United States, significant sentiment existed to establish, through law, a constitutional amendment (the Ludlow amendment) that would have required a national referendum of the American people before a declaration of war would be possible. Leon Trotsky argued support for the amendment despite his recognition that, even if it were successfully adopted, a bourgeois government would refuse to recognize the referendum. This support became embodied in the slogan.

Hell no, we won't go. This antiwar slogan was used during the Vietnam war by demonstrators and protesters. It not only marked a new level of civil disobedience by encouraging resistance to the draft ("we won't go"), but used a cadence that was particularly appropriate for marching, unlike the previous two examples.

The preparation of revolutionary slogans is an art, not a science. Over the decades, slogans have been used by the thousands, but only a few have entered historical accounts. In the United States, "Free Tom Mooney," "End the No Strike Pledge," and the more recent "Power to the People," are slogans that have disappeared into history although these were influential at the times they were used. For every important slogan, even those that have "disappeared," there are dozens of slogans that were attempted and found to be failures. Sometimes such slogans die because they are too complex, too difficult to repeat, or too easily converted into a joke.

STUDY GROUPS

Serving a variety of purposes at different times, the study group demonstrates a combination of organizing, recruiting, and mobilizing concerns. The way in which study groups have served these functions has varied considerably in different contexts.

The Old Left. Particularly within the vanguard elements of the Old Left, the study group was viewed as an important educational and training device for recruitment. Consideration of the way Lenin defined the character of the vanguard organization (see Chapter 7) shows how this conception of organization requires intermediate training grounds within which people can be educated and tested prior to admission to the revolutionary party.

Members of Old Left organizations such as the Communist Party, the Socialist Party, or the Socialist Workers Party functioned in a variety of broader organizations such as unions, public protest groups, and "front" organizations. Within such wider public environments revolutionaries sought to identify individuals who might be potential members of their group. Attempts would then be made to bring such people into study groups and other similar organizations where their education could be furthered and they could be tested through their participation in various kinds of activities.

When an individual appeared to have some potential, in the initial phases he or she was referred to as a "contact." As individual study group members became better known, often because of their participation in the group and in actions undertaken by the group, a person would become considered a "prospect," that is, a prospective member. With the continuation of activity and study, an individual might apply for or be suggested for membership.

At all stages, from contact to member, the educational development of the individual was considered of first importance. Since the vanguard concept requires a highly developed cadre of professional revolutionaries, the capability of individuals to understand and apply revolutionary theory and experience was regarded as vital. The study group constituted a major entity within which this educational process could unfold.

Old Left study groups would typically set out a course of study in the marxian classics. Beginning with *The Communist Manifesto* and some of the economic writings of Marx, *Value, Price and Profit* and *Wage Labor and Capital*, the study group would often turn to important political analyses by Marx and Engels such as *The Eighteenth Brumaire* and *The Civil War in France*. Works by Lenin such as *What Is to Be Done?* or *The State and Revolution* might also be introduced early. At a later stage, some of the more difficult writings would be undertaken such as *Capital, The German Ideology, Critique of the Gotha Program* by Marx and Engels, or Lenin on *Imperialism*. The specific works to be studied varied according to the experiences and capabilities of the students and the skill of the study group leader in recognizing how fast students could be moved into the more abstract and difficult revolutionary works. At all times, the going might become too difficult for some participants or they might find themselves in political disagreement and drop away.

Old Left study groups would often turn to current ideological issues and, in particular, the kinds of issues that delineated the specific organizational concerns of the study group sponsor. Trotskyist groups, for example, focused much discussion on the Russian Revolution, its degeneration, and the character of Stalinism. As students became sophisticated with ideas and with the special language of revolutionary analysis, the study group would move to works of increasing difficulty.

Study groups, in and of themselves, were inadequate preparation grounds. Participants, as they developed knowledge and sophistication, would be asked to translate their information into concrete action. This might range from being called on to distribute newspapers at some factory gate to representing the organization's viewpoint within one's own union. Sophisticated people were expected, in turn, to bring new contacts into the periphery of the organization and perhaps help to organize new study groups. The study group thus served the function of education, but individuals were expected to translate their new knowledge into concrete strategies for action before they could demonstrate their worthiness to belong to the vanguard organization.

The New Left. Many aspects of Old Left study groups were reproduced in those created by the New Left in the 1960s. As with the old, the primary function of study groups was seen as educational — providing opportunities for newcomers to familiarize themselves with classic socialist writers. Because the New Left was largely antivanguardist, their study groups varied in purpose and tone from the older versions.

- New Leftists were much more concerned about learning environments and the size of organization than were the older generation. One aim of New Left study groups, therefore, was to create a smaller-scale atmosphere within which people would feel more comfortable than they could in large meetings.
- Because there were few vanguard groups for which to recruit, the study groups were not considered intermediate organizations in which people learned and

were tested. Rather, these groups were intended to provide education and a linkage to action. Individual members were expected to determine their own degree of activism and involvement rather than striving for ultimate membership in the inner vanguard organization.

As with the Old Left, the New Left considered study groups to be useful but auxiliary devices to the main forms of organization and activism. The Old Left tended to be more thoroughly organized with respect to study groups and perhaps more detached from them, regarding them as necessary devices through which people could be tested. New Leftists brought spontaneous enthusiasm to their study groups so that their atmosphere was less serious and more personally engaging. Because of their lack of structure and spontaneity these groups often fell apart more easily than did Old Left study groups.

Women's Consciousness Raising Groups. The growth of the women's movement in the late 1960s saw the evolution of the study group as a distinctive form of mobilization with different intentions from either the Old or New Left. Although often ignoring a revolutionary perspective, some segments of the women's movement saw these groups as necessary for the formation of women's self-consciousness.

The women's liberation movement has argued the need for *personal liberation* groups as devices for mobilizing the energies of women for change, whether revolutionary or not. Because women tend to be isolated from each other and because of the competitiveness imposed on them by American society, women came to view the personal liberation group as the first step in mobilization and self-organization.

Generally, small groups of women (between six and twelve) would meet and begin to know each other on a personal basis. At this initial stage, women were concerned with recounting personal experiences with sexism and to release—to openly acknowledge—their bitterness, frustration, and anger. They might examine past experiences and interpret them in terms of how they felt about them. At this stage, participants strove to admit their feelings about themselves, about other women, about men. The expressions of individuals would be evaluated and discussed within the group, often by going around the room to seek comments and questions. Once individual "testimonies" were obtained, the group ideally attempted to locate common elements in the experiences.

There were often reasonable fears for the refusal to develop a higher consciousness, fears of seeing one's life as wasted and meaningless; or the fear of feeling the full weight of the uncomfortable and painful present; or despair for the prospects for change in the future. Personal liberation groups sought to articulate these fears and analyze them in terms of the objective conditions of women's situations in the past and present.

Study groups often reached a stage where they turned to a broader consideration of the sources of oppression. At this point the common experiences of other oppressed groups might be examined and the similarities to and differences from those of women would be analyzed. Broadening consciousness was regarded as important since the condition of women was recognized by most women's liberationists as only one form of systemic oppression. Again, resistance might develop to this broadening tendency. Some women might remain committed solely to a women's struggle stance; others might again experience despair; still others would recognize the broader elements of oppression and see the opportunities to join with other groups in a common struggle, while protecting the integrity of the women's struggle.

Finally, personal liberation groups often turned outward and moved toward action. In this mobilizational phase, women sought to join active struggles in their own organizations or in common organizations with others engaged in similar efforts. At this stage, women were expected to confront their oppression and deal with it openly. Activism might involve actions such as organizing new personal liberation groups for novices, learning to express oneself in public through writing and speaking, developing political campaigns on issues affecting women, and undertaking public relations activities to educate the general public.

Women's liberation study groups were distinctly different from those found in the Old and New Left. With personal liberation as a primary emphasis, they moved from individual therapeutic approaches to a broadening of consciousness before moving to public activism. Like the New Left groups, however, the emphasis was on the need to create small-scale environments within which individuals could feel comfortable and grapple with their own experience.

LEGALITY AND MORALITY

Mobilization poses, perhaps more directly than any other question, problems of morality and legality. Almost invariably, revolutionary activity gives rise to ethical questions about "ends justifying means."

Marx originally dealt with this issue by viewing law and morality as an expression of material relationships: law and morality are reflections, in bourgeois society, of bourgeois social relationships. It is for this reason that so many legal and ethical issues center on questions of property, why property rights are given so much more attention than human rights in capitalist society. Law and morality are determined by the means of production and, since socialists must be concerned with changing the means of production, two inevitable consequences derive. First, revolutionaries should not be bound by prevailing moralities; second, revolutionaries *must generate their own moral order* based on the mode of production of socialist society. While Marx never delineated the pattern of the moral order, he made clear that the failure to adhere to bourgeois morality did not represent amorality, but instead constituted a rejection of the moral rules by which exploitation was continued and justified.

Perhaps one way to concretize a long and abstract discussion is to examine morality within the context of a single specific issue — violence and nonviolence. The use of violence has generated much criticism by bourgeois and liberal critics of revolutionaries.*

---

*These critics often overlook the use of violence by instrumentalities of the state, e.g., the police, since this type of violence is regarded as "legitimate" or "moral." The response of revolutionaries to such criticism has been to argue that, if from a bourgeois point of view it is legitimate for police to defend the state, then from a revolutionary viewpoint it is moral to attack the state and its agencies and instrumentalities with whatever means are available and feasible. Revolutionaries also contend that exploitation — such as hunger — represents a form of violence exercised by the bourgeoisie over exploited classes. The acceptance of such forms of violence as legitimate is regarded by revolutionaries as a form of immorality on the part of their bourgeois critics.

Nonviolence has ancient antecedents in both the western world (in Christ, for example) and the eastern world (in Chinese philosophy). The major influences in this direction in the United States have come from Henry David Thoreau and Mahatma Gandhi. Thoreau, in his famous essay of 1846 on "Civil Disobedience," set forth the basic nonviolent orientation. Written on the occasion of being imprisoned for one night for failure to pay taxes supporting the Mexican War (and indirectly, slavery), Thoreau argued that people must dissociate themselves from governments conducting immoral acts. Thoreau contended that noncooperation with unjust laws was a moral duty to one's conscience as an individual, as well as an effective way to fight evil for those holding minority viewpoints in society:

> Abolitionists should at once . . . withdraw their support, both in person and in property, from the government of Massachusetts, and not wait till they constitute a majority of one before they suffer the right to prevail through them. I think that it is enough if they have God on their side, without waiting for that other one . . .
>
> Under a government which imprisons anyone unjustly, the true place for a just man is also a prison. . . . Cast your whole vote, not a strip of paper merely, but your whole influence. A minority is powerless while it conforms to the majority; it is not even a minority then; but it is irresistible when it clogs by its whole weight. . . . If a thousand men were not to pay their tax bills this year, that would not be a violent and bloody measure, as it would be to pay them to enable the State to commit violence and shed innocent blood. This is, in fact, the definition of a peaceful revolution, if any such is possible.

Where Thoreau's appeal was to individual conscience, it remained for Mahatma Gandhi to provide a model of the power of nonviolent *social* force in confronting British colonialism in India. In his approach, Gandhi placed great emphasis on *satyagraha* or "soul-force," a notion that has many parallels in the Christian dictum to "love your enemies." Gandhi, indeed, drew many of his ideas from Tolstoy, the Russian Christian-anarchist. He proposed that one should confront enemies lovingly, since they are more likely to see the error of their ways and would therefore be more prone to submit to true justice.

While emphasizing passive resistance, Gandhi did not believe in passivity. He encouraged active nonviolent tactics such as blocking trains with one's own body. At the same time, resisters submitted willingly to the punishments of legal authorities since this strengthened their own moral position and weakened the moral position of their exploiters. Gandhi succeeded in utilizing the morality of nonviolence to generate massive campaigns against British domination in India, campaigns which contributed to the British withdrawal from South Asia.

Nonviolence had a resurgence in the United States during the 1960s, being accepted by virtually every significant civil rights organization and most peace groups. An important articulator of this idea was Martin Luther King, Jr., who set out five important aspects of the nonviolent approach to action:

1. Nonviolence is active, not passive.

2. Nonviolence has the end of redemption and reconciliation, not the defeat or humiliation of an opponent.

3. Nonviolence is directed against forces of evil and not against persons doing the evil.

4. Nonviolence accepts suffering without retaliation since suffering has tremendous educational possibilities.

5. Nonviolence not only avoids physical violence but also moral violence; a nonviolent resister not only refuses to shoot an opponent but also refuses to hate the opponent.

While most revolutionaries do not favor nonviolence, most are not abstractly in favor of violence. Many revolutionaries, especially in recent times, support what has come to be known as "tactical nonviolence"; that is, while not subscribing to philosophical pacifism, they prefer to engage in actions that are nonviolent, looking on violence only as a last resort.

The theme of nonviolence became accepted by a broad range of civil rights groups and was manifested through sit-ins, boycotts, and vigils. As the peace movement grew in the 1960s, the same spirit prevailed. Some interesting issues were raised by many pacifists who not only condemned the United States—for its violence in Vietnam—but also the National Liberation Front and the Vietnamese communists in the north. David Dellinger, an advocate of revolutionary nonviolence (and later a defendent in the Chicago 8 conspiracy trial) argued this stance:

> We need to get back to Gandhi's insight that the best way to resist injustice is nonviolently but that it is nonetheless better to resist oppression violently than not to resist it at all. To the extent that we agree with Gandhi in this, we will remain nonviolent ourselves and will attempt to persuade others that this is the better way. It seems to be that we will also offer nonviolent assistance to those who are struggling in their own way for freedom and justice, dignity and self-liberation from Western domination.

While Dellinger represented an important stream of revolutionary nonviolence, it should be noted that most marxists have taken a different position on this issue, opposing nonviolence as an abstract morality unrelated to real conditions of life such as exploitation and power. Leon Trotsky has stated the marxist perspective on this issue:

> Under "normal" conditions a "normal" man observes the commandment: "Thou shalt not kill!" But if he kills under exceptional conditions for self-defense, the jury acquits him. . . . Insofar as the state is concerned, in peaceful times it limits itself to legalized killings of individuals so that in time of war it may transform the "obligatory" commandment, "Thou shalt not kill!" into its opposite. The most "humane" governments . . . proclaim during war that the highest duty of their armies is the extermination of the greatest possible number of people.

Trotsky continued:

> A means can be justified only by its end. But the end in its turn needs to be justified. From the marxist point of view . . . the end is justified if it leads to increasing the power of man over nature and to the abolition of the power of man over man.

The only "permissible and obligatory" means are those

> . . . which unite the revolutionary proletariat, fill their hearts with irreconcilable hostility to oppression, teach them contempt for official morality and its

democratic echoers. . . . from this it flows that *not* all means are permissible. . . . the great revolutionary end spurns those base means . . . which set one part of the working class against other parts, or attempt to make the masses happy without their participation; or lower the faith of the masses in themselves and their organization, replacing it by worship for the "leaders."

Several leaders in the struggle for civil rights during the 1960s rejected nonviolence as a limitation. Perhaps most prominent of those who wrote on this matter was Malcolm X, an influential American black nationalist. Appealing mainly to ghetto blacks for whom nonviolence was a meaningless and abstruse idea, Malcolm argued:

I *am* for violence if nonviolence means we continue postponing a solution to the American black man's problem — just to *avoid* violence. . . . If it must take violence to get the black man his human rights in this country, I'm *for* violence exactly as you know [other minority groups] would be if they were flagrantly discriminated against.

Violence, like other questions relating to the morality of political action, is not generally an issue to which revolutionaries respond with absolute answers. That revolutionaries must be prepared to respond to violence with violence is indicated by the experiences of the Chilean revolution and counterrevolution of the 1970s. Coming to power through electoral means, the socialist administration of Salvador Allende was confronted by the continual violence of bourgeois forces. This process was culminated by a military coup that annihilated the socialist forces. The failure to prepare for the eventualities of counterrevolution destroyed the promise of the Chilean revolution.

CHAPTER THIRTEEN

Mobilization at the Point of Production

Revolutionaries have traditionally concentrated much of their energies on organizing and mobilizing at the point of production — the work place. For many marxists, particularly until the 1950s, the belief that the greatest contradictions of capitalism were experienced by the rapidly growing industrial work force led them to focus more narrowly on factory workers. With the decline in the relative size of the industrial sector and the growth of service and professional sectors, there developed a tendency to broaden the definition of work-place organizing and activity to include office, shops, laboratories, and places other than factories.

The growing role of the state in affecting such "work place" questions as wage agreements has combined with an increased importance of social relations outside of the work place to make new forms of mobilization take on added significance.

Despite these dramatic changes of the past few decades, work-place organizing among the industrial proletariat continues to play an important role in the strategy of many revolutionary groups. The combination of physical concentration, direct exploitation in the production process, and the experience of common activity continue to suggest the mobilizational possibilities of the work place.

In this chapter we turn to mobilizational forms focused on the work place: to unions and industrial organization, the issues of nationalization and workers' control, soviets (councils), and the general strike as a mobilizational weapon.

Unionism and Industrial Organization

Unions represent one of the earliest forms of working-class organization for self-protection. While the initial reaction on the part of the working class to the development of capitalism occasionally took the form of trying to destroy machinery, workers quickly recognized the power of their own forms of organization on the shop floor.

Unionism did not develop immediately, however. The initial phases of organization often took the form of spontaneous upsurges (such as minor riots) before workers recognized the power of continuous organization. Most unions began when workers sought a collective response to their immediate situation with individual employers.

While revolutionaries recognized the tremendous organizational power of the unions, they also noted the tendency for unions to lose interest in the transformation of society and to concentrate on winning economic benefits for their members. Early revolutionaries therefore focused their energies on trying to win over union members to more radical programs, constantly experiencing tensions between their revolutionary goals and their desire to build a powerful constituency.

Early unionism in Europe and the United States took the form of craft unionism in which only skilled workers were organized into unions involving their individual skills or crafts. All too often these craft unions demonstrated narrow interests in protecting their members only, ignoring the large numbers of unskilled workers who were being recruited to work in the new factories. Revolutionaries came to believe that the reformist views of the existing unions were largely a function of their emphasis on a small elite of skilled workers to the exclusion of the growing mass of industrial workers. It was for this reason that radicals in the United States began to talk about *industrial organization* or *industrial unionism*, which would create unions for unskilled workers, almost from the time the craft-dominated American Federation of Labor was formed in 1888. Two approaches were taken: some believed that organization should take place within the AFL, whereas others, despairing of ever changing the AFL, argued for a new organization to bring revolutionary unionism to the unskilled workers.

FIRST ATTEMPTS: THE INDUSTRIAL WORKERS OF THE WORLD

The Industrial Workers of the World (IWW) — often known as the "Wobblies" — was formed in 1905 from a combination of militant trade unions, left-wing parties, individual revolutionaries, and others sympathetic to organizing industrial workers. After several formative years of factional fighting, the IWW became established as a radical union seeking a revolutionary transformation of society but hostile to political organization, particularly working in elections; in this respect, the IWW emerged as a revolutionary *syndicalist* union.

The high point of the IWW's existence came through its leadership of a strike of textile workers in Lawrence, Massachusetts, in 1912. The textile workers were almost entirely unskilled: new to employment and from a large variety of ethnic groups, and many were women. All experienced abysmal working conditions, meager wages, and had little potential for surviving in the mills. When the Lawrence textile workers struck — spontaneously and without prior organization — they were ignored by other unions. The IWW responded quickly by sending organizers to the scene. At this stage many of the innovative strategies of the IWW were born that were to infuriate employers.

Finding the strikers' children suffering because their parents had little money, the IWW organizers arranged to send the children to major urban centers nearby to live with strike sympathizers until the strike was over. Once arrangements had been made, the IWW organized a dramatic farewell in the form of a march to the railway station. When police attacked the mothers and children, the resulting publicity led to a huge outpouring of public support and a congressional investigation. Other similar actions demonstrated not only that the IWW had a flair for dramatically presenting the hardships of workers to other workers but that they could also organize the energies of very diverse groups of striking workers.

By the end of the Lawrence strike the IWW was seen as a threat not only to employers but also by the AFL and by those concerned about sustaining American capitalism as a whole.

But the IWW's successes at Lawrence were short-lived. The Wobblies opposed signing contracts with employers on the grounds that workers should not tie themselves down to such "illegitimate" agreements with their class enemies. This principle took away from the Lawrence textile workers the safeguards and protection that a contract with employers would have provided. Shortly after the strike was settled the employers began to fire radicals and strike leaders. By 1914 this policy, coupled with a rise in unemployment caused by a depression in the textile industry, had eliminated nearly all IWW influence among the Lawrence workers.

Between 1912 and 1916 the IWW grew in size as it addressed itself to situations in which industrial workers were seeking action against their employers. During this period the IWW learned to deal with the many different ethnic nationalities present in the mass-production industries. Foreign-language sections were organized, newspapers were started in many different languages, and organizers were trained who came from the many ethnic groups. As the United States drew closer to entry into the First World War, the IWW was viewed in government circles as a great danger because, unlike the AFL, it was unwilling to forgo the strike weapon and other instruments of class struggle during the war. The government thereupon unleashed a major attack on the IWW, persecuting and prosecuting its leadership, framing individual leaders, and harassing the organization in innumerable ways. The persecution was continued after America's entry into the war and, by its end, the IWW remained only a shell.

The IWW did not limit its appeals and activities to union organizing. When political opponents and business interests tried to limit the right of public discussion, the IWW took on continual free-speech battles in recognition that the right to such a freedom was crucial to future organizing. A free-speech fight might begin when a Wobbly organizer was thrown in jail for delivering a soapbox talk on a street corner. As the word passed along the grapevine that followed the railroads on which the Wobblies rode, hundreds of IWW members would descend on the towns. The intent was to fill the jails with free-speech fighters until the system was so clogged that the authorities would give up and let the Wobblies speak their piece. The tactic worked in some cases in which publicity attracted the support of civil libertarians, but failed in others when Wobblies were beaten, lynched, or in some cases thrown off trains in the desert and left to walk their way out.

THE CIO: SUCCESSFUL UNIONISM;
UNSUCCESSFUL REVOLUTIONARY MOBILIZATION

The destruction of the IWW during and after World War I left the United States with no organization geared to the needs of unskilled workers in the mass-production industries. This was a period in which the growth of giant factories and the spread of the assembly line transformed U.S. production. Despite some attempts at revolutionary industrial unionism by the Communist Party and the growth of some company unions, the conditions of unskilled workers was disasterously worsened by the onset of the Great Depression of the 1930s. As the depression deepened, hundreds of thousands of unskilled workers were left without any work and with no source of support. But as the economy improved slightly in 1934, the first inklings of new industrial action occurred in automotive cities such as Toledo, Ohio. Factory workers, on their own, organized temporary organizations, fought bitter strikes in which strikebreakers were imported by employers, and began to create new forms of working-class militancy.

By 1935 the attention of Americans—including revolutionaries and radicals—became focused on the dramatic events unfolding in the auto, maritime, rubber, steel, textile, and other mass-production industries. The interest of radicals was heightened by a dramatic technique invented by factory workers: the sit-down strike. This strike form developed when industrial workers occupied the factories rather than moving outside to walk the picket lines. Invented by rubber workers in Akron, Ohio, the sit-down strike spread rapidly to the auto factories of Michigan and elsewhere in the United States. Although it was not explicitly intended as such, the sit-down strikes represented the seizure of private property by the workers since it prevented the owners from doing what they wanted with their property. In hundreds of factories, strikers took their tools from the assembly lines, welded the factory doors shut, sealed most windows, established "weapons depots" on the factory roofs consisting of tools, parts, pieces of equipment, and prepared to battle the police— not in the name of revolution but in protection of their jobs and to insist that the employers recognize their new industrial unions.

Inside the factories, democratic procedures were established on the shop floor, with elected delegates for each plant forming strike committees to provide direction. And, for a short period of time before a more established union leadership moved in, rank-and-file domination of the strikes and the unions provided a measure of democratic workers' control that had hitherto been unknown in American industry.

If the employers fought unionism viciously, the new efforts at organization received a mixed reception in the AFL. Some unionists wanted to support the new organizations but others hesitated for the same reasons that had existed thirty years earlier. In particular, the jurisdictional issue—which unions would the different workers join?—posed an insoluble dilemma for the AFL. While the AFL dithered over what action to take, many radicals joined in support of the new unionism.

A significant change occurred when ten unions inside the AFL decided to create a Committee for Industrial Organization (CIO) to support the industrial workers. From this point, much of the development fell under the leadership of John L. Lewis, then head of the United Mine Workers (UMW). While Lewis was a militant, he was also a strong believer in capitalism. Lewis helped to negotiate the first contracts that provided union recognition. From then on, shop-level democracy (with which Lewis had never been sympathetic, especially in his own miners union) was discouraged and sitting-down on the job was brought to a halt.

Initially, the drive for industrial unionism held high promise for revolutionary action. Radicals had argued for decades that the movement of industrial workers into unionism would unleash vast untapped energies. As the events unfolded, not only did workers seize factories but, as the return to work began, they initiated extensive shop-level participation over grievances. If the assembly line moved too fast, the workers stopped work and went *with* their stewards to negotiate with the foremen. The strategy of the employers and top-level leadership of the unions became one of limiting participation in grievances to shop-level representatives — the shop stewards. With "representation" becoming the form through which worker dissatisfaction was expressed, it is not surprising that the initial militant thrust of organization — with its revolutionary implications — became dispersed.

The role of the left organizations in this process must be noted. Industrial unionism attracted a considerable number of revolutionaries — in the communist, socialist, and other parties — who entered the factories, established contacts with shop-level leaders, and often became workers themselves (if they were not already). Through these actions, leftists won an enduring base of support in the factories — support that lasted for several decades after the sit-down strikes. But the left was more involved in recruitment and building their organizations than in the broadening of working-class consciousness about the ultimate goal of the sit-down strikes. When the official union leadership deflected the militancy into representative bargaining, the left was unable to sustain a broad vision of the potential organization or to keep workers involved in controlling production on the assembly lines. The failure of the leftist organizations to keep attention focused on the goals of social transformation and on increased participation, meant that the radical organizations ultimately had to be satisfied with picking up some crumbs in the form of new members. While not unimportant, this failed to sustain militancy; industrial unionism soon followed the reformist direction of the AFL.

By 1939 the process of institutionalization of the new industrial unions was well advanced. Employers came to recognize that they could live with industrial unions *if* those unions could be brought under control and, in particular, management could regain control over vital processes in the factories, such as the speed of the assembly lines. Between 1938 and the U.S. entry into the Second World War in 1941, a battle went on as rank-and-file workers sought to retain the controls they had won over shop conditions. Originally, when a grievance arose, workers would stop working and move as a group to negotiate the problem with the boss; soon a formalized grievance procedure was written into the contracts that gave responsibility for negotiations to shop stewards. This not only removed workers from the negotiations process but made the "representatives" amenable to company pressures. The leadership of the industrial unions encouraged the process, since it eased their handling of the rank and file; rather than having to deal with hundreds of angry workers, the leadership could talk to a smaller number of "representatives." The sit-down technique was also abandoned by the leadership under managerial pressure when formal union recognition was granted; sit-downs were also declared illegal by the courts, and the union leadership hesitated to violate any laws.

As the United States moved into the Second World War, the militant drive of the industrial workers was eroded further. Managements insisted on emphasizing "managerial prerogatives" and wrote increasing numbers of such prerogatives into the contracts. The weakening of militancy was also accelerated by political events. While the supporters of the Communist Party inside the unions were relatively militant in the mid-1930s, they became supermilitant during the period of the Stalin-Hitler Pact in the late 1930s. This militancy fitted well with the mood of the industrial workers, but it was soon to be undermined. After Germany invaded the Soviet Union in June 1941 the American Communist Party became a vehement supporter of U.S. entry into the war against Hitler. Unionists who supported the CP now endorsed a "no-strike pledge" for American workers, contending that it was necessary to accept compromises on the shop floor in the name of increased production for the war effort. They argued that union struggles had to be put aside for the duration of the war because aiding the successful mobilization against Hitler was the prime responsibility of American workers. Other socialist unionists, however, felt that being a committed antifascist did not necessarily mean that one had to abandon the class struggle at home. As a result, wildcat strikes and other "illegal" work stoppages occurred throughout the war period.

By the end of the war, much of the old CIO militancy had largely disappeared. The new pattern of industrial relations became institutionalized; in which a trade-off was made whereby workers surrendered their participation in the determination of their work lives for an improved and relatively privileged standard of living. A potentially revolutionary weapon became little more than another established institution, somewhat concerned about producing a little more equalization in society but abandoning interest in fundamental social change.

Nationalization and Workers' Control

The twin issues of nationalization and workers' control arise, at least in part, as a result of the search by revolutionaries for mobilizational approaches that will be meaningful to workers and move them into action to undermine capitalism. Nationalization, the demand that the state take over capitalist enterprises, originated in revolutionaries' opposition to private ownership of property. Matching this demand with workers' control began as socialists recognized that nationalization, in and of itself, was inadequate as a socialist demand.

During the last part of the 19th century and the early 20th century, socialists believed that nationalization of factories and of productive enterprises would undermine capitalism by removing the profit-making capability of the bourgeoisie. By transferring productive property to state ownership, it was thought that the very foundation of capitalism would be undermined. Even if capitalists were compensated for their property—one of the issues that arose when nationalization was proposed—there would not be any place in which they could invest their funds. Nationalization would thus lay the basis for socialism.

This view of nationalization proved to be mistaken. Although state ownership of some elements of the economy became a standard feature of modern capitalism (post offices in every country; railways in many European countries), in no nation did widespread nationalization occur to the degree that the basis for capitalism was undermined. Indeed, where nationalization was instituted, it usually occurred *with* compensation to private employers and ample opportunities for reinvestment. In addition, nationalization became a procedure adopted for those segments of the economy that were defined as socially necessary but which had become unprofitable. In Great Britain, for example, railways and coal mines were nationalized when they began losing money regularly rather than when they yielded the profits that originally made the British bourgeoisie strong. Nationalization, in this form, came to be a device for socializing bankruptcy, for spreading the costs to the people of running enterprises that could no longer yield profit. In addition, when it took place, nationalization often did so as a legal form: translating one form of ownership (private) for another form of legal ownership (public) with no changes in the way in which enterprises were operated and managed. In Great Britain, when the mines were nationalized, a National Coal Board was created to operate the mines. At the level of the individual mine, managements remained the same. At the national level, a new entity was created representing management that was now even more distant from the mines than the previous private managements had been.

These experiences and others indicated to most socialists that nationalization was not, in itself, a device that would produce the socialist transition. At the same time, two facts became clear:

1. In some countries, the demand for nationalization remains an important mobilizational concept. In Great Britain, for example, militant workers continue to press for the end of private ownership of the means of production and its conversion into public ownership. Even in the United States, where nationalization has had less support as an idea than in Europe, it has the potential for becoming a significant issue during events such as the energy crisis. Many people who still might be unwilling to support socialism can see the reasonableness of the demand for nationalization of the oil corporations.

2. Nationalization should be considered as a *necessary but not sufficient condition* for the establishment of socialism. Unless private ownership is ended, the basis for socialism cannot be created; nationalization in itself, however, does not create socialism because it may leave workers as powerless as before.

In the European context many socialists have argued the need for workers' control in nationalization struggles. Although the idea of workers' control arises from other circumstances, when paired with the conception of public ownership through nationalization, it is believed to have a far more meaningful socialistic content. Before turning to workers' control as a mobilizational concept, it is worth examining some of the experiences that led to the formulation of this idea.

As has been noted, industrial unionism provided a general improvement in the economic conditions of manual workers and established a simple grievance procedure to provide a defense for workers against arbitrary management actions. These gains, while not unimportant, failed to fulfill the revolutionary promise of industrial unionism. Rather than workers participating collectively in the determination of their conditions, their representatives began to bargain with managements. Not only did this leave workers out of the key process of determining their fate, but it placed them in a continually defensive position in which they could only *react* after some managerial action had occurred. Far from creating a system in which workers had any important degree of control over their work lives, industrial unionism simply set some limits on the exercise of arbitrary managerial power.

Experience has also shown the weakness of approaches that argue for *workers' participation* within the framework of existing capitalism. In Germany, during the 1950s, the principle of codetermination (*mittbestimmungsrecht*) was legally established in which workers would *share* some control of firms through designating workers' representatives to membership on boards of directors. The consequences of such programs have produced some small reforms but have had little effect on the shop floor or on the setting of basic policies within an industry or firm.

WHAT IS WORKERS' CONTROL?

The demand for workers' control centers on the belief that workers should have control over their own existences through direct determination of working conditions, including production and distribution processes, what is to be distributed, and how. Further, it argues that workers should control conditions not only on the immediate shop floor but throughout the firm and, indeed, the industry.

Workers' control at the shop level can be thought of as beginning with the kind of situation that existed in the early days of CIO organizing. When foremen or management undertook to implement a policy—whether to increase the speed of the assembly line or to discipline a worker—the workers of that unit, in a body, stopped work to argue the case with management. The principle of workers' control, therefore, starts with the notion of workers' participating *collectively* in the determination of conditions of work. But workers' control also implies that action must be taken beyond a simple collective defense of interests. Workers must, in addition, collectively determine the way in which their work is managed; rather than permitting foremen or other supervisors to assign jobs, workers as a collectivity must organize these responsibilities. In effect, each production unit of a factory, office, hospital, or organization becomes directly involved in determining *all* policies affecting the work group.

An essential feature in thinking about workers' control is to remember that it is not something that is requested or "demanded" in the same way that unions currently make economic demands. Nor is it negotiable between unions and management or grantable by management. To be effective, workers' control must be implemented by workers whether management likes it or not. If it is "granted," it might take the ostensible form of workers' control but actually be some distortion of the process.

One big advantage of workers' control is that it permits the experience and knowledge of workers to be implemented immediately at those levels where they have greater knowledge and expertise. Most workers have a highly detailed understanding of the work processes in which they are engaged; they are often disinterested in them because of their incapability of influencing anything under the present systems of work organization. Their knowledge can be put to good use, however, not only in the organization of productive labor but in restoring their confidence in themselves. Once workers learn that they know a great deal about their own work lives, they will be able to think about issues that many currently believe unthinkable, e.g., how to organize and operate an industry and eventually a society.

Some marxists have been critical of what they see as a narrowness in the concept of workers' control. They argue that, because of a diminution of skills and the degradation of work that has characterized the capitalist mode of production, the entire productive process must be reorganized—not just the undemocratic nature of the work place. Harry Braverman has put this argument clearly:

> The conception of a democracy in the work place based simply upon the imposition of a formal structure of parliamentarism—election of directors, the making of production and other decisions by ballot, etc.—upon the existing organization of production is delusory. Without the return of requisite technical knowledge to the mass of workers and the reshaping of the organization of labor—without, in a word, a new and truly collective mode of production—balloting within factories and offices does not alter the fact that the workers remain as dependent as before upon "experts," and can only choose among them, or vote for alternatives presented by them. Thus genuine workers' control has as its prerequisite the demystifying of technology and the reorganization of the mode of production. This does not mean, of course, that the seizure of power within industry through demands for workers' control is not a revolutionary act. It means rather that a true workers' democracy cannot subsist on a purely formal parliamentary scheme.

WORKERS' CONTROL AS A MOBILIZATIONAL STRATEGY

Part of the problem of thinking about workers' control in the American context rests on the ostensible apathy of the American working class. American labor in the 1960s and 1970s appeared to be largely indifferent to larger social issues, and disinterested in work and the work place; concerns centered on economic trends only as they affected each individual's job. The organized expression of the working class, the unions, are narrow organizations interested more in the specific economic concerns of their members than in larger issues about improving society or improving the conditions of the very poor.

This analysis, however, overlooks the dissatisfaction that lies hidden in the shops, factories, and offices. In a context of uneven quiescence, industrial America has seen spontaneous revolt after revolt. The wildcat strikes and sabotage in the General Motors Vega plant in Lordstown, Ohio, in the early 1970s showed that there was a great deal of dissatisfaction operating despite the high hourly pay and the superior working conditions provided by the contract with the United Automobile Workers. The Lordstown strikes and others gave rise to a rash of studies on worker alienation, and the early 1970s saw the rediscovery of the idea that workers under capitalism were, indeed, alienated from their work—something Marx had discovered in the middle of the last century.

On the surface, the American working class would appear to be unready for an approach such as workers' control. Nevertheless, experiences elsewhere indicate that such a slogan may not be so far away from consciousness. In many countries in industrialized Europe, for example, the alienating effects of mass production have generated attempts at workers' control, including the development of situations in Italy where workers undertook to rotate themselves through different jobs. The procedure of *job rotation* was quickly seized on by some automobile managements in Europe as a solution to the problem of alienation. In the Saab factory in Sweden this has been given the form of *job enlargement*, in which small teams of workers make up a work unit, thereby eliminating the fragmentation of the division of labor and reintegrating it. In most cases, these attempts by management represent attempts to forestall workers' control by substituting a limited form of control over relatively unimportant issues. When management implements job enlargement it is done by a superior force in industry saying to an inferior one: "This is good for you and as a result you will feel better (and therefore produce better)." In fact, of course, job enlargement may or may not resolve workers' problems. The point is that workers should decide for themselves which processes they prefer and to change them as they prefer. Until such preferences can develop through the collective action of workers on the shop floor, the old hierarchical patterns of industry will continue to stifle the creative energies of individuals.

While workers' control currently may seem far from the experience of many American workers, the actions of the 1930s show that the concept has been meaningful historically and can become real again.

Soviets and Other Councils

Soviets or councils represent a mobilizational form that developed in Europe in various revolutionary situations: originally in Russia in 1905 and again in 1917; in northern Italy in 1920; and in scattered circumstances in Germany, France, and Hungary. As a mobilizational device, councils are an interesting social form since they not only increase revolutionary energies but can serve as transitional social institutions to the socialist period.

Soviets were invented during the 1905 revolution in Russia and spread widely throughout the country. Because of a number of working-class disturbances, a government commission was organized in 1905 which called for working-class representation through elections in factories and workshops. Although the commission was subsequently canceled, the principle of electing a representative (called "deputy") for each five hundred workers and the councils of such deputies meeting and deciding on various actions spread rapidly. Although the 1905 revolution was suppressed, soviets sprang up again during the March 1917 revolution. Their popularity as an organizational form was confirmed by their rapid acceptance by the Russian armed forces and the peasant villages.

The soviets became popular not simply because of their representational character but because they drew large numbers of people immediately into the political process. This was accomplished through the relations between the soviets themselves — which met continually and took an increasingly broad number of decisions — and the local levels of institutions: factories, military units, villages. The formal device enforcing this interrelationship was the principle of *immediate recall*: deputies could be recalled by their constituents at a moment's notice; they did not hold their position as deputies for any specified period but only at the pleasure of their supporters. This not only meant that deputies had to report back on a continuing basis (often daily) but that they had to defend and argue the positions being taken in the debates in the soviets, what their stances were, and what they should be.

As a device for revolutionary transition, the soviets emerged as significant because they defined increasing areas of life as within the competence of workers, peasants, and soldiers. In the 1917 Russian Revolution, issues continually arose such as "Shall General Korniloy be permitted to move his troops around at his will?" Because of their mistrust of Kornilov, the Executive Committee of the Soviets determined that there would be no troop movements without its permission. Similarly, irritated by the monarchist press, the Executive Committee closed it down. In these and in hundreds of other actions, the soviets had an impact on day-to-day politics.

The operations of the soviets countered, almost immediately, the work of the weak provisional government which replaced czarist authority. The coexistence of two forms of power is referred to by marxists as *dual power*—a highly unstable political relationship in which the pressures of each claimant to power leads to collision. This is what happened in Russia. Conflicts occurred over issues as fundamental as "Shall the war continue?" The provisional government wished to keep Russia in the war against Germany; the troops, bled by inefficient generals and the collapse of the supply system, opposed the war. When the Bolsheviks formulated the slogan "All Power to the Soviets" they were arguing for a transition to a single popular and responsive form of rule.

While the soviets failed as a transitional device in Russia—their role was preempted by the Bolsheviks and they became simple instrumentalities of the party—the significance of the soviets as institutions that reflect a different way by which people organize themselves must not be overlooked. The important principles embodied in the soviets—immediate recall and representation based on occupational attachment or economic interest—were soon to become a model for development in other circumstances. In Italy, in 1919 and 1920, as the war ended and the working class began a period of increased militancy, the soviets became the model for expanding an originally indigenous Italian development.

The factory councils in Italy had a long history even if they had not emerged as important entities at the factory level as compared to the unions. It was to these organizations that Antonio Gramsci, an Italian socialist (and later one of the founders of the Italian Communist Party), turned to seek ways to develop soviets in Italy. These groups became extremely important in 1920 in Turin and, to a lesser degree, in other industrial centers in Italy.

The factory council concept is, at one and the same time, close to, yet different from, the soviet idea. For one thing, Gramsci stressed the importance of factory-level organization (the factory committees) and their role in affecting production immediately. Second, Gramsci saw the councils not only as a means to organize workers at the point of production and to enhance revolutionary energies, but also as a vital training ground where workers could develop the requisite skills for future self-management of factories and production units. Gramsci viewed the factory councils as transitional instrumentalities in the political and economic struggle for power—in committees on the shop floor with the employers; and in the nation, through councils, following the example of the Russian soviets. Third, Gramsci envisioned factory committees and councils as important devices for the development of proletarian culture. A new form of culture was essential, Gramsci believed, if the intellectual *hegemony* or domination of capitalism was to be overcome. It was naive to expect socialist consciousness to grow overnight with the transition of power; bourgeois domination—the legacy of capitalistic ideas, of personal greed and advancement, of selfishness, of competition—would have to be overcome through the growth of proletarian ideological hegemony. The growth of proletarian culture would take place, Gramsci argued, through the formation of factory committees and councils. As they developed organically within capitalist factories, the new movement would lay the basis for the New Order (*Nuovo Ordine*—the name of Gramsci's newspaper and group).

If the factory committee and council movement did not develop appropriately, it was to a large extent because of the jealousy of the unions and the political party of the working class. The factory council movement in the north of Italy was permitted by the unions and left parties to languish in a general strike in 1920, helping to lay the basis for the successful takeover of power by Mussolini and the fascists. Gramsci's theoretical contributions to the conceptualization of dual power as a means of transition are nevertheless important. They leave, however, three crucial theoretical questions unresolved:

1. Both the Russian and Italian experiences pose questions about the relations of the soviets/councils to the revolutionary party. In the former case, the party undermined the soviets and removed effective grassroots control; in the latter situation the party worried about losing control of the working class because of the importance of the factory council movement.

2. While Gramsci argued that the factory councils should take on a multiplicity of functions including the development of a proletarian culture, other organizational experiences raise questions about the feasibility of multifunctional organization. Can proletarian culture develop within entities dedicated to economic concerns such as control over production? The experience with the syndicalist *bourses de travail* (chambers of labor) movement in France argues that such institutions can handle only a single major function. Created through syndicalist initiatives, the *bourses de travail* were intended to be multifaceted institutions serving as agencies for the protection of workers and as entities within which proletarian culture could develop. They were eventually co-opted into the machinery of the state as employment agencies. This historical experience raises the question as to whether the councils projected by Gramsci would have been any more successful.

3. Soviets/councils deliberately pose the issue of dual power. Dual power is fundamentally unstable. No two entities, each claiming for itself complete legitimacy, can tolerate the existence of competing bodies in the domination of the state. Because dual power is unstable, the question of how long it can be maintained—a week, a month, a year—is inevitably raised. Perhaps even more important are the questions: When shall the revolutionary forces embodied in the soviets/councils move to take power? And how shall the move be made?

In the Russian experience, a Military Revolutionary Committee of the soviets was organized by the Bolsheviks as the instrument through which the insurrection would occur. But Gramsci provided no clear answer to this question in the Italian context, and modern revolution theorists have been unable to resolve it further.

Soviets/councils represent a mobilizational and transitional form that takes on particular meaning when the revolutionary process is already fairly advanced. In the context of present-day America these approaches may sound almost inconceivable. However, experience elsewhere shows that when revolutionary energies begin to be generated, soviets/councils are forms that make good sense for integrating the energies of workers at the point of production with larger-scale political events.

The General Strike

The general strike is the most romantic, elusive, and powerful mobilizational device for challenging the authority of a ruling class. Historically, national general strikes have their origins in the call in 1832 for a Grand National Holiday by William Benbow, a radical from Manchester, England. The cataclysmic view of the general strike and its function to effect a transition in power from the unproductive to the productive classes can be seen in the endorsement of the idea by Glasgow workers in 1833:

> There will not be insurrection; it will simply be passive resistance. The men may remain at leisure; there is and can be no law to compel men to work against their will. They may walk the streets and fields with their arms folded, they will wear no swords, carry no muskets; they will present no multitude for the riot act to disperse. They merely abstain, when their funds are sufficient, from going to work for one week or one month; and what happens in consequence? Bills are dishonored, the *Gazette* teems with bankruptcies, capital is destroyed, the revenue fails, the system of government falls into confusion, and every link in the chain which binds society together is broken in a moment by this inert conspiracy of the poor against the rich.

Unfortunately, the simple transition of power projected in this view has proven to be ephemeral. Experience over one hundred years has revealed three basic types of general strikes:

1. Economic general strikes involve the winning of economic gains from employers in circumstances that go beyond an individual employer. Examples of such strikes are the British general strike of 1926 and the San Francisco general strike of 1934. In the former, British workers joined a strike that had begun among the miners on economic grounds. In the latter, the entire San Francisco waterfront was closed when the unions in the city supported a strike by longshoremen.

2. Political general strikes are actions taken by workers either to extract political concessions from the state or to reject a political seizure of power by a reactionary group. An example of the former is found in the proposal for a general strike in Germany to win equality in the electoral process (see Chapter 8); the latter kind of political general strike occurred in Germany in 1923 when a small right-wing group seized power in what is known as the *"Kapp Putsch."*

Downing their tools in a general strike, the workers forced the collapse of the putsch and the return to the parliamentary democratic regime.

3. Revolutionary general strikes represent the type of transition originally contemplated in the idea of the Grand National Holiday. In syndicalist and anarchist thinking, revolutionary general strikes usually originate in economic or political strikes and may become revolutionary as the center of coordination and control shifts from established centers of power to strike centers. Examples of revolutionary general strikes can be found in the Russian revolution of 1905.

In the view of anarchists and syndicalists of the last century, the general strike was the primary mechanism through which the destruction of capitalism would occur. At once paralyzing the existing system of production and domination, the revolutionary general strike would reveal the weakness of the bourgeoisie and permit the working class to establish its control over the system of production. For the anarchists, the general strike should be accompanied by armed revolt. As the power of central governments increased, however, the general strike came to be seen as a strike "with folded arms" where the life of the country could be paralyzed and government forced to capitulate to the superior power of the proletariat. The general strike would be even more effective than in earlier times because the division of labor meant that even a small number of workers could stop all of industry. Nor could the power of the military break a general strike, since the strike would be so widespread as to require too great a dispersal of the army.

The syndicalist view of the general strike was perhaps best articulated by Georges Sorel, a leading French theoretician. Sorel argued that the social myth of the general strike was indispensible to the revolutionary working-class movement, having "such power behind it that it drags into the revolutionary track everything it touches." The idea of the general strike encourages workers to fight in intermediate struggles, looking at them as temporary stages before the decisive battle occurs.

Marx and the early marxists were skeptical of the general strike and often criticized the views of the anarchists and syndicalists. Engels argued, for example, that the bourgeoisie would hardly remain inactive while the workers went on a general strike. Nor did he consider it possible for the working class to amass the reserves necessary to sustain a strike long enough to damage the bourgeoisie. The capitalists would either starve out the workers or let loose their troops upon them. While general strikes might be a useful tactic to supplement other, more political, approaches, they should not be regarded as *the* means to effect the revolution.

The Russian revolution of 1905 caused many socialists to change their views of the general strike. Anticipating these events by a year, in 1904 Trotsky drew up a plan of action that would develop from a general strike:

> Tear the workers away from the machines and workshops; lead them through the factory gate out into the street; direct them to neighboring factories; proclaim a stoppage there; and carry new masses into the street. Thus, moving from factory to factory, from workshop to workshop, growing under way and sweeping away police obstacles, haranguing and attracting passers-by, absorbing groups that come from the opposite direction, filling the streets, taking possession of the first suitable buildings for public meetings, entrenching yourselves in those

buildings, using them for uninterrupted revolutionary meetings with a permanently shifting and changing audience, you shall bring order into the movement of the masses, raise their confidence, explain to them the purpose and the sense of events; and thus you shall eventually transform the city into a revolutionary camp — this, by and large, is the plan of action.

Trotsky's scenario for the general strike was based on earlier strikes which had been springing up in Russia for over a decade. The 1905 strikes developed after troops gunned down peaceful demonstrators marching to petition the czar. A mass sympathy strike rapidly unfolded in working-class centers in Russia, Poland, and Lithuania which broadened into an economic strike. Although the strike waned during the summer of 1905, it intensified in the autumn. During the strike, soviets were organized inside the factories as the device to provide organized expression for the workers. Trotsky viewed the general strike as the main weapon of the soviets:

> The power of the strike lies in disorganizing the power of the government. The greater the "anarchy" created by a strike, the nearer its victory. This is true only when "anarchy" is not being created by anarchic actions. The class that puts into motion, day in and day out, the industrial apparatus and the governmental apparatus; the class that is able, by a sudden stoppage of work, to paralyze both industry and government, must be organized enough not to fall the first victim of the very "anarchy" it has created. The more effective the disorganization of government caused by a strike, the more the strike organization is compelled to assume governmental functions.

Rosa Luxemburg also saw in the Russian events of 1905 a tremendous lesson, and she repudiated the earlier marxist rejection of the general strike. Recognizing that the conditions giving rise to a general strike were what the marxists should study, Luxemburg also criticized the unreal expectations of its outcomes that the anarchists had accepted. Most important, she argued that there was a unity between the economic and political struggles implicit in general strikes:

> . . . the economic struggle is the transmitter from one political center to another; the political struggle is the periodic fertilization of the soil for the economic struggle. Cause and effect here continually change places; and thus the economic and the political factor in the period of the mass strike, now widely removed, completely separated or even mutually exclusive, as the theoretical plan would have them, merely form the two interlacing sides of the proletarian class struggle in Russia.

Luxemburg also attached great importance to the spontaneity that accompanied general strikes. She viewed spontaneity as part of the creative energies of the workers responding to their conditions and life experiences. Revolutions were too important to permit any group or party to play the role of "schoolmaster" to the workers (i.e., to dominate them). The primeval energies of the people could be released creatively through the general strike and would increase revolutionary energies.

General strikes have had a widespread history in this century. From the 1905 Russian general strike that saw the spontaneous invention of the soviets to the general strike in France in 1968 precipitated by students but given greater power by the French working class, general strikes have terrified governments. Although they often do not become revolutionary, the general strike always poses the issue of fundamental power. Even in economic strikes, decisions must be made about which essential services are maintained. When a general strike committee decides, for example, that fire services must be maintained and that hospitals should not be closed, existing governments properly feel that they are being supplanted.

The general strike, as a mobilizational device, transcends the limitations of the factory and work place. While its base rests on the proletariat, and organization takes place at the point of production, the *general* character of the strike pits the working class as a class against employers and the state.

Conclusion

In Chapter 12, four elements of mobilization were set out: raising consciousness, increasing participation, undermining the system, and building the revolutionary organization. Each of these elements was related to the goal of socialist transition if they were to provide mobilization for revolutionary transition.

How have the various approaches discussed in the present chapter fulfilled these four elements? Industrial organization, for example, was long regarded as important for drawing the new unskilled workers into the revolutionary process. In fact, this approach was deflected from revolutionary mobilization by the loss of focus of the entire purpose of the sit-down strikes—to win some control over life in the work place. Similarly, nationalization, once regarded as a socialist panacea, has been found to be lacking in and of itself. Without being accompanied by a meaningful form of workers' control, nationalization simply reemerges as another form of domination over the working class with bureaucrats reaping the benefits and exercising the power.

Workers' control can be a meaningful revolutionary device or it can be deflected into relatively minor concessions. What difference does it make to the management of the Saab automobile factories if the workers, in their work group, decide who will do what job? Unless those workers begin to exercise control over the product they produce, workers' control, like industrial unionism, can become a simple reform, unthreatening to capitalism. Yet linked to the idea of a socialist transformation, in a strategy which relates workers' control explicitly to that goal, an approach such as workers' control can be meaningful to workers and the first step in their movement in revolutionary directions.

Each of the approaches discussed has considerable potential for fulfilling all four of the elements of mobilization. Concrete implementation, however, is not easy and represents the major problem for revolutionaries to accomplish.

CHAPTER FOURTEEN

Mobilizational Forms in the General Society

Not everyone is exploited at the point of production; indeed, considerable numbers of people experience the overbearing character of a system without being directly exploited by it. Housewives represent an important example: while oppressed, their exploitation is individualized and isolated within the context of the household. They have few opportunities to respond to their experiences in a collective manner. And the same applies to others who may not work: older and retired people, young people, and the unemployed.

At the same time, workers undergo exploitative experiences in contexts other than the work place. As consumers, for example, they are exploited but they can respond through organization and mobilization. While some revolutionaries may be skeptical about electoral transitions to socialism, elections offer opportunities for revolutionaries to reach large numbers of people.

Similarly, cases of persecution on race and class grounds are continually arising that can demonstrate the iniquities of capitalist justice. Not only must such cases be fought on their own grounds but they can serve as opportunities to mobilize segments of the population and to educate others. Ultimately, all power in capitalist society, including private property as an institution, flows from the power of the state and the institutions it dominates—educational, judicial, administrative, police and military—and such power must be challenged wherever it is exercised and whenever feasible.

Another reason for interest in other forms of mobilization is that much can be learned by examining the approaches and techniques of some social reformers—people who are nonrevolutionary but who have undertaken to effect social change within the context of the system. The approaches of certain reformers have been utilized by some revolutionary and radical elements and can contribute to our understanding of mobilizational theory.

Many of the approaches discussed in this chapter are characteristic of relatively unrevolutionary periods. As was pointed out in Chapter 12, revolutionary energy does not consist of a constant force: there are periods in which workers and large parts of the population are "in motion" and other periods where they are relatively quiet. Revolutionaries have to live through quiet periods and cope with them as best they can. During such periods some individuals may become discouraged and give up their attempts to actively intervene in the political process; others may shift toward reformism.

Periods of relative inactivity are not without value. There can be times, for example, in which activists turn to study and analysis, familiarizing themselves with the work of theorists and the practical actions — successes and failures — of other revolutionary situations. These are also times in which individuals can develop nonrevolutionary, activist experiences and gain a better knowledge of the problems of working with different kinds of people. An individual can learn to test his or her capabilities, and organized movements can learn the strengths and weaknesses of individual members.

Periods of quiescence give rise to hundreds of adaptations. Revolutionary activity in such periods depends heavily on the existence of local options. In Russia during the repressive period that followed the 1905 revolution, activists went underground and into exile. Underground activity involved clandestine meetings, and the writing and distribution of materials. Exile, while permitting individual freedom of movement and expression, often involved a detached observation of the world that could be extremely demoralizing.

"Quiet" periods occur, of course, in a variety of forms. Some quiet periods are marked with extreme inaction. The early 1950s in the United States was such a time when the influence of McCarthyism and the infiltration by the FBI into various radical organizations led to a hesitancy by most people to become politically involved. There are other times in which activism increases but does not reach wide segments of the population. This was characteristic of the later 1950s and early 1960s in the United States. Blacks, students, and others became active, but a base of involvement in the rest of the population was not generated. Despite the activism of the late 1960s and early 1970s the situation then was not revolutionary. Large numbers of people became involved in a variety of movements, but the scope of these movements tended to be narrowly focused on single issues rather than directing participants toward a definition of the need for systemic change.

In this chapter we turn to forms of mobilization other than at the point of production, as well as to forms that are often characterized by a nonrevolutionary approach. In examining campaigns, community organizing, and confrontations we emphasize the need to learn from these experiences and apply them to the development of a theory of revolutionary mobilization. As technique, each of these approaches may dissolve into mindless activism or simple reform; the intent here is to abstract the essential qualities of the approach and suggest ways in which each can be utilized for revolutionary mobilization.

Campaigns

Campaigns are large-scale activities intended to create broad public environments within which leftists can reach wider sectors than are normally reached through everyday activities. Basically, campaigns seek to:

- Bring issues home — make them relevant — to a larger number of people than normally are reached through leftist groups (that are usually somewhat sectarian in their approach and ingrown in their attitudes).
- Focus on a limited number of issues rather than on an entire gamut of problems.
- Make these issues immediately and directly relevant, and propose practical means for their solution, so that people do not have to wait until capitalism has been eliminated in order to resolve the problem at hand.
- Identify potential members and future revolutionaries.

DEFENSE COMMITTEES

One specific type of campaign takes the form of the *defense committee*. This approach is used when someone is victimized by the government for ostensibly criminal activities, where leftist groups believe the underlying cause for the persecution rests on political grounds.

The history of the left in the United States is filled with such cases. In the 1920s the Sacco and Vanzetti case created tremendous publicity and stirred international protest when two Italian immigrant anarchists were accused of robbing a bank and murdering a guard. International protest failed to stop their execution. A similar protest on a more modest scale ensued when Tom Mooney and Warren K. Billings were accused of setting a bomb during a 1916 Preparedness Day parade in San Francisco. Both men were active unionists, and leftists believed they were victimized for their unionism rather than for any substantive crime. In more recent times, cases such as those of Huey Newton, Angela Davis, the Chicago 8, the Catonsville 9, the Harrisburg 6, and Joan Little have given rise to defense campaigns for people involved in the black and the antiwar movements. While governments often seek to victimize individual radicals and groups, such repressive campaigns also serve to tie up the resources and energies of radicals, a not inconsequential spin-off from the point of view of the repressive state.

Defense committees tend to raise the specter of revolutionaries becoming involved in struggles more to promote their own interests than to serve the cause of defendants — although both struggles may often mesh well together. In the early 1930s, the case of the Scottsboro Boys, a group of young blacks accused of raping two white women in Alabama, raised this problem. Some leftists contended that the Communist Party's heavy involvement in the defense was for the purpose of capitalizing on the case rather than to defend the accused. Others have argued that, with the Scottsboro case as with the Black Panthers in the 1960s, a "political trial" was the only way to bring justice to a case already overwhelmed by the prejudices of the locale.

Defense committees have three basic functions:

1. Committees are involved in the substantive issues of defense of a person or persons with respect to the specific accusation. Defense committees must not only be concerned with the political elements of a case but with raising funds and with providing the legal services necessary to defend the accused.

2. Committees are often concerned not only with the defense of the accused as such but with demonstrating the difficulties or impossibilities of obtaining substantive justice within the framework of capitalist law. The Scottsboro case revealed the depth of race prejudice in the juries of southern towns.

3. Committees can become instrumentalities that are the first initiation of sympathetic people into a more conscious political criticism of capitalist society. As liberals see the system of justice exposed, some may become critical of the entire system and of the basis for justice under capitalism. It is this function that has brought the defense committee under some suspicion as being a "front" for political groups rather than being substantively concerned wth the victims.

The organization of a defense committee confronts a radical political group with a set of strains in choosing between these three distinctive functions. Proper legal defense for a victim is an appropriate goal in itself, especially where those being victimized are people who have conducted a struggle for revolutionary change. However, to the extent that such a defense becomes popular, it becomes difficult for political groups to resist utilizing a legal-defense approach either to expose the inequities of capitalism or to recruit potential members. Such strains are never easily resolved. Where political groups shift from the first to the second and third functions, however, they become vulnerable to accusations of using the defense campaign for their political interests — rather than for solely obtaining substantive justice or the defense of the victims involved.

Beyond these dilemmas, defense committees have on occasion served as mass mobilizational devices. Campaigns for Sacco and Vanzetti had international consequences; the Mooney and Billings campaign was a major national issue in the 1930s. Most campaigns have less impact but their utilization as a mobilizational and educative approach has been tested and proven relatively successful.

ELECTORAL CAMPAIGNS

Electoral campaigns try to reach broader numbers of people by translating general political programs into immediate political issues. Such campaigns can be mounted locally, statewide, or nationally. In deciding on an electoral campaign, a revolutionary group must weigh the amount of energy to be invested in a campaign against the potential political payoffs. In many cases revolutionary groups have been less concerned with actually electing individuals than in using the campaign and the timeliness of a program as a device for political education, broadening criticism of the system, and creating a more sympathetic political environment.

Although the experience of most social-democratic parties discussed in Chapter 8 was to move in a nonrevolutionary direction as they became influential in their countries, theoretically there is no need for a loss of revolutionary principles in following an electoral strategy.

Most Americans view elections as the legitimate arena in which access to political power is obtained. Although more and more people see politicians as corrupt (a view that is reflected in large-scale absenteeism from the polls), left strategies that avoid elections are often viewed by many people as being antidemocratic, or one by which a minority seeks to impose its will upon the majority. No doubt the legacy of Russian communism has added greatly to this popular impression of the left as antidemocratic; for some leftists, the only way to counter that is to contest for power openly.

There is no inherent reason why a revolutionary organization making gains at the polls should compromise its principles. Rather, by convincing people that a socialist society is the only alternative to the problems of capitalism, it is conceivable that the socialists would eventually achieve control of the executive and legislative branches. At some point a more complete taking of power would need to occur, one resulting in the elimination of large private enterprise.

Once a left movement is successful in winning electoral office, the most serious problem facing it may not be opportunism, but the threat of rightist counterrevolution, usually taking the form of a military coup. The 1973 Chilean coup provides the clearest example of a successful left electoral strategy that was unable to deal effectively with the military question.

Much of the Chilean left saw the revolutionary process as proceeding in two stages, even after the initial electoral victory of the popular front. The first stage was anti-imperialist, a lengthy transitional period in which adherence to constitutional norms was to be sustained as Chile regained its political and economic independence from imperialism. During this period, it was hoped that constitutionalism would keep the support of, or at least neutralize, the middle strata of the population and the military. The problem was for the left forces to administer a capitalist economy while trying to transform it at the same time. While this stage was developing, some parties on the left called for stronger measures to be taken—to move into a second and more revolutionary phase—such as seizing land for distribution among the peasants, taking over factories and passing control to the workers and, indeed, to arming the people. Most of the left resisted these tendencies for fear of provoking a coup by the military. However, without some countervailing power to that of the military, there was little to prevent the military intervention that decimated the Chilean left. But was the alternative to abstain from the elections that produced the victories for the left? The defeat in Chile shows the problems of an electoral strategy overshadowing other forms of revolutionary activity, but nothing theoretically prevents them from coexisting.

The political campaign remains a popular device used by many leftist groups. Because a general political program can be translated into a number of localized issues that will hopefully be more meaningful to most people than "the abolition of capitalism," it represents an important device for broadening the political consciousness of the people.

One important aspect of electoral campaigns in the United States is that, under existing arrangements, such campaigns offer broad opportunities to reach large numbers of otherwise unreachable people. Not only is publicity generated through the legal requirements of the electoral system (such as the equal time provisions on radio and television, even if they are violated) but it is often provided to minority parties as a relief from the tedium of continuous coverage of normal candidates of the major parties.

Electoral campaigns absorb enormous amounts of energy, however, and leftist parties are often reluctant to engage in campaigns that are aimed at a very diffuse audience: the people. Many leftist groups therefore avoid electoral campaigns. Other leftist groups engage in them tactically from time to time, depending on their assessment of the time and the temper of the people. Wide differences continue to exist over whether electoral campaigns should emphasize education, actual success in gaining office, or various combinations of the two purposes.

LARGE-SCALE CAMPAIGNS

At different stages in national history, governments may undertake broadly unpopular or morally repugnant actions. Or institutional arrangements are created which are found to be suppressive of popular rights and liberties. An example of the latter is the no-strike pledge during World War II. This was a pledge by the unions to give up the right to strike for the duration of the war "in the national interest." When profit-making increased and managements began to take advantage of the no-strike pledge by pushing workers even harder than they had in the past, disenchantment grew among the rank and file. This took the form of a popular campaign to eliminate the no-strike pledge. Although the movement did not succeed, it shook up a number of unions such as the United Automobile Workers and reintroduced popular participation into union politics.

A broader popular movement grew in the United States in the 1960s as a result of American involvement in the Vietnam war. Although based initially on U.S. campuses, the antiwar movement eventually reached most segments of American society. The pressures generated through vigils, marches, national gatherings and protests were so powerful that they contributed to the U.S. withdrawal.

The antiwar movement of the 1960s was largely the product of leftist action. It represents an interesting campaign since most of the groups involved, particularly those of the New Left, were less concerned with recruitment than with obtaining the substantive purpose of the campaign: the end of American involvement in Vietnam. Within the antiwar movement, however, organizations such as Students for a Democratic Society flourished and grew.

Campaigns of the scale of the antiwar movement often come close to moving the whole society toward a prerevolutionary direction. This is not to suggest that, because of the breadth of involvement of the American population in the antiwar movement, that the United States was in a prerevolutionary situation; many people continued to support the government in its prosecution of the war. In particular, large sections of the unionized working class rejected the criticism offered by the antiwar movement. However, the peak of the movement in 1969–70 coincided with a general turn toward radicalism by significant segments of the population, particularly the young. At the same time, most of these same elements did not make any association between American involvement in the war and the character of American capitalism. The inability of various radical groups to clarify this relationship dissipated the spirit of the antiwar movement once direct American involvement ended — despite the fact that the United States continued to provide the economic and technological base for the south Vietnamese. Thus, broad protest is not necessarily equivalent to a prerevolutionary situation. There are three salient features of large-scale campaigns:

1. They are largely unpredictable as to timing; often radical groups begin an action and find strong popular support. They continue to energize the campaign until major public involvement develops.

2. The essence of campaigns is often embodied in a single slogan such as "U.S. Out of Vietnam," "Free Sacco and Vanzetti," or "No Nukes."

3. Campaigns are organizationally anomalous. In some cases, the guiding organizational thrust will come from a single political group, or a single organization will attempt to take over the campaign. In other cases, direction may come from a coalition of political groups and/or from nonrevolutionary but politicized individuals.

Community Organization

While community organizing has been found in other times and places, its development has been more an American phenomenon than anything else. At different times, primitive forms of community organizing have been undertaken. One example is a very early attempt by a group of Russian revolutionaries, the *Narodniki*, to "go to the people." Their belief was that, by joining the peasants and adapting to their life-style, the revolutionaries could bring revolutionary consciousness to the peasants and create a new egalitarian society based upon traditional forms of land sharing. Other attempts have been made in southeast Asia and in the southern United States.

The most prominent recent attempts at community organization were those begun by Saul Alinsky, a radical who moved into mobilizing local neighborhoods before the Second World War. The "Back of the Yards" movement of residents near the Chicago stockyards proved to be highly successful. Alinsky went on to other organizing campaigns that included the Community Services Organization of Mexican-Americans in California, and FIGHT, a black organization in Rochester, New York. Modeling themselves somewhat on Alinsky but struggling for a more radical approach, Students for a Democratic Society (SDS) undertook a number of community action campaigns in low-income areas in Newark, Chicago, and a number of other cities. A major spin-off of the Alinsky approach developed with farm workers in California when Cesar Chavez, moving out of the Community Services Organization, created the National Farm Workers Association. The NFWA later evolved into the United Farm Workers Union.

The basic assumptions of the community organization approach to mobilization involve a set of beliefs that

- Power is unequally distributed in a community; only by organizing those at the bottom can a significant redistribution of power take place.

- Society should be truly democratic and people should be involved in controlling the local decisions that affect their lives.
- The process of organizing powerless groups increases the intransigence of powerful groups; this increases the militancy and the consciousness of the powerless.

While these assumptions have a somewhat radical content, in and of themselves they do not necessarily lead participants in revolutionary directions. Indeed, the major problem with most efforts at community organization is that they have not related local issues to the overall character of the system and have therefore bogged down in localism. In effect, community organization represents a form of economism in the neighborhood similar to what Lenin criticized with respect to factories (see Chapter 7), since it seldom develops consciousness of the overall system of exploitation.

Considerable differences exist in styles—and assumptions—of community organizers. The approaches that can be used by revolutionaries with respect to community organization would emphasize the following:

- Focusing on a localized geographic area. Community organizers mobilize people on the basis of their residence, emphasizing problems that are particularly important in certain locales. This can provide great strength, in that the problems concentrated on are most meaningful, graspable, and tractable in a personal sense. On the other hand, unless related to broader issues, a local focus may degenerate into relatively meaningless actions that leave the system untouched.
- Mobilization of the constituency begins from the experiences of the constituency and not of the organizer. The function of the organizer is to bring to consciousness the grievances and problems of those to be organized. All too often revolutionary organizers approach a constituency with a full analysis and a set of solutions. The community organization approach calls for the organizers to facilitate the constituency's articulation of their own grievances.
- Defining a resolvable problem. Once the constituents begin to articulate their dissatisfactions, the organizer moves toward getting them to define one or a few problems that are potentially resolvable. Again, this represents both potential strength and weakness from a revolutionary point of view. Revolutionaries often develop approaches that are so global as to be meaningless to many people; defining resolvable problems that can be won can give people a sense of confidence and efficacy. Such problems are often minuscule and unimportant, however, and the revolutionary organizer must continually seek to broaden localized issues to more systemic concerns.
- The organizer must encourage constituents to act for themselves. If the organizer becomes the major source of activity, this permits the constituents to sit back and wait; instead, the constitutents must be encouraged to undertake action on their own behalf, to develop confidence in themselves and in their capabilities to plan and carry through actions.

Great varieties of styles and approaches can be found among community organizers, but most of the experiments in this direction have not been very successful. Revolutionary critics point to a number of difficulties in the approach:

1. Some community organizing attempts have become limited, self-serving, and racist. Alinsky's "Back of the Yards" movement is a good example, degen-

erating into a major support group for Chicago's establishment mayor, Richard Daley. This is a product of the narrow definition given to the goals of the organization.

2. Community organizations seem fated to remain localized. Because of the practice by organizers to concentrate on manageable problems at the outset, the tendency all too frequently is to remain stuck with such a concentration. As a result, the organizations rarely relate to national or systemic problems affecting their members.

3. Community organization deals, therefore, only with illusions of power and not with its realities. Power is organized nationally — and internationally — and a series of local successes have little impact on the exploitative character of the overall system. Even when a local group wins power, it cannot confront the overwhelming power of the national government.

These criticisms from the left of community organization are accurate. However, much of the criticism by the left is of community organization approaches that are explicitly nonsocialist — such as that of Saul Alinsky. Just as mobilization at the point of production does not automatically produce socialist consciousness as Lenin recognized, mobilization within the community may not produce such consciousness. But some of the approaches to community organization with a socialist perspective hold potential for this mobilizational technique to be used for revolutionary purposes.

Confrontation

A scenario similar to the following developed at many universities in the United States during the late 1960s.

At the beginning of the school year, the local chapter of Students for a Democratic Society (SDS) discovers that the School of Engineering (or some other unit) is doing research under contract to the Department of Defense. SDS members begin writing articles in the campus newspaper criticizing university complicity with the war effort. After several weeks, the students arrange a meeting with the dean of students who tells them he has no jurisdiction over the matter. SDS then schedules a meeting with the president of the university who tells them that the university is dependent on many sources, including the federal goverment, for its research funds and that, in any case, the amount of federal funds is negligible.

The students pass out leaflets denouncing the administration's reply and calling a rally to protest research being used to destroy Vietnamese peasants. Over 1,000 students attend the rally. Sympathetic faculty members attend a faculty meeting, which most of them rarely do, to raise the issue. The president responds by appointing a commission to study the matter. He selects five professors (one radical, one liberal, and three sturdy types who can be depended on), five students (the president of student government, the editor of the campus newspaper, the head of the interfraternity council, the freshman class secretary [the token woman], and a leftist-liberalish but non-SDS student), and five administrators. SDS attacks the commission as "loaded," biased, and as an attempt to co-opt and defuse the issue. The fall semester ends.

About a month into the spring semester, SDS renews its campaign and demands that the university end the contract with the Defense Department. The president replies that it would be inappropriate to take action until the commission completes its work and reports to him. SDS increases the agitation and, as the weather improves, schedules several rallies with audiences of varying sizes. Finally SDS demands a reply by May 6 or threatens militant (but unspecified) action. On May 4 the president's commission reports — 11 to 4 — in favor of continuing the research. The next day, the president thanks the commission for their enormous effort and announces that, as a believer in the democratic process, he will abide by their recommendation.

SDS denounces the report and the decision and calls a rally for May 7 after having met continuously for forty-eight hours since the commission's report became public. It will continue to meet continuously until the start of the rally, arguing strategy and tactics, while participants will vary from several hundred around noon to only several handfuls around 4 A.M. Three thousand students attend the rally and, in response to a "spontaneous" suggestion from one of the more militant SDSers, 1,000 students march to the administration building to "talk" to the president. When they get there, there are so many that they take over the building, the staff having previously been alerted and evacuated. The protesters, now barricaded inside the building, issue a list of six demands: the first requires an end to the Defense Department contract; the second calls for an end to the war in Vietnam; the last is concerned with complete amnesty for all protesters. The president turns down the demands and calls in the police to clear the building. After a day of ultimatums back and forth, with several thousand students watching outside, the police clear the building, indiscriminately chasing all students and beating up anyone they can reach. Three hundred and fifty students are arrested and 12 hospitalized, while a rumor sweeps the campus that another 130 were treated surreptitiously for beatings and wounds.

SDS now calls another rally to protest police brutality and to insist on the end of the defense research. Four thousand students and 130 faculty members attend and by a near-unanimous vote condemn the police brutality and support the six SDS demands. A strike of classes is proposed and begins immediately.

The strike is quite successful, with 7,000 students (somewhat more than half of the student body) refusing to attend regular classes, but instead taking part in unofficial classes taught by sympathetic faculty moving off-campus or "reconstituting" to discuss relevant issues rather than the scheduled class material. With so many students on strike, the administration tacitly concedes the effectiveness of the strike and cancels final exams and papers while suspending 12 of the SDS leaders. SDS calls a further rally to protest the suspensions but too many students have already left the campus for the summer and others are too tired to do anything. The protest fizzles.

Six months later, the president resigns to take a position with a large foundation. The charges against the 350 arrested students are dropped with no explanation. Six of the suspended SDSers return to school while the other six are now working full-time for the organization. The contract with the Defense Department is quietly permitted to expire.

This scenario was typical of many instances in the 1960s; with only a few changes in details, it could describe hundreds of similar actions in a broad range of American universities. Confrontation protests such as these took place in the context of the Vietnam war — a war regarded by leftists in the United States as a concrete manifestation of American imperialism taking its most brutal form through the physical destruction of a large part of the Vietnamese population.

Confrontations are standard fare for radical and revolutionary movements. They have been used in such diverse instances as Mahatma Gandhi in India refusing to pay a salt tax to the British and in the free-speech fights of the American Industrial Workers of the World. In the particular format they took in the 1960s, they had their origins in the nonviolent lunch-counter sit-ins of southern black college students in the early 1960s. These sit-ins followed the principles of civil disobedience practiced by Gandhi and Martin Luther King, Jr. Intended to break down discrimination against blacks who were refused service in public restaurants, the sit-in students were told by their leaders:

> Do show yourself friendly on the counter at all times. Do sit straight and always face the counter. Don't strike back, or curse back if attacked. Don't laugh out. Don't hold conversations. Don't block entrances.

As the antiwar movement grew during the 1960s, many of these nonviolent but action-oriented techniques were absorbed. Tactics such as sit-ins, marches, picket lines, and vigils—always based on nonviolence—were used to raise the issue of American involvement in Vietnam. The hopes were that, through peaceful and nonviolent protest, neutral people would see the wrongness of American policy. More and more actions were taken against agencies of government and corporations furthering the war effort. Sit-ins at draft boards were held in numerous areas and other actions (on a smaller scale) were aimed at destroying or defacing draft-board files. Despite its being illegal, hundreds of people burned their draft cards in public demonstrations and thousands more returned their cards to the Selective Service System.

As the war continued, local protests mounted and moved toward national confrontations such as that which took place at the Pentagon in Washington, D.C. on October 21, 1967. Here the mood shifted toward a more serious and determined effort to literally pull the United States out of Vietnam. With thousands maintaining an all-night sit-in on the steps of the Pentagon, hundreds sought to surge through the ranks of military police to get into the building (and in some cases succeeded). The numbers arrested approximated one thousand. Protests continued on the campuses against military training (demanding an end to ROTC on campus), military recruiting of students, and the recruitment of students for employment by corporations doing defense work—Dow Chemical, the manufacturer of napalm, being the most hated.

The tactics used by students during this period were diverse and imaginative. Carl Davidson, writing in SDS's *New Left Notes*, provided an extensive list of the tactics commonly used by student radicals:

1. individual vocal dissension, questions, and speeches at recruiting areas.
2. attending, officially or unofficially, training classes and "teaching-in," either on a one-shot basis or for the duration of the course.
3. leafletting training classes with counterinformation, counterreadings, and counterexams and/or holding counter classes.
4. leafletting recruiting areas and research sites.

5. exposing secret research and/or exposing clandestine connections of open research, recruiting, or training institutes in campus and national news media.

6. making appointments with recruiters in order to debate, harass, and/or take up their time.

7. obtaining favorable resolutions against current and future recruiting, research and/or training from student government, faculty senates, and other groups.

8. placing "war crimes" and other dramatic posters at recruiting sites or training classrooms.

9. setting up counter tables next to recruiting tables or training classrooms.

10. picketing recruiting areas or training classrooms.

11. staging "guerrilla theater" with death masks, posters, props and pictures in recruiting areas and training classrooms.

12. holding teach-ins before, during, and after recruiting, training, or research work.

13. holding "war crimes trials" for recruiters, trainees, and researchers.

14. holding a "guerrilla siege" of buildings during counterinsurgency classes.

15. holding speaking forums, questionings, and rallies drawing sufficient numbers into recruiting or training areas in order to indirectly stop or disrupt the recruiting or training process.

16. holding nonobstructive sit-ins at recruiting sites, leaving a pathway cleared for recruitees.

17. holding obstructive sit-ins at recruiting sites to prevent recruiting:

(a) passive: recruitee or others can pass if they use force.

(b) active: recruitee or others using force to pass will be met with counterforce by those sitting-in.

18. holding obstructive or non-obstructive sit-ins at administration offices to bring pressure for the cancelation of recruiting, training, or research.

19. holding obstructive sit-ins around automobiles and/or campus entrances to prevent recruiters and/or police cars or paddy wagons containing arrested students from leaving.

20. tipping over recruiting tables and/or seizing recruiting literature.

21. removing recruiters and/or police from campus by force or threat of force.

22. organizing a student strike until administrators stop the activity of certain recruiters, researchers, training classes, police action, or their own reprisals.

The mobilizational elements comprising confrontations include:

- Relating everyday issues to global issues—e.g., linking a local university's military research to the war in Vietnam.
- Building an increasing pace or tempo from smaller-scale to larger-scale.
- Exposing participants to a wide variety of potential tactics from which spontaneous decisions for action can emerge.
- Creating a generalized political environment which permits continuing, high-level participation for increasing numbers of people.

Mobilization through confrontation proved to be a powerful device during the Vietnam war period. Hundreds of thousands of students were exposed to political action for the first time in their lives and were brought into contact with a panoply of ideas. There were a number of major weaknesses in the confrontational approach, however. As protests grew larger, they also became more and more disruptive and violent. This was caused both by an escalation of militancy by demonstrators and an increase in the level of repressive violence used by college administrators and the police. Increased violence had the effect of scaring off many protesters. It also led the movement into a tactical impasse: either escalate or develop a new strategy. Although some tried to advance the level of militancy, most radicals were forced to reconsider their approach.

Another weakness with confrontation politics was that, as the antiwar movement grew, so did the opposition to the war within "legitimate" channels of government. As public officials and candidates for high office came to oppose the war, the arena for antiwar activity shifted for many to the Democratic Party, thus reducing the desireability and popularity of confrontational politics.

Finally, the confrontational approach tended to be focused narrowly on the university and its culpability in the Vietnam war. In a sense, once the university began to shed some of its more direct relationships to the war, much of the momentum of the student movement was lost. Once American involvement in the ground war came to an end, the antiwar movement went into serious decline. The confrontations, in other words, never succeeded in making clear to large numbers of students the relationship of the war to capitalism as a system, and serious revolutionary mobilization never emerged as a consequence of the student rebellion.

Conclusion

The mobilizational approaches discussed in this chapter have the common characteristic of being focused on people in their locations other than as producers, and of occurring in relatively quiet, nonrevolutionary periods. Each of the three forms discussed have largely developed under conditions of reformism rather than revolution, but each has important lessons for revolutionaries. The point to be emphasized is that any mobilizational approach *must* relate specific goals to the more general understanding of the overall system that gives rise to the specific problem. Unless this broadening is developed, as soon as a specific goal is attained—or even partially implemented—a movement can easily lose its impetus. This permits the system that gives rise to generic problems to resolve a specific problem without changing itself. The function of revolutionaries in utilizing these mobilizational forms is always to relate the specific to the general; without such a relationship these approaches inevitably lead to reformism.

CHAPTER FIFTEEN

Revolutionary Warfare as Mobilizational

Ever since Marx and Engels wrote "The Communists . . . openly declare that their ends can be attained only by the forcible overthrow of all existing conditions," in *The Communist Manifesto*, revolutionaries have considered insurrection and warfare as legitimate means to take and hold power. This approach to revolutionary warfare has been reinforced by experiences that have shown how reluctant the ruling class is to surrender power through peaceful electoral means.

Although both Marx and Engels — the latter more than the former — addressed themselves to military issues in their writings, most revolutionary theory on questions of warfare has been done by those who have been directly involved in military struggles. Without exception, these writers have maintained that revolutionary warfare is preeminently a question of political and social relationships and not simply a matter of technology or military skill.

In contrast to other forms of warfare, revolutionary warfare is always directed not only at defeating the enemy by military means but at the mass involvement of the people as a crucial part of the process. This chapter begins with a discussion of the political and social character of revolutionary warfare and its mobilizational aspects. We then examine forms of revolutionary war that have emerged historically including insurrection, protracted war, and rural and urban guerrilla warfare.

Revolutionary Warfare and the People

Revolutionary warfare was initiated as a topic of discussion by theoreticians as a result of the experience of the urban working class in Europe. Subsequently, with the development of rural revolutions based on the peasantry, the character of the discussion changed and focused on such issues as guerrilla warfare and protracted war.

The subject of revolutionary warfare makes sense, however, in the context of the liberal, democratic capitalist countries of Europe and North America only in terms of the existence or nonexistence of democratic possibilities. As long as such possibilities exist and as long as the bulk of the population believe in democratic opportunities to change the system within its existing rules, revolutionary warfare has little relevance. It is only when no significant legal opportunities exist for change *and the population realizes this* that revolutionary warfare becomes a potential mobilizational approach for revolutionaries. Any discussion of such warfare must be considered within this context.

The crucial distinction between revolutionary warfare and standard warfare is that the former is dedicated to involving the people directly in most aspects of military and political action. Rather than leaving warfare to soldiers as specialists, revolutionaries regard the involvement of the population in *all* aspects of war, fighting, and production, as a vital element. Mao Zedong has argued the relationship between military power and the people:

> Weapons are an important factor in war, but not the decisive factor; it is people, not things, that are decisive. The contest of strength is not only a contest of military and economic power, but also a contest of human power and morale. Military and economic power are necessarily wielded by people.

The necessity for popular support was underlined continually by Mao. In 1936, arguing the *Problems of Strategy in China's Revolutionary War*, Mao listed six conditions that must exist before the Red Army could move from defensive to offensive. "The first condition, active support of the population, is the most important one for the Red Army . . . given this condition, it is easy to achieve conditions 4, 5 and 6." (These three conditions included the discovery of the enemy's weak spots, the reduction of the enemy to fatigue and demoralization, and the development of mistakes by the enemy.)

Popular support permits revolutionary forces to operate in conditions that are impossible for conventional military forces functioning without such support. Discussing the relationship between the Red Army and the Nationalist army of the Kuomintang, Mao quotes one of the Kuomintang commanders as saying: "Everywhere the National Army gropes in the dark, while the Red Army walks in broad daylight." By this Mao meant that the Red Army had means to move, to operate, to set ambushes and traps, since the population continually provided it with information and support. In contrast, the Kuomintang armies had few information sources, rarely knew when an ambush would be sprung, nor whether, in questioning a village elder, they might not be talking to an important person in the communist forces.

The relationship between the army and the people involves one of continuous political engagement, frankness, and honesty between the revolutionaries and the army and people:

> . . . we should tell the Red Army and the people in the base area clearly, resolutely and fully that the enemy's offensive is inevitable and imminent and will do serious harm to the people, but at the same time, we should tell them about his weaknesses, the factors favorable to the Red Army, our indomitable will to victory, and our general plan of work. . . . Except where military secrets are con-

cerned, political mobilization must be carried on openly and, what is more, every effort should be made to extend it to all who might possibly support the revolutionary cause.

Mao developed the metaphor which has classically delineated the role of guerrillas with respect to population. Mao saw political mobilization as creating "a vast sea in which to drown the enemy . . ." A variant of this metaphor was used by Vo Nguyen Giap in Indo-China: "The people are to the army what water is to fish."*

Political mobilization, according to Mao, consisted of four distinctive elements:

1. It involves the education of soldiers and civilians in the political aims of the revolutionary war. It is insufficient to simply fight; all of the participants must be brought to a level of consciousness and understanding about the purposes of the war, whether it is to take land from the landlords or to drive out the invading Japanese.

2. A political program must be formulated and explained by the revolutionary party that sets out what the revolutionary struggle is all about. Thus, while the first element explains the reason for the war, the second sets out a program to deal with the problems creating the war.

3. Mobilization involves a wide range of communications, utilizing every means available and appropriate to the people involved. If they are illiterate, word of mouth; where they are literate, through newspapers, books, pamphlets; through dramatic performances; utilizing the educational system and the organizations that the revolutionaries have created or that have been formed spontaneously by the people. No means of education should remain untouched since each means reinforces the others.

4. Continuity is essential to political mobilization. The setting out of a program is not sufficient. Programs must be explained and reexplained and their appropriateness must be reinterpreted with each new event or battle, victorious or defeated. Without continuity, people fail to grasp the meaning of warfare and withdraw to normal pursuits (to personal and private business rather than the public business of revolutionary change).

Mobilization does not involve conveying abstract ideas. Peasants are ordinary human beings who understand their self-interest. Unless mobilization can occur

*Ho Chi Minh and Vo Nguyen Giap, in what was then French Indo-China, emerged during the 1930s and 1940s as brilliant political-military strategists of revolutionary warfare. Adopting a view of flexible warfare akin to that of Mao, the Vietnamese communists also developed Mao's notion of the national bloc of progressive classes. A major Vietnamese innovation, however, consisted of the formulation of an approach to politics and warfare that produced a better integration between the peasants and the fighting forces. In China, these two elements were distinct even though the soldiers supported themselves and "served the people." In Vietnam, in contrast, during most of the war against the French and later against the United States, the fighting forces and the peasantry were interrelated; many people were peasants by day and fighters by night. In this way, at the village level the anti-imperialist forces exercised political authority as long as the troops of the imperialists were not physically present. This process of "out-administering" the imperialists, by creating parallel hierarchies, also became a key element in the revolutionary war against the French in Algeria.

within a context they can understand and is meaningful to their life experience, it will not be successful.

We must lead the peasants' struggle for land and distribute the land to them, heighten their labor enthusiasm and increase agricultural production, safeguard the interests of the workers, establish cooperatives, develop trade with outside areas, and solve the problems facing the masses — food, shelter and clothing, fuel, rice, cooking oil and salt, sickness and hygiene, and marriage. . . . If we attend to these problems, solve them and satisfy the needs of the masses, we shall really become organizers of the well-being of the masses, and they will truly rally round us and give us warm support. Comrades, will we then be able to arouse them to take part in the revolutionary war? Yes, indeed we will.

It is inadequate to simply fight and propagandize: revolutionary warfare requires the solution of the problems of the people so that they will bring their enthusiasm and energy to the struggle. Only by tapping this enormous resource does it become possible for the revolutionary armed forces to overcome the handicaps of inadequate training and inferior equipment.

Revolutionary Warfare as a Mobilizational Approach

Revolutionary warfare is regarded by its advocates as an important form for mobilizing populations as well as laying the basis for the destruction of oppressive regimes. The degree to which it accomplishes mobilization can be seen by applying the four criteria set out in Chapter 12.

RAISING AND DEVELOPING CONSCIOUSNESS

Revolutionary warfare can potentially accomplish this end, but in different ways for differing fighting forces. In China, consciousness was developed in the peasantry through the formation of peasant organizations, through the seizure of land from the landlords, and through the creation of social forms that demonstrated to peasants what could be accomplished to resolve everyday problems. For Mao, revolutionary military struggle involved two distinct set of forces. First, there were the military forces associated with the Communist Party — the Red Army — which battled against the forces of reaction and demonstrated, by example, how peasants can be defended. Second, there were the defense forces created and staffed by the peasants themselves (the militia) which protected the land seizures and the peasant organizations.

In Cuba, in contrast, consciousness developed when the peasants (and others) saw how weak the reactionaries really were, how small bands of warriors could resist them, and how the possibilities for change could become conceivable. Thus, revolutionary warfare can increase and improve consciousness through exemplary action by the revolutionary armed forces.

INCREASING PARTICIPATION

Participation of the people increases differentially during revolutionary warfare. In protracted and civil wars, revolutionaries want to involve the population in all aspects of the war. This includes participation in the armed forces, whether the army or the militia (self-defense units); production for the war itself; and defense and protection of the fighters. The aim is to move the people from passivity to action. Originally, the population may take a wait-and-see attitude toward combat. To the extent that warfare involves them in the determination of their lives, however, and to the extent that they begin to see possibilities for overthrowing the exploitative system, people can begin to participate more actively.

In some circumstances, guerrillas prefer a less direct involvement of the population, as in Cuba in the initial phases of the struggle when the protection of the peasants was considered to be paramount. Ultimately, however, unless the population participates, guerrilla warfare degenerates into the guerrilla-ism of the restricted band, isolated from the people and doomed to ultimate destruction.

UNDERMINING THE SYSTEM

It is in this respect that *successful* revolutionary warfare is perhaps most important since victorious actions weaken the ruling forces and open the opportunities for the new revolutionary society to emerge. Not only is the intent of revolutionary warfare to demonstrate the weakness of the reactionary forces but it undermines the entire system of authority and acceptance.

RECRUITMENT

Mao Zedong argued forcefully on the importance of using the circumstances of revolutionary warfare to recruit people to the revolutionary forces and the party. Peasants must be brought into their own organizations to protect the land they seized or that which was seized on their behalf. Some of them will join the armed forces. All of them can become involved in the Communist Party.

Forms of Revolutionary Warfare

Until the Paris Commune of 1871 most revolutionaries considered the urban insurrection to be the prevailing mode of social transition. In the French Revolution of 1789, as well as the revolutions of 1830 and 1848, the insurrection emerged as the dramatic means through which change could be effected rapidly. The bloody defeat of the Commune, however, led many revolutionaries, including Engels, to conclude that insurrection was no longer feasible as a means to overcome the bourgeois state. Nevertheless, the experiences in Russia in 1905 showed that insurrection remained worthy of serious consideration by revolutionaries.

The Russian revolutions of 1917 and their aftermath set out the basic approaches that were to develop in revolutionary warfare, making clear to revolutionaries the utility of planned, armed insurrection. The first revolution of March 1917 was a spontaneous insurrection that overthrew the czar. A weak, liberal, bourgeois government was established that found itself unable to govern as the soviets of workers, soldiers, and peasants formed and took over increased decision-making powers. In November 1917 Leon Trotsky, leader of the St. Petersburg soviet, directed a planned insurrection on behalf of the Bolshevik Party. With a few exceptions, power was taken by force but without great loss of life. This experience reestablished the impor-tance of the insurrection for most revolutionaries.

Subsequently a lengthy civil war was fought between the Bolsheviks and the czarist forces supported by foreign troops from Great Britain, France, Japan, the United States, and elsewhere. A Red Army, built by Trotsky from scratch, demonstrated its capability by destroying the counterrevolutionary forces.

Protracted war, as it was called by Mao Zedong, became the vital element in the battle for power in China. Directed first in a civil war against the reactionary Kuomintang party, then against Japanese invaders, and again against the Kuomin-tang after the Second World War, Mao has provided the most extended commentary on warfare by any revolutionary writer.

Because the war was fought for over twenty years and covered thousands of miles of territory, considerable time was available for the analysis of warfare from a revolutionary point of view. Subsequently, many of the developments in China were independently discovered in Cuba and incorporated as approaches in Indo-China, Algeria, and elsewhere.

Revolutionaries note the existence of two distinctive types of revolutionary war-fare:

1. The insurrection. A rapid mobilization of military force accompanied by mass action, the insurrection is epitomized by the Paris Commune of 1871 and the Russian revolutions of 1917. The insurrection should not be confused with the *coup* or *golpe* in which a select and restricted band of conspirators seizes power without mass participation (although they may contend that they are doing so on behalf of the people).

2. Protracted war. Insurrections, as a means for taking power, are often not feasible, but military actions over a long period of time may be possible or necessary. The conditions for such warfare vary greatly: they may range from a situation in which power has already been won but the revolution must be de-fended, as in the case of the civil war that followed the Bolshevik seizure of power, to one in which national self-determination requires military action against an invading force, such as in the case of China's war against Japanese ag-gression or in the anticolonial wars that occurred in Vietnam, Algeria, Cuba, and the Philippines.

Despite the universal agreement by revolutionaries about the need for *flexibility* in revolutionary tactics, they all too frequently argue from the immediate successes and failures toward generalizations that may or may not be applicable in varying cir-cumstances. Engels saw great difficulties, for example, in barricade warfare due to the development of the rapid-firing breech-loading rifle, the revised architecture of city planning that permitted the mounting of artillery to annihilate the barricaders, and the invention of high-powered explosives such as dynamite. Despite this, bar-ricades reemerged during the Russian revolution of 1905 and proved to be a signifi-cant device. Similarly, Mao Zedong argued that revolutionary guerrilla warfare and protracted war were possible only in the enormous spaces available in China. Fidel Castro and his comrades however had not read Mao, but they demonstrated that it was feasible to conduct protracted guerrilla warfare on the constricted island of

Cuba. Che Guevara, in turn, contended that guerrilla warfare was essentially rural, agrarian warfare and was not feasible in urban centers. However, the sometime success of the Tupamaros, an urban guerrilla movement in Uruguay (despite their ultimate defeat), and the activity of the Irish Republican Army in southern Ireland, and more recently in Northern Ireland, have shown that urban guerrilla warfare is also possible.

In the following discussion on the forms of revolutionary warfare, it is crucial that no rigid dogmas be developed; flexibility in application of theory to practice is essential to the conduct of revolutionary warfare.

INSURRECTIONARY WARFARE

Rebellion by masses of people is a common historical phenomenon. History records innumerable instances in which peasants or urban dwellers have rioted against their conditions. In China, for example, rebellions of peasants against localized oppression were widely known. However, in most cases, where successful rebellions occurred, they simply reproduced the former social system so that no social revolution accompanied them. Similarly, the temper of urban populations was for centuries a matter of concern for rulers of societies containing large cities; however, when city dwellers rioted they rarely produced anything more profound than some temporary alleviation of conditions.

Revolutionary upsurges such as the slave insurrection led by Spartacus against Rome—a potential social revolution that was defeated—are, in contrast to the many rebellions, rare in world history. The Age of Revolution was ushered in with the development of capitalism in Europe: the Industrial Revolution in England and the French Revolution of 1789 produced changes in the character of the ruling classes and in class domination. In turn, the rise of capitalism created the proletariat and introduced into advanced capitalist societies the potential for revolutionary upsurge by the urban working class. After the revolutions of 1830 and 1848 the working class emerged as a serious contender for political power and as a key social entity over which control had to be established and maintained.

The major difference, therefore, between the rebellions of precapitalist societies and those of capitalism is that the earlier rebellions, while threatening specific individuals and families, never challenged the character of class rule although some late medieval revolts shook the class organization of the society of the time.

If the revolutions of 1830 and 1848 in France alerted the now-ruling bourgeois class (and Marx) to the potential significance of the proletariat, the Paris Commune put them on warning. The 1871 Commune demonstrated the capacity of the working class to seize control of the capital, rule it, but not survive against the military power of the state. The lesson was clear to the developing proletarian forces: it was inadequate to simply seize the capital city to win success in revolutionary action; revolutionary action had to be more widespread. This lesson was reinforced by the events in Russia in 1905. Here the strength of the urban working class in Petrograd, Moscow, and other centers, was inadequate to combat an army that continued to support the czarist regime.

When the revolution was crushed by the czar's police and troops, a period of reaction set in. Lenin turned to a consideration of the forms of struggle appropriate to the draconian circumstances. Drawing from experiences developed over previous decades, Lenin argued that, among other forms of armed struggle, two types of warfare were justifiable under the political conditions then existing: assassinations of important persons and seizure of funds. Assassination had been one of the earliest forms of political action by Russia's revolutionaries; the robbery of banks—expropriations, as they were more commonly called—was also a device by which revolutionaries could support themselves and their movements during the czarist repression. Lenin argued that these actions had to take place within a context of political direction by a revolutionary party and *not* as individualistic acts. When conditions changed, however, Lenin preferred other forms of armed struggle as better able to involve the working class.

The revolution of 1917 reinforced the utility of the insurrection as the main device for the seizure of power from which the revolution against the entire system could be expanded. The experiences of Western Europe, then, form the basis for the first and earliest conception of the transition from capitalism to socialism. The concept emerged from the spontaneous actions of the early and undeveloped working class in France (and elsewhere) in 1830 and 1848 and emerged in its fullness with the October Revolution in Russia in 1917.

The key elements of this approach to the taking of power involved:

- A short burst of insurrection involving large numbers of people in urban centers, supported later by an outpouring of mass support in the rural areas.
- The physical seizure of the major centers of communications and control: government buildings, post offices and telegraph stations, newspapers (and later, radio stations and television stations).
- Development of control through a set of auxiliary revolutionary institutions (such as soviets) rather than physically replacing leadership at the top of existing governmental institutions.
- Mobilizing military power as necessary to ensure continuity of physical control of communications and production centers, dispersing potential and real opposition especially of a military character, and, if necessary, fighting a civil war to oppose attempts to reestablish the *status quo.*

The insurrection, then, was conceived as a transition of power that was very rapid, like the French Revolution of 1789. The crucial features involved not only speed but the physical taking control of administrative centers and holding them. The civil war that might follow the seizure of power could be protracted, but had to be fought from the base of overall control; otherwise, it was believed, the revolutionary transition could neither be successful nor completed.

This conception of revolutionary transition dominated the thinking of revolutionaries for the last half of the 19th century and was the preeminent approach to revolutionary transition for much of the present century as well.

PROTRACTED WARFARE: THE STRATEGIES AND TACTICS OF MAO ZEDONG

The Russian civil war was a short episode compared to the lengthy struggle by China's communists. Forced to withdraw to the rural hinterland following the defeat of the urban proletariat, the Chinese communists developed a successful political-military system based on the peasantry. Only once was the existence of this new social form seriously threatened — and then at a time when the usual flexibility in military warfare was replaced by acceptance of more traditional military theory. The result was the major defeat that forced the evacuation of the Soviet base area in southern China and the Long March to the northwest where the communists established a new base from which they resisted the Japanese during the Second World War and ultimately conquered China's mainland.

The major theoretical contribution that Mao made to revolutionary warfare consisted in clarifying the different forms of warfare and their relationship to each other. To begin with, Mao deplored "guerrilla-ism", spontaneous warfare by roving bands of fighters. This form of warfare existed sporadically in China through the centuries; Mao saw it as wasteful of revolutionary resources. The failure to place such action within a firm political context and thereby give it political direction dooms guerrilla-ism to defeat. Unless a political base has been developed, any military defeat tends to wipe out such groups. They fight on an all-or-nothing principle; either they win or they are wiped out.

Revolutionary warfare, Mao argued, requires that a social base must be created that not only can sustain the revolutionary fighters in quiet times but provide the basis for their continuance in times of defeat. The establishment of *base areas* is the key idea (that will be developed in greater detail below). The important point to be noted now is that while guerrilla-ism is to be deplored, guerrilla warfare is an important component of every revolutionary struggle and protracted war.

Mao made a second important point about guerrilla actions, distinguishing between proper guerrilla warfare and mobile warfare. Guerrilla warfare is a form of warfare that emphasizes *mobility in small groups*. It is utilized when revolutionary forces are weak; once forces grow in strength, other forms become equally or more important.

The prime task of guerrillas is to weaken the enemy forces, erode their bases, take their weaponry, and recruit new troops from within their forces. Mao summarized the work of true guerrilla forces in his famous "sixteen character formula:"

The enemy advances, we retreat;
The enemy camps, we harass;
The enemy tires, we attack;
The enemy retreats, we pursue.

While guerrilla warfare is important, it contrasts with guerrilla-ism in that the former maintains a centralized command without which, according to Mao, no guerrilla warfare can be successful. While guerrilla warfare cannot be as centralized as other forms, some degree of centralization is necessary and this can be obtained by centralized strategic command and decentralized command in campaigns and battles.

For Mao, guerrilla warfare was a necessary form — necessary to be used even after more regular forms of warfare become possible and feasible. It is vital, however, that more stabilized forms of military organization be developed.

As the Red Army reaches a higher stage, we must (eliminate guerrilla-ism) . . . so as to make the Red Army more centralized, more unified, more disciplined and more thorough in its work — in short, more regular in character . . . we should also gradually and consciously reduce such guerrilla characteristics as are no longer required at a higher stage.

Mao set out the conditions under which guerrilla units are converted into regular army units waging mobile warfare. Most important is the development and elaboration of a base area from which regular troops can operate and from which guerrilla actions can be mounted. Base areas are "the strategic bases on which guerrilla forces rely in performing their strategic tasks and achieving the object of preserving and expanding themselves and destroying and driving out the enemy."

Mao contended that the process of "regularization" of warfare had two stages:

1. The creation of guerrilla zones, the first stage, consists of setting out areas held when the guerrillas are physically present and by the enemy when *they* are present. This is a condition in which two military forces are present in the same area at the same time and in which contention between the two forces can occur.

2. The second stage consists of the conversion of the guerrilla zones into base areas. This occurs ". . . when large numbers of enemy troops have been annihilated or defeated there, the puppet regime has been destroyed, the masses have been roused to activity, anti-Japanese mass organizations have been formed, people's local armed forces have been developed, and anti-Japanese political power has been established. . . . the transformation of a guerrilla zone into a base area is an arduous creative process, and its accomplishment depends on the extent to which the enemy is destroyed and the masses are aroused."

Mao further reinforced the base area concept by setting out three conditions necessary for their establishment:

1. The formation of regular armed forces.

2. The coordination of the armed forces and the people in defeating the enemy.

3. Arousing the people, in every way, to fight the enemy. This involves arming the population, organizing self-defense and guerrilla units, forming mass organizations, organizing workers, peasants, youth, women, children, merchants, professionals. "Without organization, the people cannot give effect to their anti-Japanese strength."

The base areas embrace rural districts and small towns. Particularly in the early phases of warfare, before substantial bases have been set up, they should be regarded as small and flexible. Base areas are strategic locations that revolutionary forces rely on from which to operate and from which guerrilla forces can be mounted. Guerrilla units cannot maintain a rear since they are surrounded by the enemy; the base area becomes the "rear" to which they must withdraw to be replenished although guerrillas must seek to sustain themselves without this area.

The base area is also the place from which more regularized forms of warfare, mobile and positional, can be mounted. Beyond warfare, however, the base provides the space within which the revolutionary forces can not only replenish themselves but also mobilize the population. Through their example of participation in the war *and* in the construction of socialist social forms they demonstrate to the peasantry the possibilities for revolutionary action.

A key element in mobilizing the support of the population is that the revolutionary army must depend on its own resources rather than skim the peasantry for support. Self-sufficiency by the army is vital to setting an example and winning support. Peasants who can barely survive under normal conditions should not have the burden of feeding soldiers.

Mao continually stressed the idea that the function of the Red Army is not simply to fight:

> . . . the Chinese Red Army is an armed body for carrying out the political tasks of the revolution. . . . The Red Army should certainly not confine itself to fighting; . . . it should shoulder such important tasks as doing propaganda among the masses, organizing the masses, arming them, helping them to establish revolutionary political power and setting up Party organizations.

Stressing the nonprofessional character of the army Mao stated:

> The army is not only a fighting force, it is mainly a working force. All army cadres should learn how to take over and administer cities. In urban work they should learn how to be good at dealing with the imperialists and Kuomintang reactionaries, good at dealing with the bourgeoisie, good at leading the workers and organizing trade unions, good at mobilizing and organizing youth, good at uniting with and training cadres in the new Liberated Areas, good at managing industry and commerce, good at running schools, newspapers, new agencies, and broadcasting stations, good at handling foreign affairs, good at handling problems relating to the democratic parties and people's organizations, good at adjusting the relations betwen the cities and the rural areas and solving the problems of food, coal, and other daily necessities, and good at handling monetary and financial problems. In short, all urban problems, with which in the past our army cadres and fighters were unfamiliar, should from now on be shouldered by them. . . . The army is still a fighting force, and in this respect there must be absolutely no relaxing; to relax would be a mistake. Nevertheless, the time has come for us to set ourselves the task of turning the army into a working force.

As the Second World War came near its end, Mao argued that self-support was not only vital to sustaining the very large military forces then in existence but as an improvement over the situations in which a standing military force is divorced from production. Mao listed the benefits of being self-supporting as including:

- Improved relations between officers and men.
- Better attitudes toward work.
- Stronger discipline.
- Improved relations between the army and the people.
- Less grumbling.

Production, therefore, is not only necessary to support the army but creates better relationships with the people and provides them with examples of what can be done, and shows them what is possible in organizing work, relationships, and organizations among themselves.

The salient character of revolutionary warfare, Mao stressed, is flexibility. Accordingly, it is necessary to overcome various errors in thinking (Mao refers to them as "deviations"): one is to belittle the enemy, the second is to be terrified of them. By correctly assessing the enemy's strength and concentrating one's own forces, it becomes possible for numerically and technically inferior forces to overcome larger and better equipped forces. "Our strategy is 'pit one against ten' and our tactics are 'pit ten against one . . .' " by which Mao means that, in the long run, concentrated forces can destroy pieces of the enemy's larger armies. "Fight when you can win, move away when you can't win." And "Injuring all of a man's ten fingers is not as effective as chopping off one, and routing ten enemy divisions is not as effective as annihilating one of them."

The crucial element is to concentrate one's own forces tactically to produce a victory.

> We should strike only when positively certain that the enemy's situation, the terrain and popular support are all in our favor and not in his. Otherwise we should rather fall back and carefully bide our time. There will always be opportunities; we should not rashly accept battle . . .
> . . . it is inadvisable to fight when the force confronting us is too large; second, it is sometimes inadvisable to fight when the force confronting us, though not so large, is very close to other enemy forces; third, it is generally inadvisable to fight an enemy force that is not isolated and is strongly entrenched; fourth, it is inadvisable to continue an engagement in which there is no prospect for victory.

It should be noted that, even when Mao was emphasizing the relationship of military forces, he never forgot the involvement of the people. Thus, he explicated war as a mobilizing activity and the military forces of the revolutionary army as key production units, exemplars of behavior, and therefore of forces for political mobilization.

Mao outlined three stages in protracted war. In the first stage, the enemy is stronger and takes the strategic offensive. During this period, the revolutionary army emphasizes mobile warfare, which is supplemented by guerrilla warfare and positional warfare. In no case does the revolutionary army permit any tactical advantage to the enemy; wherever the enemy has such advantage, the Red Army withdraws. In the second stage, during the enemy's period of consolidation, the revolutionary forces prepare for a counteroffensive by engaging the enemy at their border areas and working behind their borders with guerrilla forces that undermine their supplies, troops, and morale. In the final stage, the revolutionary army begins a strategic counteroffensive to force the enemy to retreat. Even in this phase, mobile war is given priority over positional warfare. Guerrilla warfare declines in significance, however, giving way to positional war.

Mao's contributions to military thinking is much more complex and detailed than has been presented here. Confronting many enemies, including a far superior Japanese military force, for so long a period provided an opportunity to test his thinking and that of his colleagues, especially Zhu De (Chu Teh), in a broad variety of circumstances. This summary of Mao has focused as much as possible on the mobilizational elements of Mao's writing, since he believes that this aspect is vital to success in revolutionary warfare.

Guerrilla Warfare and Revolutionary Mobilization

The relationship of guerrilla warfare to revolutionary mobilization has, perhaps, best been set out by Che Guevara, the lengendary Argentinian guerrilla who played a vital role in the Cuban revolution and who perished in an attempt to develop a guerrilla movement in Bolivia. In the initial "general principles" of his book *Guerrilla Warfare*, Che Guevara makes clear that guerrilla activity develops only after the possibilities of peaceful struggle have been exhausted.

> Where a government has come into power through some form of popular vote, fraudulent or not, and maintains at least an appearance of constitutional legality, the guerrilla outbreak cannot be promoted, since the possibilities of peaceful struggle have not yet been exhausted.

In other words, as long as the population sees social change occurring potentially through peaceful means, the development of guerrilla warfare is impossible since the necessary base in the population cannot be built. This would explain, for example, the inability of the Weatherman organization to generate revolutionary mobilization through its underground activities in the United States after 1970.

An examination of Chinese and Cuban guerrilla warfare demonstrates the existence of some distinctive differences but, at the same time, a number of important similarities. Chinese guerrilla warfare, developing under conditions of enormous territorial expanse, tended to be more open than Cuban. Where Mao argued for a continually open relationship to the masses, Regis Debray, examining the Cuban situation, contended that underground operations were required:

> The revolutionary guerrilla force is clandestine. It is born and develops secretly. The fighters . . . keep out of sight, and when they allow themselves to be seen it is at a time and place chosen by their chief. The guerrilla force is independent of the civilian population, in action as well as in military organization; . . . The protection of the population depends on the progressive destruction of the enemy's military potential.

This view of guerrilla warfare not only postulated a separation of the guerrillas from the population but maintained a relationship of secrecy between the guerrillas and the peasants. Secrecy was a function of the special features of Cuba, in which the smaller scale initially permitted the government forces to move with impunity anywhere they wanted. Thus, secrecy accomplished two purposes:

> 1. Protection of the population from the repressive army, because the population had no information about the guerrillas. Even if the army tortured peasants for information, the army would eventually learn that there existed no such information and they would stop their tortures. Secrecy is seen as a device to protect the peasants.
>
> 2. Protection of the guerrilla force itself. The "three golden rules," according to Debray, were: "Constant vigilance, constant mistrust, constant mobility." Debray argued: "Various considerations of common sense necessitate wariness toward the civilian population and the maintenance of a certain aloofness."

Despite the secrecy and the isolation of the Cuban guerrillas, the function of guerrilla warfare as a mobilizational device were clear to Che Guevara:

> . . . guerrilla warfare is a war of the masses, a war of the people. The guerrilla band is an armed nucleus, the fighting vanguard of the people. It draws its great force from the mass of the people themselves . . . Guerrilla warfare is used by the

side which is supported by a majority but which possesses a much smaller number of arms for use in defense against oppression.

If we look for the similarities between the Chinese and Cuban cases, we can see the following points of convergence:

1. The role of the guerrillas as revolutionary agents of change in society.

2. The importance of guerrilla warfare for exemplary action — in China, to demonstrate to the peasants the capabilities for revolution; in Cuba, to demonstrate to the peasants the weakness of the reactionary government.

3. The importance of flexibility in military approaches.

4. The necessity to concentrate forces against a given military target so that "No battle, combat, or skirmish is to be fought unless it will be won" (Che Guevara) and "Fight when you can win, move away when you can't win" (Mao Zedong).

Urban Guerrilla Warfare

Traditionally, guerrilla warfare occurred in rural rather than urban environments as, for example, in China, Cuba, and Vietnam. There have been mixed types, however, in places such as Algeria where the urban struggle culminated, during the "Battle of Algiers," in the destruction of most of the urban guerrillas when they permitted themselves to be isolated in a positional battle. The rural guerrillas in Algeria were able to continue the military struggle after the loss of the Battle of Algiers.

In the 1960s and 1970s and on into the 1980s, guerrilla warfare has been found increasingly in urban locales. These recent urban guerrilla movements have developed in two types: popular-based movements in which mobilization and raising class consciousness are paramount considerations; and elite movements concerned with demonstrating, in action, the vulnerability of the system even though they are not effective at raising consciousness or mobilizing support activities.

POPULAR-BASED GUERRILLA WARFARE

There has been a wide range of popular-based movements whose major manifestation has involved the support and sustenance of guerrilla bands. The guerrillas, while concentrating on military action, have been concerned with the development of broad-based support organizations.

In France during the Second World War, the Maquis or Resistance engaged in guerrilla warfare against the occupying army of Germany.

In Nicaragua, the Sandinista movement developed support in rural and urban populations and, in 1979, overturned the repressive Somoza government.

One exclusively urban movement, the Tupamaros, was based in Montevideo, the capital of Uruguay. This city encompasses over half of Uruguay's population and dominates the country's economic, political, and cultural life. The presence of an urban complex permitted the Tupamaros to mount a variety of guerrilla actions against a reactionary regime with the guerrillas "disappearing" into the population after each action. Ultimately the movement was broken by government repression.

In Northern Ireland, following patterns established in the south decades before, the Irish Republican Army and its various wings and split-offs have maintained continuous guerrilla combat against the dominating Protestant majority and the British army. This example involves nationalist guerrilla warfare, although issues of revolutionary transition have also been raised by some of the groups concerned.

ELITE GUERRILLA WARFARE

In the United States in the early 1970s, the Weatherman organization, a splinter group of Students for a Democratic Society, represented an elite guerrilla organization. Their paramilitary activities generated little popular support and their actions lost their revolutionary character rapidly, ultimately becoming ends in themselves. Once the mobilizational and consciousness-raising functions of the guerrilla activity is lost, it resembles terrorism rather than revolutionary warfare.

In Italy the Red Brigades largely became separated from a broad popular base during the late 1970s. The ability of the Brigades to continue sporadic operations indicate that they were able to maintain some base of support outside of their own military action groups. The Red Brigades differed from Weatherman in that the latter group targeted property for their actions; the Red Brigades made examples of individuals through kidnapping or acts of violence against individuals.

Urban guerrilla warfare follows techniques of rural warfare. As in Cuba,

> The urban guerrilla is an implacable enemy of the government, and systematically works against the authorities, and those who rule the country and wield power. His major job is to baffle, discredit and harass the military and other forces of repression, and to destroy or loot goods belonging to North Americans, the heads of foreign firms, or the Brazilian upper classes.

The limited forms of political action that exist in a repressive system such as Brazil's lead to two objectives of armed struggle that are very close to those discussed by Lenin in the aftermath of the 1905 revolution when the repressive czarist regime left open few options for political activity. Carlos Marighella, the theorist of the Brazilian urban guerrillas, calls for:

> (1) The physical liquidation of the high- and low-ranking officers of both the armed forces and the police; (2) The expropriation of arms and goods belonging to the government, the large capitalists, the *latifundiarios*, and the imperialists. Small expropriations will provide for the urban guerrilla's personal livelihood; the larger ones will assist the revolution.

The tactics of urban guerrillas must be adapted to the particular conditions of urban life. Rather than concentrating military forces for armed battles against smaller units of the government, urban guerrillas utilize techniques that permit a greater facility for disappearing into the population. Besides assassination and expropriations, urban guerrillas utilize assaults and raids (that strike quickly, and from which the guerrillas disappear rapidly), ambushes, armed attacks on commercial and government installations, sabotage, and kidnappings — especially of government officials, foreign business people, and ambassadors of great powers.

As with rural guerrillas, the success of urban guerrillas depends on the support they receive from the people. The guerrillas count on the supporters to hide them and provide them with information:

> The government's chances of identifying and liquidating the guerrillas grow poorer as enemies of the dictatorship increase among the population at large. Such people will inform us about the activities of police and government agents, whereas they will not inform them about ours. In fact, they may try to confuse them by giving them false information. In any case, the urban guerrilla has potentially far greater sources of information than have the police. Though the latter realize that the people are watching them, they are unaware who is on the side of the guerrillas, and to the extent that they behave with injustice and violence toward ordinary people, they present the guerrillas with more and more allies.

The Brazilians and the Tupamaros based their strategy on the popular discontent felt toward their respective governments. By attacking local wealthy people and the corporations of foreign powers, the guerrillas were able to win considerable popular support. The guerrillas counted on the dislike of the people for the status quo to be a supportive factor:

> It is fundamental that the greater part of the population, although not ready to rise up in insurrection, is at the same time not going to let itself be killed by a regime that oppresses it.

The Dangers and Dilemmas of Guerrilla Warfare

Guerrilla warfare is a dangerous approach to mobilization, one whose utility is limited; it is brutal, deadly, and often unsuccessful, as the fatal experience of Che Guevara in Bolivia testifies. Four distinct dangers and dilemmas must be confronted in thinking about revolutionary warfare and, in particular, its initial form, guerrilla warfare.

1. Revolutionary or guerrilla warfare is feasible only when a population has no democratic illusions. As long as people believe that democratic forms exist, open warfare produces negative results. This can be seen in the situation of the Weatherman group in the United States in the early 1970s where guerrilla action had negative consequences because of the belief in democratic possibilities.

2. Guerrilla warfare can become a substitute for widespread participation by the population. Some guerrillas become so involved in their own struggle that they overlook the purpose of revolutionary warfare—to relate the revolutionary struggle to the people and involve them in it. Because guerrilla warfare is limited in form and requires great secrecy and an underground existence, the struggle itself often becomes the end rather than the involvement of the people. Unless guerrillas encourage wide popular participation, their movements are reduced to guerrilla-ism and move toward military coups rather than popular revolutions.

3. Participants in revolutionary and guerrilla warfare can become preoccupied with technique. This is a corollary of the previous dilemma. A practitioner such as Che Guevara spent considerable space discussing technical details in his book *Guerrilla Warfare* and comparatively little space dealing with the more important

political issues despite the fact that he himself recognized the preeminence of political factors.

4. Revolutionary or guerrilla warfare can decimate the population. Despite the approach of the Cuban guerrillas who sought to protect the population from punishment by providing them with no information, a ruthless and determined repressive force will decimate the population base which sustains guerrilla forces.

This has been the experience in a variety of countries where the government forces have learned that the people were contributing to the survival of the guerrillas. It has led to the development of a variety of techniques intended to disrupt the base — "emptying the fishbowl" — which sustains the guerrillas.

Ecocide and partial genocide. On a number of occasions repressive forces have decimated parts of the population to eliminate the social base of revolutionary warfare. This policy was followed by the United States in defoliating enormous areas of Vietnam and in creating "free-fire" zones.

Population control through concentration. Guerrillas can often be sustained in circumstances of low population densities of peasants when there are extensive land masses. This has led governments to implement policies of population concentration under circumstances that limit the access of guerrillas to the people. This policy, used by many ruling groups against rebellious populations, was first applied systematically by the British in Malaya and later adapted to repress the Mau Mau rebellion in Kenya in the 1950s.

It was also used by the United States in Vietnam where "strategic hamlets" were created as concentration points for the rural population. While the Vietnamese were originally village dwellers, reconcentration in newly formed villages forced them to mix with people outside their traditional village structure. This led to a breakdown in trust in village organization, a heightening of surveillance, and the maintenance of more direct control over the population. Indiscriminate bombing in the so-called "free fire" zones made life outside of the strategic hamlets so dangerous that people uprooted themselves and fled "voluntarily" into the controlled circumstance.

Such base-disrupting techniques are devastating but have been used by antipopular governments to maintain control. Any moves toward guerrilla or revolutionary warfare must take account of the limits and dangers of such an approach and assess it in terms of existing popular consciousness and against the possibilities of other forms of revolutionary mobilization.

PART FOUR

Theories of
Future Arrangements

While revolutionary thinkers have been thorough and detailed in their analyses of society and the revolutionary process, they have been sparing in their delineation of the transition to socialism and the character of future society. This reluctance to predict the future was a product of the context within which marxism developed: Marx believed it incorrect to set out detailed programs which might serve as a fetter on the development of revolutionary energy; he saw little hope in attempting to create a socialist utopia within the bosom of existing capitalism.

In his debates with various utopian socialists and the anarchists, Marx mentioned several characteristics of future socialist society. His conception of socialism as egalitarian and classless was clear; he was equally definitive on the need for a revolution to upset the existing arrangements of the state. And, at various times he discussed the existence of two stages in the postrevolutionary epoch, a transitional stage with a proletarian state of socialism and one of communism in which the state would wither away.

It was not until the success of the Russian Revolution that the detailed problems of giving day-to-day meaning to what socialism represents had to be confronted. Part IV turns first to the historical experience and then to the specific lessons that have been learned in attempting to build socialist societies, concentrating primarily on the lessons to be learned through the experiences of Russia and China. Drawing on these experiences, some of the problems that will have to be confronted by revolutionaries seeking to develop socialism in the United States and other advanced capitalist societies will become clearer.

CHAPTER SIXTEEN

Theoretical Elements of the Postrevolutionary Period

Marx and Future Arrangements

In examining the way in which revolutionaries have thought about the future, the approach developed by Marx has been utilized more than that of the anarchists. The anarchists believed that immediately after the revolution a new stage of stateless society could be entered. In contrast, Marx contended that a transitional period would be necessary. This transitional phase, which Marx referred to on occasion as "socialism," was different from the ultimate "communist" period in which the state would no longer be needed.

As a critical analyst of capitalist society, Marx was neither the first nor, during his lifetime, necessarily the most influential of socialists. Early socialist thought was dominated by utopian and anarchist thinkers and experimenters in England and France such as Robert Owen, Saint-Simon, Fourier, and Proudhon. Marx was reluctant to specify the future for a variety of reasons. First, he believed that events would unveil themselves through the specific actions of revolutionary struggle; he felt it inappropriate to set out blueprints when the proletariat would have to develop its own future through its own action. But beyond this, Marx was hesitant to provide specifications because of the intellectual battles between the critics of capitalism.

The earliest critics of capitalism were often individuals who had strong ties to and interests in capitalism as a system. Some, like Robert Owen, were successful manufacturers who believed it necessary to introduce more humane and less exploitative forms of production and social organization. Others, like the followers of Saint-Simon, anxious to produce a new world, became leading elements in the French bourgeoisie. Most early critics lacked a specific analysis of the class forces of capitalist society. Unlike Marx, they did not see the bourgeoisie as a specifically revolutionary *and* exploitative class; nor did they grasp the crucial role of the working class that Marx described. Many, indeed, were idealists who believed in the power of ideas alone to change history, unlike Marx who held that class forces and class conflict produce history.

The earliest socialists — those whom Marx called "utopians" — sought to implement change by focusing on the development of specific social experiments — piecemeal attempts that would demonstrate the superiority of such social arrangements — and thereby convince the public of the need for such experiments to grow, develop, and spread. The turn of the 19th century saw the proliferation of experiments intended to create living utopias. From Robert Owen's New Harmony in Indiana to fourierist experiments such as Brook Farm, a wide variety of utopian communities were built to show the way to the future. Many experiments focused on collective property and communal living; some were democratic and others were authoritarian; some attempted to eliminate marriage as a private institution while others held a more puritanical perspective. Most such communities required closing off the experimental group from the larger society and living in isolation — which was why many were constructed in the developing United States rather than in settled Europe. Almost all died within a relatively short period of time.

Marx regarded these experiments as futile. Not only did they fail to grasp the importance of a class analysis but, he argued, none could survive within the milieu of capitalism. Capitalist forces would organize economically against such experiments, which were also politically vulnerable. Further, the intellectual milieu that surrounded these experiments doomed them to extinction. Some of the utopians recognized the hegemonic power of surrounding capitalist society and, like Robert Owen, attempted to move their experiments to relatively pristine and undisturbed environments in the New World.

Marx rejected these experiments for their piecemeal approach, for their failures to understand the systemic character of capitalist exploitation, and for their inability to recognize that new social forms could grow only through the process of revolutionary action.

Marx's critique of anarchism followed similar lines. From Proudhon to Bakunin and into the 20th century, anarchists recognized the exploitative character of the state and projected a future society without a state. In their orientation to a stateless and uncoercive world, the anarchists shared with the marxists a common view of an ultimate society. But the anarchists, in the main, did not accept the class analysis that Marx put forth. In some cases, as with Proudhon and later with Kropotkin, the future was projected on the basis of existing low-technology peasant society, with its institutions of sharing and equality. Later, many anarchists adopted marxian class analysis to formulate the approach of revolutionary syndicalism but held a vision in which there would be an immediate transformation of capitalist exploitation into an egalitarian stateless world.

The marxist reluctance to predict the future was born out of a rejection of the utopian and anarchist specifications. Marx believed that the revolutionary proletariat would begin the development of its own institutions in the postrevolutionary period as a result of its experiences in the revolutionary process, rather than having theorists specify for them what the future would look like. Socialist institutions would be adapted to implementing the various stages of development that Marx saw as inevitable after the transition of power from the bourgeoisie to the working class. And it should be noted that, with the exception of the Soviet Union and other countries that have actually had to confront the problems of running postrevolutionary societies, the reluctance to speculate about the details of arrangements has been deeply engrained in most marxists and their movements. In addition, many modern revolutionaries view the actual experience of countries like the Soviet Union as gross distortions of the socialist ideal, a tendency that has led to demoralization or withdrawal *or* a continued reluctance to specify details about the future.

In polemicizing against the views projected by the utopians and anarchists, Marx did suggest some characteristics of future socialist society. First, there would be a period of transition which Marx called "socialism." This would be a stage in which the many aspects of bourgeois life would have to be overcome. Counterrevolutionary attempts to reestablish bourgeois society and bourgeois ideas would have to be fought. During the socialist phase, Marx contended, the state would continue to exist. The state has always existed as a mechanism of domination of one class by another class; the same would be true in the period of socialism. The proletarian state would continue to control the bourgeoisie and ensure that they did not return — either through counterrevolutionary action or through the engrained habits people had developed. Not only would overt bourgeois ideas such as individual profit have to be overcome; but concepts about the superiority of one sex or of different racial groups would also have to be slowly dispersed. Social problems such as sexism and racism would require time to be surmounted and the continued existence of a proletarian state would ensure that no one social group rose to exploit any others.

An essential feature of this transition would be to break the dependence of the proletariat on bourgeois domination. Therefore, Marx argued, it was inappropriate for the revolutionary proletariat simply to seize the existing instrumentalities of the state and use them as implements of domination. Instead, Marx contended, it was necessary for the working class to destroy the existing state, set aside existing systems of coercion such as the army and the police, and establish a new state mechanism accompanied by the armed people as the primary instrument of coercion. Institutions of force should neither be specialized nor isolated from the mass of the population; as long as it was, exploitation could be continued. Instead, Marx contended, the armed people would provide the power to protect the new society and form the group that determined the shape of future society.

Socialism would be a transition period moving toward the eventual goal of free human production, in which each individual participated in social production because of its inherent reward as a social activity. During the socialist transition, differential material rewards would continue to play a significant, but diminishing, role. Unlike capitalism, however, economic security would be guaranteed to all and production itself would be oriented toward meeting social needs and not the creation of profit for a small, powerful class. Because there would be no economic exploitation, individual competition would be reduced and people would not find themselves wanting an endless succession of commodities.

Because of the reduction in waste production, the returns to producers would be so considerable that the psychological need for accumulation — commodity fetishism – would begin to disappear. Once individuals responded to social norms of everyday life rather than to the pressures to be better than their neighbors, the coercive mechanism of the state would decline. Thus would begin the withering away of the state. This would be a gradual process (Marx never specified how long it would take – a year, a decade, a century – but he was clear that it would take considerable time) leading to the final stage that Marx called "communism."

In the communist phase, class antagonisms would cease since social classes would no longer exist. There would be no state. Individuals would work voluntarily as necessary, wanting to perform tasks out of a sense of social responsibility rather than coercion. No individual would occupy a single occupation for all or part of his or her life. Instead, individuals would work at different occupations continuously. Marx argued:

> . . . in communist society, where nobody has one exclusive sphere of activity but each can become accomplished in any branch he wishes, society regulates the general production and thus makes it possible for me to do one thing today and another tomorrow, to hunt in the morning, fish in the afternoon, rear cattle in the evening, criticise after dinner, just as I have a mind, without ever becoming hunter, fisherman, shepherd or critic.

The coordination of economic production would be a function of all and not left in the hands of specialists, just as the actual process of production would involve everyone in society. Instead of the administration of people, there would begin an administration of things. During this stage, the state would wither away and differential economic incentives would disappear; there would begin the implementation of Marx's famous dictum: "From each according to his ability; to each according to his need."

These relatively few suggestions about the character of postrevolutionary society remained the main intellectual heritage on future arrangements that marxians maintained until the Russian Revolution of 1917. During the revolutionary period, but before the October Revolution, Lenin addressed himself to the future in *The State and Revolution*. This work added only a little to the earlier arguments by Marx and Engels. As the revolution began to unfold, however, a number of important issues became clear that were subsequently reinforced by the victory of the Chinese (and other revolutions) and the defeats of others.

First, the pattern of future arrangements must inevitably follow from the character of the revolutionary process. In Russia, for example, because the soviets, the Bolshevik Party, and the insurrection played important roles in the transition to power, social, political, and economic arrangements took a very different form from those that emerged in China. China's revolution was characterized by protracted war and the development of a rural, agricultural, peasant base. Still a different form was projected by Antonio Gramsci for Italy. Although the party would continue to play a central role, Gramsci foresaw an organic growth of working-class institutions within the factories, seeing it moving toward increasing control over factory life and the development of a proletarian culture. This movement would culminate in an insurrection that would complete the process of proletarian transformation. Although this movement did not take place, in theory it suggested an outcome which might have been significantly different from either the Soviet Union or China.

Second, the experience of the Russian Revolution — the decline of the soviets, the growing domination of Russian society by the Bolshevik Party, and the ultimate domination of the party by Stalin — raised issues about the future of proletarian democracy. When major segments of the Bolshevik Party were physically annihilated during the purges of the 1930s, the question of the viability of differing views within the successful revolutionary party had to be confronted. This issue was resolved, at least partially, by the careful form given to "rectification" in the ideological struggles inside the Chinese Communist Party. Physical purges were placed outside of party processes, on the whole, at least until the Cultural Revolution. Emphasis was given instead to convincing opponents through debate and discussion. The Chinese example established "rectification," to some degree, as an alternative to the conception of a dictatorship that ruthlessly destroyed not only enemies of the regime but internal dissidents.

The experience of the successful overthrow of oppressive regimes in a number of countries not only has laid the basis for beginning an examination of future socialist institutions but has demonstrated that this future might consist not only of a single form of socialism. The remainder of this chapter will be devoted to examining specific examples of the meaning of a socialist society in terms of the ostensible and proclaimed experiences of past revolutions.

Given the experiences of past revolutionary transitions, it is necessary to emphasize the need for maintaining a critical stance toward such events. For example, the Great Proletarian Cultural Revolution of Communist China will be mentioned below, but the meaning of this part of the Chinese experience is still *very* unclear, even to sympathetic observers. On the one hand, it may be viewed as an attempt to develop a continuing revolution; on the other, as the romantic notion of an aging revolutionary leader approaching senility. It can also be interpreted as part of the ideological propaganda used by one faction of the party against another. These issues will not be resolved here for they can only be judged when there is greater evidence and a better historical perspective.

The notions about future socialist arrangements are suggested here as representing possibilities. Future socialist realities, if and when they unfold in advanced capitalist countries, may be very different.

Issues and Solutions of the Postrevolutionary Period

EXPLOITATION AND NATIONALIZATION

The basis of class formation and exploitation rest on the forms of ownership and control of the means of production. This point, developed in Marx's analysis of capitalism (see Chapter 1), remains basic to implementing the socialist period.

The emphasis on breaking the back of bourgeois power through the elimination of private property became, historically, the prime means focused on by marxians in the latter part of the 19th century and the first part of the 20th. Since this issue has been discussed as a mobilizational question (in Chapter 13) we will only note that most revolutionaries regard nationalization as a necessary but not sufficient condition for the establishment of socialism and the end of exploitation.

SMASHING THE STATE*

Marx believed that the creation of a socialist society depended upon the destruction of the bourgeois state which existed to support the overall interests of the capitalist class. The bourgeois state must be replaced by a transitional state to serve the interests of the working classes in their struggle to create the classless communist society.

Marx's key idea here was that the structure of government would have to be transformed to enable the proletariat to reach its goals. In the place of the bureaucratized and distant political apparatus of capitalism, the socialist state would rest upon forms of power, management, and decision-making involving the bulk of the population directly and actively. The socialist state had to serve, first, as the instrument of the working classes in their struggle for a new, truly human, society. At the same time, the new state would provide the necessary forms of control and coercion to prevent a revival of capitalism. This could occur either through counter-revolutionary action (e.g., the bourgeoisie organizing a civil war against the socialist society) or through the gradual reestablishment of a capitalist class as a result of the retention of bourgeois ideology, habits, or practices.

Marx was explicit that the socialist phase was not the classless utopia envisaged in the final stages of communism. As long as bourgeois individuals and ideas (competition, narrowly conceived self-interest, profit and accumulation motives, racism, sexism, privilege, etc.) existed, the working class would have to consciously organize and use the state to protect the gains of their revolutionary struggles. The difficult problem, as subsequent events have shown, is to ensure that "smashing" the bourgeois state does not in turn destroy the democratic freedoms of speech, expression, assembly, and organization that must be maintained in a truly socialist society.

---

*Engels wrote, in his "Introduction" to Marx's *The Civil War in France*: ". . . the Commune was compelled to recognize that the working class, once come to power, could not go on managing with the old state machine; . . . this working class . . . must do away with all of the old repressive machinery previously used against itself." The issue of "smashing the machinery of the state" is inevitably discussed along with another concept spoken about by Marx, the "dictatorship of the proletariat." This term was mentioned fleetingly by Marx several times in his writings but was never given specific meaning. See, for example, reference to this concept in *Critique of the Gotha Program*. Engels later argued that the dictatorship of the proletariat was embodied in the Paris Commune of 1871. The specific manifestation provided by the Paris Commune was far more democratic than the bourgeois state in existence at the time. It must be remembered that Marx regarded bourgeois liberal governments as representing a "dictatorship" of the bourgeoisie over the proletariat in the sense that the bourgeois class dominated the proletariat. The meaning Marx and Engels gave to the dictatorship of the proletariat can be interpreted as referring to the existence of a state in which the proletariat dominates the bourgeoisie without necessarily being undemocratic, i.e., without restricting suffrage and other forms of political participation. It was the post-Marx embodiment of the dictatorship of the proletariat after the Russian Revolution that provided a different meaning to the notion of dictatorship—one consonant with today's meaning of the term as authoritarian and monolithic. Nowhere in Marx is this definition found, however, and we have therefore avoided this term while retaining the essence of Marx's conception of the state after the revolutionary transition.

While Marx was reluctant to specify the exact form of the socialist state, in *The Civil War In France* he outlined in a favorable light the elements of the proletarian government of the Paris Commune during its extended, though ultimately unsuccessful, insurrection. These consisted of:

1. Overthrowing the machinery of the bourgeois state by organizing a totally new machinery, the Commune.
2. Abolition of the army as a standing body of troops and its replacement by the armed populace.
3. Universal suffrage and immediate recall of representatives.
4. Payment for public service by workingmen's wages.
5. Disestablishment and disendowing of the church.
6. Free and open education for all.
7. An elected judiciary subject to recall.

While the Commune provides a good example of the superseding of the bourgeois state by a new organizational form, its representational procedures still hewed to the basic forms established in bourgeois democracy: representation through geographic units. It was not until the invention of the soviets in Russia in 1905 that a new principle of organization emerged through revolutionary action. The soviet basis for representation—and therefore for all decision-making—rested on the economic unit to which workers were attached. The soviet form subsequently spread to the armed forces where the military unit became the basis for the soviet. As it spread to the peasants, the village became the basis for the soviet.

Because it is organized around institutions which intimately affect daily life, the soviet or council can be seen as an essential element in the struggle to make all crucial issues subject to the power of the united working classes. Rather than focusing on personalities or trivial issues, or ignoring real problems and needs as is so often the case in bourgeois politics, a socialist state based on representation through production units and other institutions of daily life should promote a public politics which touches the real concerns of all people. As a result of their organization around institutions that directly affect peoples' daily lives, soviets, at least conceptually, permit the idea of full democratic participation (one person, one vote) while maintaining the power of one class (the proletariat) against another (the bourgeoisie).

In itself, however, historical experience shows that the soviet form is inadequate for the development of a democratic socialist phase. Additional devices are required to ensure fulfillment of the intent of the socialist period. These would possibly include:

- Ensuring broad participation on all political, social, and economic issues. Without broad popular participation on a sustained and continuing basis, the tendency will be for those with superior education and greater endurance to dominate decision-making. Participation must be based on all of the institutions of daily life. Not only must this be accomplished, but regular turnover of representation at each successive level of organization is necessary. This is required not only to develop and spread administrative skills (to be discussed below) but to emphasize the importance of participation of everyone in controlling all aspects of their lives.

- "Workingmen's wages" should be emphasized in rewarding public service. The wage levels of those who hold administrative positions in the socialist period should be geared at the same levels of ordinary workers and should not be remunerated at levels that provide distinctive material returns to those holding such positions. All too often the fringe benefits and material perquisites of office produce advantageous circumstances for bureaucrats. Office holders should not only rotate, but their rewards must be carefully controlled.

UNDERMINING BOURGEOIS HEGEMONY
AND DEVELOPING A SOCIALIST HEGEMONY

Capitalist hegemony (or ideological domination) exists not simply in the open exercise of naked coercion and violence. Of course, at the most basic level, the state always depends on its monopoly of violence to sustain itself. Beyond that, however, most states are maintained because the idea systems that underlie them are ground into the minds of those they dominate. This is true not only of dictatorial states but of democratic ones. Americans, for example, respect the state not only because of their ultimate fears of taking up opposition to it but because they believe that it is legitimate for people to compete with each other and for rich people to have 100 to 500 times the incomes of poor people.

Similarly, the urge to buy things and accumulate them and hold them for one's own individual possession represents another aspect of bourgeois hegemony. This commodity fetishism — in which we all wish to accumulate as many material possessions as possible — leads to mindless competition and social waste. Overcoming this represents a major challenge for socialist hegemony.

No perfect means appear readily available for the development of a cooperative hegemony to replace that of bourgeois society but the experiences of the Chinese Revolution may, perhaps, provide some guidelines for future projections. The principle that seems to have emerged in China is based on the establishment of collective psychological and personal support systems that encourage cooperation and teamwork and discourage competitiveness. An essential feature of this process consists of people being able to make critical assessments of themselves and of others without feeling threatened by the process. "Criticism/self-criticism/transformation" involves continuing discussion and evaluation of each person's work. But criticism and self-criticism are seen as educative and supportive approaches and not as destructive. At its most basic level, criticism/self-criticism is supportive by not resulting in the physical annihilation of those who make mistakes. Beyond that, however, is the need to establish confidence in a system which permits people to be undefensive about themselves. Our own system, based on bourgeois hegemony, insists on private self-criticism and public self-defense; the results can be found in personal dilemmas of "the organization man" or "the organizational personality." When individuals compete with each other, no psychologically supportive capability exists; indeed, there are advantages in cutting other people down in organizational life.

Unless criticism/self-criticism can be maintained in a supportive way, the development of a new hegemony will become impossible. But this approach should not be conceived of as requiring and insisting upon only a single way of resolving problems.

It is essential that the development of a new hegemony encourage a multiplicity of approaches. The development of new social forms that will encourage criticism and self-criticism and a broad approach to experimentation has been given only some preliminary indications through the Chinese experience. Additional analysis and criticism of that Chinese example is necessary as will be the development and adaptation of our own cultural and social experience with new supportive, self-critical forms of organization.

HIGH PRODUCTION LEVELS AND WORK SATISFACTION

Marx continually argued that bourgeois production was revolutionary in that it created the basis for socialist society by unleashing productive capacities hitherto unknown in human history. At the same time, the alienating effects of this form of production led workers to seek satisfaction outside of their work experience. Rather than discovering some intrinsic creative capability in their work, the proletariat learned to ignore work itself and find its pleasures in an alienated consumption, in the accumulation of useless commodities. Marx and his successors argued that the new socialist phase would create an interest in the intrinsic character of work as well as to unleash the productive capacities of society far beyond what capitalism had achieved. Dialectically, it was argued, because so much could be available, people would lose much of their desire to accumulate. The satisfaction of *doing*, and particularly *doing with others* in the community, would replace the alienated satisfaction of *having*.

Some aspects of this analysis have been proven to be true. It is worth noting that the children of middle-income Americans often are willing to forgo the possession of some material commodities that their parents have very much taken for granted. Indeed, one basis for the so-called generation gap in the United States during the 1960s was that parents, who had struggled to provide a high material standard of life for their children, sometimes found their children alienated from them and their material possessions. This phenomenon is most notable in circumstances where poverty is a long distance from people; where people are less affluent the tendency is often to try to accumulate as much and as rapidly as possible.

But the circumstances of some children of middle-income sectors do not hold for all social classes. The very rich, for example, have shown infinite capacities for accumulation and acquisition and therefore for demonstrating to their neighbors (and the world) their ostensible superiority. The lesson is that the setting in motion of a highly productive system does not automatically ensure the development of modesty with respect to material accumulation.

In the initial phases of socialism, the problem of unleasing the productive capacity of the people is seen as requiring two basic approaches. First, through the instrumentality of workers' control, the skills developed through experience in production can be released rather than hoarded as an instrument of class warfare. Secondly, there has been general agreement among marxists that some form of *differential material rewards* will be necessary for some period of time. Thus, the slogan for this period is *not* "From each according to his ability; to each according to his need;" rather the slogan might be: "From each according to ability; to each according to what is produced." Often, collective incentives provide returns on the output of an entire production unit or some *collective* subsection of it.

Workers' control can unleash productive capacity because workers have an intimate knowledge of the production process. Frequently, in bourgeois production, workers are primarily concerned with not letting their knowledge be translated into productive changes lest these be used to exploit them further. The issue of "restriction of output" has been one which has involved bourgeois managers for over a century; this represents an understanding of the real relationships that exist between workers and owners at the point of production. And managers and owners have sought for years to overcome this restrictiveness through incentive systems, suggestion plans, and individual reward mechanisms.

Most of these attempts have been less than successful: workers continue to restrict production. Office workers generally prefer to spend more time on the coffee break and at the water fountain than on improving their output. When control and the fruits of the production process shift to the workers themselves, many of these restrictive tendencies should start to wither. In addition, as workers begin to develop their skills, move to different occupations, begin to participate in the totality of the production process and in political, economic, and social decision-making, it is reasonable to expect an efflorescence of productivity. That such a flowering is not necessarily automatic can be seen by the experience of Yugoslavia, where "self-management" has produced tendencies toward parochial factory and workshop concerns. The need, therefore, for structural forces that transcend the work place to bring together localized pressures through central planning is necessary. That there therefore exists a contradiction between tendencies toward local control and those of central planning is obvious; this contradiction remains one of the unresolved problems of the socialist transition.

The question of unequal rewards is generally seen, in the socialist period, as a necessary motivational device to serve the transfer from bourgeois to socialist hegemony. Unequal rewards need not be unlimitedly unequal — as shall be discussed below — but the concept of unequal reward seems necessary to provide a transition to the ultimate stage when "From each according to ability; to each according to need" can prevail. Some material benefits, it is expected, will accrue to some occupations and for some performances. More effective workers might be differentially rewarded than inefficient ones; occupations requiring greater skills may have to be better rewarded than those with fewer skills. These discrepancies are more likely to stand out in technologically underdeveloped societies where low material levels of existence are prevalent. In technologically developed societies, the size of such differentials may very well be much smaller.

The issue of the degree of reward is, however, of great importance. In capitalist society, it is common for farm workers to earn about $4,000 a year, while corporate executives make in excess of $400,000. The ratio of 100 to 1 — of executive to farm worker — is, from a socialist perspective, scandalous. Much lower ratios would be implemented in future social arrangements. Experience in China and Cuba, with ratios approximating 3.5 to 1, indicate that reduction in income differentials can be substantial without destroying motivation. More modest differential rates of return can provide incentives for those operating within a bourgeois hegemony that insists on some discrepancies in material returns. Yet by decreasing the ratio between top and bottom, the basis will be laid for a full transition to communist thinking—where no differentials need be made since people will control their accumulation. This control will ensure that neither commodity fetishism nor individual self-display occur.

PREVENTING THE DEVELOPMENT OF A NEW RULING CLASS

"Who says organization says oligarchy."

The central thrust of Robert Michels's analysis of the working-class movement in Europe before the First World War dealt with a paradox: the organizations created to struggle for democracy had themselves become bureaucratic oligarchies. The "iron law of oligarchy" led Michels to a pessimistic view of the future: there was no hope for industrialized socialism without complex organization; and there was no hope for democracy because leadership would dominate the people and allocate material wealth to themselves.

Michels's analysis was more than fulfilled by the growth of a bureaucracy in Russia after the soviet revolution. Although originally paid "workingmen's wages," the bureaucracy soon became increasingly privileged until it constituted, in its turn, a new ruling class. These tendencies toward oligarchy based on superior technical skills and coordinative functions have tended to be overlooked as a significant issue in many socialist circles.

While the "michelsian dilemma" is far from resolved, several real situations indicate that the problem of oligarchy during the socialist period is not insurmountable, and that there are ways to resist oligarchy and the emergence of a new dominating social class.

These might include:

- "Workingmen's wages"—the existence of some wage differentials between occupations with modest ratios of no more than 7 to 1, rather than the massive ratios found in capitalist society.
- Stringent limitations on the capability of transmitting material wealth between generations (through a confiscatory inheritance tax).
- Increasing use of prestige and symbolic rewards and other moral incentives in place of material rewards.
- Developing collective rewards for the production group as a whole rather than for individual members.
- Rotation through occupations, and the simplification of administrative tasks so that an increasing segment of the population can handle these responsibilities. These help to prevent the "crystallization" of individuals in important occupational roles and reduces their vested interest in remunerating such roles disproportionately.
- Broadening educational opportunities to facilitate the spread of skills so that rotation through various occupations and administrative positions can occur.

The experience of China's Cultural Revolution is appropriate here. Confronted by tendencies in which the Communist Party began to dominate all aspects of life—and party bureaucrats were becoming increasingly significant as decision-makers—the Cultural Revolution produced a crude form of occupational rotation. Party officials were removed from their positions and given ordinary productive roles in factories and agricultural communes, and students were sent into the countryside to work in agriculture. One legacy of the Cultural Revolution is the occasional return of officials to factories and fields for periods of time. Some may spend one day a week in factories working on assembly lines; others may return to agricultural communes for several weeks or more extended periods.

The principle established here is clear: it is vital that individuals fulfilling integrative and coordinative functions be rotated to ordinary production roles. Institutionalizing the process involves difficulties, but the process is necessary to minimize the tendencies toward oligarchical development.

One empirical case study in the United States is worth noting as an example of a trade union that has resisted oligarchical tendencies. While the analysis of this union — the International Typographical Union — would be too long to undertake here, the main features that have led to its resistance to oligarchy can be seen in two devices: first, officers are not paid significantly higher salaries than members; second, an occupational community exists within which people can find fulfillment even if they have lost election to union office. These devices serve to protect union democracy by not making officership so important that individuals would be willing to violate the norms of democratic behavior. The "iron law," though constituting a problem to which socialists must address their attention, is not of such a character, therefore, that it dooms all future revolutions to bureaucratic degeneration.

OVERCOMING THE DIFFERENCE BETWEEN TOWN AND COUNTRY

While the issue of town-country relations has been posed dramatically as a result of the success of socialist revolutions in technologically underdeveloped countries, these relationships pose problems for highly industrialized countries making the socialist transition as well.

The problem emerged dramatically following the Bolshevik revolution, when the issue arose as to how to make an industrial transformation from a society that was overwhelmingly peasant based. The course that was undertaken called for forced collectivization of the land and maintenance of highly favorable prices for industrial commodities and low rates for agricultural products. These policies engendered a crisis between town and country in which the peasantry slaughtered its livestock and refused to produce; a reaction that was met in turn by rigid totalitarian measures in which millions of peasants were moved into concentration camps. This policy resulted in forced urbanization and industrialization in which the countryside paid an enormously high social cost.

The contrast in China is remarkable. It was recognized that a highly favorable relationship toward industrial prices might facilitate the process of socialist accumulation of capital but would antagonize the 90 percent of the population that drew its sustenance from agriculture. Accordingly agricultural prices have been maintained in a favorable relationship with respect to industrial commodities. Capital accumulation has been smaller as a result, but the normative involvement of the population in the system has also been more profound.

This experience suggests the continued relevance of Marx's call for breaking down the distinction between town and country. It involves:

- Limitations on urban growth, whether in underdeveloped or industrially developed societies. In the latter, it should mean a redistribution of population away from the cities, since the dependence of 95 percent of the population of industrial producers on the 5 percent in agricultural production can potentially be exploitative of urban dwellers.
- Development of highly complex agricultural systems based on collective direction. In underdeveloped countries this means passing through a transition of peasant small-ownership (as was the case in China) to voluntary aggregation in cooperatives to large-scale collective units. In agriculturally industrialized countries such as the United States it means making a transition in the form of control from individual and corporate ownership to collective direction by workers themselves.
- Dispersal of industry. At present, industry tends to be concentrated, as do centers of distribution and control. Some dispersal of industry has taken place within the framework of capitalism as, for example, when industry has moved to new sites in search of cheap labor. The dispersal of industry should take place in terms of its integration with agricultural production. It should be feasible to develop many industrial enterprises within the context of agricultural collectives. Producers need not be limited in occupational rotation to industrial and urban occupations; rather it should be possible to spend time growing crops as well as emptying garbage cans and performing surgery.

While some economies of scale may still prevail in certain industries (steel can probably best be produced in concentrated capital formations), many industrial enterprises can be operated more successfully through dispersal. In the socialist phase, many of these enterprises would probably relocate into industrial-agricultural centers.

The Communist Phase

While countless writers have manufactured various versions of utopias (or their logical extension, antiutopias), it has been difficult to delineate a final phase of social development when competition has ended, individual development flourishes, and material production is so affluent that material items are regarded as insignificant. Marx himself did not treat this subject consistently, originally making a distinct separation between the socialist and communist phases but later blurring them.

Unlike the transitional phase of socialism, there are not even inadequate models of the communist period. At least a small number of countries have passed through the revolutionary transition and have struggled to implement socialism; these examples provide some basis for understanding the mistakes, difficulties, and problems of the socialist phase. But communism has no similar parallel; here we must depend on the logical extension of the theoretical analysis of Marx and others and operate in a realm of speculation. While speculation has perfectly good antecedents, this volume has set out to utilize not only theoretical developments and concrete examples but to apply those pieces of scientific information that are available and relevant. Accordingly, speculation — the construction of imaginery utopias — is not acceptable and we must seek to deal with the *probable* realities of communism.

Four basic elements of the communist phase have emerged from the original brief comments by Marx and Engels and by subsequent revolutionary thinkers. These involve (1) the withering away of the state as a classless society develops, (2) a virtual complete interchangeability in the division of labor, (3) a full flourishing of a non-competitive individualism, and (4) the abolition of all economic privilege. Each of these four orientations is integrally related to the others; no full individual personality can develop, according to revolutionary thinking, in a society characterized by the coerciveness of a state. The state is, in turn, a product of the conflict between classes which originates in the division of labor that produces economic privilege and the concentration of power and prestige.

The transition from the socialist to communist phase is one which does not take place abruptly: the state withers gradually as classlessness develops. The state becomes less significant as greater interchangeability in the division of labor produces fewer tendencies toward status and class crystallization. While the four basic tendencies in communism are discussed separately, their interrelationship and mutual dependence must be emphasized.

THE WITHERING AWAY OF THE STATE

This concept was stressed by Marx and Engels as a result of the various misconceptions they saw developing in early socialist and anarchist thinking about the anticapitalist revolution. Marx, like Bakunin, projected an ultimate future in which no coercive political system would operate, but he argued against the illusion that statelessness could be achieved immediately through the revolutionary process.

If the revolution would produce a proletarian state requiring coercion to ensure that the bourgeois system would not return, it would at the same time initiate a process of its own destruction as every element of the population began to engage in productive labor. To the extent that classes are abolished, the need declines for a state which functions as an instrumentality of coercion to enforce the domination by one class (which owns and controls the means of production). With private ownership and control eliminated, and with *all* participating in productive activities, the need for state power declines and ultimately withers.

INTERCHANGEABILITY IN THE DIVISION OF LABOR

In our discussion of the socialist period, the need to rotate occupational and administrative tasks was pointed out. Basic to the withering away of the state is not only the elimination of classes and the engagement of all in production, but the further development of a division of labor that permits interchangeability. This process is, to a considerable degree, a consequence of the advanced technology created by capitalism. Not only can we "hunt in the morning, fish in the afternoon, rear cattle in the evening, criticise after dinner," as Marx put it, but we can engage in many additional occupations as well.

Part of the problem in grasping the concept of very high interchangeability in the division of labor rests on the experience we have in capitalist society that still emphasizes the development of "lifetime careers" requiring long periods of training and education. And there is no doubt that many occupations still require relatively long periods of socialization and training.

Yet the concept of the "lifetime occupational career" has become increasingly outdated and less attractive in capitalist society as many individuals now make major career shifts during their work lives. While working a second job or "moonlighting" is produced by economic need and/or the pressures within capitalism to accumulate, the fact remains that many people have very diverse sets of skills. Many Americans, for example, have the ability to do repairs around their homes, and have learned various skills of automobile maintenance, carpentry, craft activities, and so forth.

The point here is not to argue that *each* individual will become a plumber, electrician, carpenter, or sheet-metal worker, or that certain specialized occupations will not still be necessary and useful in the communist phase (though such specialization can still be practiced along with a mix of other occupational activities). Rather, a high degree of interchangeability in the labor force can reduce the tendencies toward status and class crystallization discussed above and, at the same time, bring greater fulfillment to all workers.

Perhaps more significantly, even where "specialities" continue to exist in terms of sectors of employment, e.g. plumbers versus electricians, the distinctions between mental and manual labor, e.g. managers versus custodians, will begin to erode as collective management becomes the norm. Office managers will type and typists will manage offices.

Interchangeability in the division of labor can be accelerated during the socialist phase as parts and pieces of manufactured items move toward standardization. Much of the failures of standardization are a function of the anarchy of capitalism that requires competitiveness to produce "unique" elements out of very ordinary production. Taillights on automobiles, for example, come in a large variety of types, shapes, and forms, each of which is mounted in a different way and sealed with different kinds of gaskets. Similarly, variations in circuitbreakers make it difficult for ordinary people to make electrical repairs and we must fall back upon specialists. With a standardization of many productive elements, many of us can accumulate a still-wider variety of skills. And just as individuals now enjoy a break from the routine of even the most creative work into some other economic activity, in communist society people will appreciate the opportunity to undertake a wide variety of occupations in relatively short periods of time, continually learning new skills.

NONCOMPETITIVE INDIVIDUALISM

One of the great fears about socialism has been that a collective form of ownership produces a "single gray mass" with no individualism. This theme of uniformity in thought and action has been an important concern of critics of socialism and has formed the theme of many antiutopian novels. Since socialism produces collective ownership and collective ways of doing things, the fear has arisen that individual freedom will decline as a result of a successful socialist revolution.

These legitimate fears were exacerbated by the experiences of the Russian Revolution in which the repression of creativity and criticism became a standing feature of everyday life. Not only were people herded into meetings in which they had to publicly express agreement with their leadership, but art and culture became dominated by a single ruling group. Criticism of any kind—literary, artistic, musical, or political—became impossible. The domination of cultural and scientific work became so pervasive that science was given an "official" character, as when a set of biological theories—having no basis in fact and later repudiated—was sanctioned by the state and criticism of such views was forbidden. Art was reduced to limited forms of "proletarian realism" and experimentation was prohibited. While less is known about China, the tendency from the outside is to see a somewhat similar sterility and conformity: uniform clothing, a homogeneous culture represented by "proletarian opera" and art, and little tendency toward open criticism. Although Mao Zedong called for "one hundred flowers" to bloom, when criticism was forthcoming this campaign was soon brought to a halt.

Thinking about full individual development in noncompetitive terms is difficult because of the impression that bourgeois society makes on us. Individualism is, for many, a product of the pursuit of personal ends irrespective of social consequences. Yet even within the framework of capitalist society, tendencies toward uncompetitive individualism can be noted. One might consider, for example, the encouragement given within the New Left of the 1960s to individualism. During this period there was a flowering of individual and collective actions at a variety of levels: political, economic, intellectual, and social. Various elements in the New Left encouraged collective living in different forms, growth centers and personal liberation actions, the formation of a wide variety of organizational forms to publish books, write poetry, or maintain child-care cooperatives.

Marx and Engels continually emphasized their beliefs that, without socialism, true individual development and freedom could not occur. The state dominates individuals and constrains their growth and thought, they argued. Class divisions and the rigid limitations placed on those within each class, religion, sex, and race also serve to limit full human potential. The creativity of people forced to spend long hours in dull, repetitive, and alienated labor obviously suffers. Significant universal individual development can only take place as a result of the proletarian revolution. This process should begin immediately after the revolution. And it is possible to find examples of this in Russia in the flowering of writing and film making in the 1920s. Russian movies, for example, influenced film makers throughout the world because of their experimentalism and originality, although, after 1929, cultural production became stodgy as official intervention penalized those who failed to conform to official delineations of what was "good."

THE ELIMINATION OF PRIVILEGE

As material production improves and makes available commodities both in sufficient quantity and which no longer contain built-in obsolescence, the tendencies toward accumulation should begin to decline. The need for differential material rewards will become unnecessary when each one can have reasonable amounts of everything. Questions may, of course, be raised about what is "reasonable." Just as a strong movement has developed within capitalist society to cease endless utilization of resources until their extinction, social definitions of "reasonableness" will emerge through daily practice. What is most important in implementing this concept will be the capability of overcoming the need to feel superior to other people and to manifest this through some tangible symbolic manifestation (better homes, more clothes, finer art, etc.).

"From each according to his ability; to each according to his need." The celebrated slogan coined by Marx and Engels characterizes the ultimate phase of communism with respect to privilege. Just as individuals, even within capitalism, can escape commodity fetishism, once material possession becomes less significant, the need for making distinctions between people in terms of material return for their labor should end.

Similarly, there should also be less need for symbolic rewards in the form of prestige and honor. People will wish to work for the social good and for their own personal self-fulfillment; these orientations will provide adequate motivation for labor and adequate rewards intrinsic to the individual.

Unresolved Issues of the Postrevolutionary Period

Two major issues of the postrevolutionary period remain unresolved theoretically despite the experience of past socialist revolutions: the integration of workers' control, which emphasizes local level action and decision-making, with planning that concerns large-scale national and international organization; and the development of an internal dynamic to ensure that no class reemerges to dominate participation and reprivilege itself. In other words, how can the revolution continue "after" the revolution?

THE DILEMMA OF WORKERS' CONTROL AND CENTRAL PLANNING

If workers' control is a vital element in the process whereby individuals take control over a major part of their lives—the economic and productive aspect—it entails focusing critical day-to-day decisions at the level of the immediate face-to-face productive unit. While workers' control can be somewhat meaningful in larger contexts, once large-scale production units become involved, control can only be manifested through representatives rather than through the workers themselves. While it is clear that representation will be essential for the operation of many large-scale production units, it is equally clear that shop, office, or community-level control must be maintained by face-to-face groups of workers. In the demands between these two levels of production lies the potential for many difficulties.

More profound problems will develop in integrating the views of shop-level and production-unit-level approaches to production with the overall needs and demands of a society. The anarchy of capitalism, which encourages overproduction and waste through a lack of planning, must not be reproduced through the anarchy of syndicalism in which each production unit decides how it will produce, of what quality, and by what schedule. Unless coordination can take place among production units, high levels of production will not be sustained (thereby leading, once again, back toward commodity fetishism, as individuals seek to accumulate scarce commodities) and waste will occur when objects are made which are not desired except by the workers that want to produce them. A socialist society, in other words, requires the development of extensive planning and coordination: planning to determine overall levels of production needed to satisfy demand; and coordination to ensure that distribution occurs.

In an ideal situation all production units would participate in the planning process. Experience in production tells us, however, that participation will lead to a political process in which different groups bargain with each other. The need for some overall mechanism to reconcile differences, and particularly differences that manifest parochial concerns of local interests, will therefore be necessary.

Similarly, the coordinative functions of large-scale industrialized societies require that some central agencies undertake the responsibility for ensuring that partly manufactured goods get from one unit to another, and that completed goods get from their place of origin to centers of distribution where consumers can have access to them.

The tendency toward the development of central locations with people who conduct planning and integration as a full-time activity is therefore quite strong. While many planning and coordinating decisions are of a simple administrative character, the overall impact of many such decisions not only have implications for politics and economics but, in addition, such decisions can come into conflict with decisions made by committees implementing the principle of workers' control.

If and when administrative planning and control functions can be developed to the extent that there is a regular turnover of the workers involved in such agencies, one major tendency toward degeneration — the perpetuity of individuals in powerful and privileged positions — can be somewhat controlled. That is, if a continuing revolution occurs in which individuals rotate through planning, coordinative, *and* productive activities, the tendencies for individuals to make decisions which benefit them in their planning capacities may be reduced.

This does not resolve the issue of power being allocated over time to the central planning agency even if individuals rotate through it. What the consequences might be in such a circumstance is unclear, but the theoretical possibility exists and its potential for undermining workers' control remains an unresolved dilemma of the socialist phase.

STRUCTURING A CONTINUING REVOLUTION

The experience of the Russian Revolution is one of degeneration into bureaucratic control and the development of a specialized and privileged elite.

It is this experience that appeared to underlie the development of the Cultural Revolution in China between 1966 and 1969. The Cultural Revolution represented an amazing phenomenon of a country having undergone one major *social* revolution, initiating a second *political* revolution two decades after taking power.

From the viewpoint of revolutionary theory, the character and the consequences of the Cultural Revolution are fairly clear, and include the following:

- The bulk of the population, relatively quiescent over the years, were suddenly and dramatically brought into action on the streets. This mobilization was not *pro forma*; action represented a genuine attack on the key institutions that dominated Chinese political life, the Chinese Communist Party and the Red Army.
- In the conflict over ideas and ideologies, the party was actually weakened as the tendency toward the development of key individuals holding powerful positions was undercut.
- Large numbers of people in powerful and relatively privileged positions were recycled into production in factories and agricultural communes. While many returned to their posts or similar ones after the Cultural Revolution ended, a tendency can be noted for such individuals to maintain some contacts with production units and to engage in production activities for periods of time.
- The Cultural Revolution, while marked by some violence, tended to be relatively peaceful. Most violence was a function more of battles between groups espousing different points of view than of the intervention of the state.
- Finally, while considerable ferment existed among workers and students before it began, the Cultural Revolution was not actually initiated through internal dynamics in the social process. Unlike the kind of dynamic that Marx thought would lead the working class into revolutionary opposition to capitalism, the Cultural Revolution was unleashed by Mao Zedong and essentially harnessed by him through the instrumentality of the army.

The theoretical problem with the continuance of the revolution rests in this case on its starting (and stopping) through the agency of an external force, a *deus ex machina*, rather than through the existence of internal dynamics. The dangers are obvious: if we must depend on the good offices of some individual to trigger the continuance of the revolution, what happens when such individuals fail to impose themselves or die? In the long run, while the various protective institutions and procedures that have been discussed earlier are important to ensure that no privileged group reappears, the best guarantee rests in the resuscitation in each new generation of a revolutionary impulse in ensure that old habits do not recur, that older elements do not arrogate to themselves the making of decisions and other aspects of privilege.

The need for structuring a continuing revolution or a revolutionary upsurge in each generation is clear, but the internal mechanisms giving rise to the institutionalization of such a revolutionary impulse are far from obvious. This central issue remains as a key dilemma of the postrevolutionary period.

An Afterword on Theories
of Future Arrangements

Why Marx's Hesitations Were Right
and Why They Must Be Transcended

The discussion in Part IV has shown that many aspects of the future of socialism were far from clear in the minds of revolutionaries. This matter is complicated by the fact that, at the present time, a significant segment of the world's population lives in countries which have labeled themselves "socialist" or "communist," having experienced a major revolutionary transition. Yet the failure of virtually all of these countries to defend civil liberties and human rights — in other words, to build socialist *democracies* — raises important issues as to the future of socialism and the purpose of socialist revolutions.

This study has been less concerned with assessing the outcome of the revolutionary process, which we labeled "theories of revolution" instead of "revolutionary theory" at the very beginning of this book, and more interested in setting out the theoretical orientations of revolutionaries themselves. We have attempted to do this sympathetically, in part because we agree with much of the analysis about the character of capitalism and the need for a new kind of society, and in part because of our belief that the best way to understand a perspective is to "enter" it without losing one's own critical perspective.

The massive polemics between revolutionaries indicate that there are problems in delineating the "true" character of the revolutionary enterprise. Indeed, the experience of successful revolutionary transitions in countries such as Russia and China requires the recognition that important theoretical problems exist for those interested in revolutionary change in advanced capitalist countries.

All successful revolutionary transitions have occurred in countries and economies that were primitive by comparison to the more advanced capitalist countries in which revolutionaries expected the revolution to be first accomplished. Yet when comparing the two world-class revolutions of Russia and China, we see fundamentally different revolutionary processes occurring even though both were backward with respect to capitalist development. In Russia the revolution was accomplished more as a result of the capacity of a highly organized, tiny group being able to mobilize large numbers of disaffected people to seize a relatively small number of centers of power and control. In China, in contrast, a mass party had to be created under desperate conditions, and a relatively lengthy war had to be fought before a transition could occur. Thus, the Russian Revolution followed the cataclysmic model of the Paris Commune whereas the Chinese Revolution was characterized by protracted war over time and space.

A second important distinction derives from the assessement that has been made after each revolutionary transition by revolutionaries themselves, both in the country involved and externally. Each revolution has generated groups that have regarded the transition as a major one in the development of world history. And each revolution has also generated antagonisms, not simply by bourgeois forces, but in socialist circles. When it is recognized that in Stalin's Russia literally millions of people perished in concentration camps and that the *gulag* remains an important institution in Russian society, it is legitimate for those people identifying themselves as socialists to raise questions such as "Is this really socialism?"

If the elimination of private ownership of the means of production alone defined socialism, then Russia and China clearly are socialist. However, even the most casual glance at each society demonstrates significant imbalances in the distribution of material resources and power. To that extent, neither country can be defined as socialist. Arguments may be given that they are "on the road to socialism." It then becomes incumbent to define what socialism means in order to determine whether this is so.

The sheer fact of taking physical power in a society by a revolutionary socialist organization, and even changing the class structure, does not necessarily produce a socialist outcome. Revolutionaries may set out to eliminate capitalism and succeed in eliminating capitalist social relationships, but this does not necessarily prove that they have eliminated class privilege and exploitation.

For us, socialism connotes the elimination of privilege and exploitation. No revolution, no matter how it designates itself, can be regarded as socialist unless it moves rapidly to accomplish these purposes. And these purposes are never accomplished if, in fact, the state becomes more powerful, more oppressive, and more exploitative, even if private ownership of the means of production has been formally eliminated.

The setting out of revolutionary theory, for us, thus does not constitute the end of a process. Rather it signifies the beginning. We are left with two major dilemmas which we believe have *not* been resolved in advanced capitalist countries.

First, much of the theoretical development with respect to revolutionary processes has been the product of experiences in underdeveloped countries. Although revolutionary experience elsewhere may be illuminating, it cannot, in and of itself, tell us very much about the process of revolutionary transition in advanced capitalist countries. We require a *What Is to Be Done?* to be written for our societies and our times. The importance of Lenin's work lies more in understanding the conditions and circumstances in which he invented the vanguard theory of organization than in insisting that the vanguard theory is appropriate for our transition. Our *What Is to Be Done?* must recognize the staggering differences in populations, state of knowledge and understanding, communications systems and institutions, *and* the revolutionary experiences and disappointments elsewhere.

Second, we do not believe that it is feasible any longer to simply offer "socialism," undefined and undelineated, as the solution to the nightmares of capitalism as we experience them. "Socialism" in advanced capitalist countries requires operational definition and programmatic specification. After learning of the horrors of the *gulags*, most people do not want to launch an act of faith into the future. They are worried, justifiably, about elitist parties and undemocratic orientations.

The work of revolutionaries in advanced capitalist societies in our time requires, therefore, not only the development of different kinds of theory but a conscious and deliberate effort to deal with some of the hesitations Marx had about delineating the character of the future. Unless socialists can convince people that a socialist future is genuinely democratic, permits fuller expression of individual interests and concerns, and reduces the horrors of exploitation, people will prefer to live with what they know and understand rather than make an unquestioning leap into the future.

Chronology of
Major Events and People

YEAR	EVENTS
1776	The American Revolution
1789	The French Revolution
1848	Revolutions across Europe
1850–1866	Taiping rebellion in China
1861–1865	Civil War in the United States
1861	Emancipation of the serfs in Russia
1863	Lassalle forms the Universal German Workingman's Association
1864–1871	The International Workingmen's Association (the First International)
1871	The Paris Commune
1875	The German Social-Democratic Party formed
1878	The German Social-Democratic Party illegalized
1882	Plekhanov organizes the first marxist circle in Russia
1889	Second International formed
1890	The German Social-Democratic Party legalized
1903	Reformism condemned at the congress of the German party
	Bolshevik-Menshevik split at Russian party congress
1905	Mass strike and revolution in Russia
	Industrial Workers of the World formed
1912	Lawrence (Massachusetts) strike
1912	Eugene Victor Debs polls 897,000 votes for president of the United States
1914	First World War
	European socialists vote for war credits
1916	Preparedness Day bombing in San Francisco; arrest and trial of Tom Mooney and Warren K. Billings
1917	February–October: revolutions in Russia
1919	Rosa Luxemburg and Karl Liebknecht assassinated in Germany
	Communist (Third) International formed
	U.S. Socialist Party splits; Communist Party formed
1920	Baku Congress

1920–1934	Unsuccessful revolutions in Germany, Hungary, Italy
1922–1949	Chinese Revolution
1927	Shanghai massacre
1930s	Stalin purges in Russia
1935–1937	Organization of the CIO in the United States
1939–1945	Second World War
1946–1974	Vietnamese revolution
1947	Cold war begins
1956	Hungarian revolution
1959	Cuban revolution
1960	Student Nonviolent Coordinating Committee formed in the United States
	Students for a Democratic Society organized
1962	SDS Port Huron Statement
1964–1972	Antiwar Vietnam movement in the United States and elsewhere
1966	Black Panther Party formed
1969	SDS split; Weatherman formed
1973	Chilean coup against Allende regime

YEAR	PEOPLE
1760–1825	Henri Saint-Simon
1771–1858	Robert Owen
1772–1837	Charles Fourier
1805–1881	Louis August Blanqui
1809–1864	Pierre Joseph Proudhon
1814–1876	Mikhail Bakunin
1815–1898	Otto von Bismarck
1817–1862	Henry David Thoreau
1818–1883	Karl Marx
1820–1895	Friedrich Engels
1825–1864	Ferdinand Lassalle
1840–1913	August Bebel
1842–1921	Peter Kropotkin
1850–1932	Eduard Bernstein
1855–1916	Eugene Victor Debs
1856–1918	Georgi Plekhanov
1869–1928	William ("Big Bill") Haywood
1869–1948	Mahatma Gandhi
1870–1919	Rosa Luxemburg
1870–1924	V. I. Lenin
1879–1940	Leon Trotsky
1880–1969	Ho Chi Minh
1891–1937	Antonio Gramsci
1893–1976	Mao Zedong
1909–1972	Saul Alinsky
1912–	Vo Nguyen Giap
1925–1965	Malcolm X
1928–1967	Ernesto "Che" Guevara
1929–1968	Martin Luther King, Jr.

Suggested Source Readings

In each chapter of this book we have drawn from a number of sources. Where the sources are primary in contributing to the material discussed in the chapter, we have listed them below as suggested reading for those who wish to consult the original sources. Readers may also wish to examine the additional sources cited in the references. In citing sources, we provide here only the author and title; readers will find full bibliographical information in the bibliography.

Chapter 1: Classical Marxian Theory

On Marx's concept of alienation see *Capital*, Vol. 1, Part 4, Chapters 13–15; also the "First Manuscript" of Marx's *Economic and Philosophical Manuscripts* in Karl Marx, *Early Writings*, T. B. Bottomore (ed.). For an application of Marx to modern production see Blauner, *Alienation and Freedom*.

On concentration of classes and proletarianization see Marx, *Capital*, Vol. 3, Part 3; the "First Manuscript" of the *Economic and Philosophical Manuscripts; The Eighteenth Brumaire Of Louis Napoleon; The Grundrisse*, David McLellan (ed.), 94–96.

On the anarchy of capital, see the "First Manuscript" of the *Economic and Philosophical Manuscripts*, 97–98.

Chapter 2: Stages of Development

For the earliest discussion of the theory of stages, see Marx and Engels, *The German Ideology*, and Marx, *The Grundrisse*.

The 1905 revolution in Russia accelerated marxian discussions about the issue of stages. For a discussion on how the revolution changed Lenin's views see Marcel Liebman, "Lenin in 1905: A Revolution That Shook a Doctrine," *Monthly Review*, April 1970; also Louis Menashe, "Vladimir Ilyitch Bakunin: An Essay on Lenin," *Socialist Revolution*, No. 18, Nov.-Dec. 1973: 9–54.

The main writer on the subject of stages was Leon Trotsky. His main work will be found in *The Permanent Revolution and Results and Prospects* and Chapter 1 of *The History of the Russian Revolution*. An excellent summary of Trotsky's arguments is in Isaac Deutscher, *The Prophet Armed: Trotsky* 1879–1921, Chapter 6.

Mao Zedong's writings on stages can be found in "Win the Masses in Their Millions for the Anti-Japanese United Front," "On Protracted War," and "The Chinese Revolution and the Chinese Communist Party." See also Brandt, Schwartz, and Fairbank, *A Documentary History of Chinese Communism*. For a good summary of Mao on the theory of stages see Stuart R. Schram, *The Political Thought of Mao Tse-tung*, "Introduction," Section C. See also, Benjamin I. Schwartz, *Chinese Communism and the Rise of Mao*; John E. Rue, *Mao Tse-tung in Opposition 1927-1935;* Stuart R. Schram, "Mao Tse-tung and the Theory of Permanent Revolution," in *China Quarterly,* No. 46.

Chapter 3: Peasants

For a discussion of the analytical problems that confronted Marx and Engels in dealing with the peasants see Friedrich Engels, "The Peasant Question in Germany," in Marx and Engels, *Selected Works*, 1968: 633-650. Lenin wrote extensively on the peasant question. See especially his articles and monographs, "The Agrarian Question in Russia at the End of the 19th Century," *The Development of Capitalism in Russia,* and *The Agrarian Programme of Social-Democracy in the First Russian Revolution, 1905-1907*. Mao Zedong has written extensively on the peasantry as a revolutionary force. See his "Report on an Investigation of the Peasant Movement in Hunan," "The Chinese Revolution and the Chinese Communist Party," and "Analysis of Classes in Chinese Society," in Vols. 1 and 2 of his *Selected Works*. An excellent discussion of Lenin's and Mao's practice in mobilizing peasants can be found in Alavi's, "Peasants and Revolution." A substantial literature has developed in recent years on underdevelopment (and the underdevelopment of the periphery by the core nations), unequal exchange, and on the significance of agrarian revolution. On underdevelopment see Paul Baran, "On the Political Economy of Backwardness"; Oliver C. Cox, Chapter 1 of *Capitalism as a System*; and André Gunder Frank, *Capitalism and Underdevelopment in Latin America*. On unequal exchange see Arghiri Emmanuel, *Unequal Exchange: A Study of the Imperialism of Trade*; and Samir Amin, *Accumulation on a World Scale: A Critique of the Theory of Underdevelopment*. For agrarian revolution see Jeffrey M. Paige, *Agrarian Revolution: Social Movements and Export Agriculture in the Underdeveloped Nations*.

Chapter 4: New Revolutionary Groups: Women, Blacks, Youth

For discussions of women in the Socialist Party see Bruce Dancis, "Socialism and Women in the United States," in *Socialist Revolution*; and James Weinstein, *The Decline of Socialism in America, 1912-1925*. On women in the Communist Party see Robert Shaffer, "Women and the Communist Party, USA, 1930-1940," in *Socialist Review*. On the development of feminist thinking in the New Left see Sara Evans, *Personal Politics: The Roots of Women's Liberation in the Civil Rights Movement and the New Left*.

For discussions on current feminist thinking, especially about the sex-gender system, see Sheila Rowbotham, *Women's Consciousness, Man's World*; Zillah Eisenstein (ed.), *Capitalist Patriarchy and the Case for Socialist Feminism*, especially her "Developing a Theory of Capitalist Patriarchy and Socialist Feminism," and chapters by Nancy Chodorow, Jean Gardiner, and Heidi Hartman; Gayle Rubin, "The Traffic in Women: Notes on the 'Political Economy' of Sex," in Rayna R. Reiter, *Toward An Anthropology of Women*; and Michele Zimbalist Rosaldo, "Women, Culture, and Society: A Theoretical Overview," in Michele Zimbalist Rosaldo and Louise Lamphere (eds.), *Women, Culture, and Society*; Shulamith Firestone, *The Dialectics of Sex: The Case for Feminist Revolution*; and Juliet Mitchell, *Women's Estate*.

For a discussion of blacks and the Old Left see James Weinstein, *The Decline of Socialism in America*, 1912-1925, 63-74; Wilson Record, *The Negro and the Communist Party*; and Harold Cruse, *The Crisis of the Negro Intellectual*. On the Black Panthers see Huey Newton, *Revolutionary Suicide*, and Bobby Seale, *Seize The Time*.

On the Old Left view of youth see Lewis Feuer, *The Conflict of Generations*. On more recent views of youth as revolutionary see Richard Flacks, "The Liberated Generation," in *Journal of Social Issues*; Irving Louis Horowitz and William H. Friedland, *The Knowledge Factory: Student Power and Academic Politics in America*; and Kirkpatrick Sale, *SDS*.

Chapter 5: New Working Class

See Herbert Gintis, "The New Working Class and Revolutionary Youth;" André Gorz, *Strategy for Labor* and "Capitalist Relations of Production and The Socially Necessary Labor Force"; Serge Mallet, "Socialism and the New Working Class"; Martin Oppenheimer, "What Is the New Working Class?"

Chapter 6: Organization: Basic Models

See Monty Johnstone, "Marx and Engels and the Concept of the Party," in *The Socialist Register 1967*.

Chapter 7: The Vanguard Party

This chapter is drawn from Lenin's *What Is to Be Done?* and *One Step Forward, Two Steps Back*. A useful but unsympathetic examination of the vanguard party based on Bolshevik practice will be found in Philip Selznick, *The Organizational Weapon*.

Chapter 8: Mass Party

On German social democracy, see Carl Landauer, *European Socialism*, Vol. 1, Chapters 6, 7, 9, 12; Carl E. Schorske, *German Social Democracy, 1905-1917*; Harry W. Laidler, *History of Socialism*, Chapter 19 and 20; and G. D. H. Cole, *A History of Socialist Thought*, Vol. 3, Part I, Chapters 5 and 6. On Eduard Bernstein's views see his *Evolutionary Socialism*. On the Socialist Party of the United States see Ira Kipnis, *The American Socialist Movement: 1897-1912*; James Weinstein, *The Decline of Socialism in America 1912-1925*; see also Ronald Radosh (ed.), *Debs*.

Rosa Luxemburg's main writings are available in English in *Selected Political Writings;* Dick Howard (ed.), *The Mass Strike, The Political Party and the Trade Unions and the Junius Pamphlet; The Accumulation of Capital*. For biographies of Luxemburg see Paul Froelich, *Rosa Luxemburg: Ideas in Action*, and J. P. Nettl, *Rosa Luxemburg*.

Chapter 9: Anarchism

On anarchism see George Woodcock, *Anarchism*; or Daniel Guerin, *Anarchism*; Leonard I. Krimerman and Lewis Perry (eds.), *Patterns of Anarchism*; Irving Louis Horowitz (ed.), *The Anarchists*. Major writings by Bakunin will be found in Sam Dolgoff (ed.), *Bakunin on Anarchy*. Prince Peter Kropotkin is available in *Selected Writings on Anarchism and Revolution*. For communist anarchism see Alexander Berkman, *What Is Communist Anarchism*? and Emma Goldman, *Anarchism and Other Essays*. On revolutionary syndicalism see Georges Sorel, *Reflections on Violence*; also Irving Louis Horowitz, *Radicalism and the Revolt Against Reason: The Social Theories of Georges Sorel*. On modern manifestations of anarchism see Daniel and Gabriel Cohn-Bendit, *Obsolete Communism*; David E. Apter and James Joll (eds.), *Anarchism Today*.

Chapter 10: Modern American Left

For an overview of the American left in the 20th century see James Weinstein, *Ambiguous Legacy: The Left in American Politics.*

On SNCC see Howard Zinn, *SNCC: The New Abolitionists;* James Forman, *The Making of Black Revolutionaries.* For SDS see Kirkpatrick Sale, *SDS*; Massimo Teodori, *The New Left: A Documentary History.* For Weatherman see Harold Jacobs (ed.), *Weatherman.*

Chapter 11: Mobilization in Historical Context

Marx's relevant writings are scattered. See Marx and Engels, *The Communist Manifesto, The German Ideology,* and Marx, *Critique of the Gotha Program*, and Saul K. Padover (ed.), *Karl Marx on the First International.* For Lenin on mobilization see "The Tasks of the Proletariat in the Present Revolution," "Lessons of the Revolution," and "Marxism and Insurrection." For Trotsky on the transitional program see *The Transitional Program for Socialist Revolution.* Mao's writings on mobilization are embedded in this discussions on revolutionary warfare, see Chapter 15 of this book. On exemplary behavior see his "Spread the Campaigns to Reduce Rent, Increase Production and 'Support The Government and Cherish the People' In the Base Areas." An excellent summary of three mobilizational campaigns undertaken during the development of the Yenan base will be found in Mark Selden, *The Yenan Way in Revolutionary China.*

Chapter 12: Mobilization Theory and Practice

For a discussion of slogans in the context of the Russian Revolution see V. I. Lenin, "On Slogans." An unsympathetic book that provides an extensive analysis of Communist Party slogans in the United States has been written by Lasswell and Blumenstock, 1939; see Chapter 7, "The Technique of Slogans."

On revolutionary nonviolence see David Dellinger, *Revolutionary Nonviolence.* For a marxist view of morality see Leon Trotsky, *Their Morals and Ours.*

Chapter 13: Mobilization at the Point of Production

On early trade unionism in Great Britain see Sidney and Beatrice Webb, *Industrial Democracy*; see also E. P. Thompson, *The Making of the English Working Class.* For an overall early history of American unionism see Joseph Raybach, *A History of American Labor.* For the IWW see Melvyn Dubofsky, *We Shall Be All: A History of the Industrial Workers of the World*; Joyce L. Kornbluh (ed.), *Rebel Voices: An IWW Anthology*; James Weinstein, "The IWW and American Socialism," in *Socialist Revolution,* Sept.–Oct. 1970.

On the CIO see Art Preis, *Labor's Giant Step: Twenty Years of the CIO* from a trotskyist view; for a contrasting view see Len De Caux, *Labor Radical: From the Wobblies to the CIO.* A social history giving the context of the formation of the CIO is the book by Irving Bernstein, *Turbulent Years: A History of the American Workers 1933-1941.* On the struggle against the no-strike pledge during the Second World War see Martin Glaberman, *Wartime Strikes.*

On nationalization, there are a number of discussions especially reflecting bourgeois points of view. See Eldon Barry, *Nationalization in British Politics: The Historical Background;* Mario Einaudi, et al., *Nationalization in France and Italy.*

On workers' control see Gerry Hunnius, G. David Carson, and John Case (eds.), *Workers' Control: A Reader on Labor and Social Change*; Ken Coates and Tony Topham, *The New Unionism: The Case for Workers' Control*; André Gorz, *Strategy for Labor.*

On soviets, see Oskar Anweiler, *The Soviets: The Russian Workers, Peasants and Soldiers Councils 1905-1921*. For Italy, see Antonio Gramsci, *Soviets in Italy.*
On the general strike see Rosa Luxemburg, *The Mass Strike*; Wilfred H. Crook, *Communism and the General Strike.* On the British general strike of 1926 see Christopher Farman, *The General Strike, May 1926.* On the San Francisco strike of 1934 see Charles Larrowe, *Harry Bridges: The Rise and Fall of Radical Labor in the U.S.*

Chapter 14: Mobilization in Other Contexts

A fairly extensive literature is available describing the Sacco and Vanzetti case and others. For Sacco and Vanzetti, see Herbert B. Ehrman, *The Case That Will Not Die: Commonwealth vs. Sacco and Vanzetti*; Frances Russell, *Tragedy at Dedham: The Story of Sacco and Vanzetti.* For the Mooney-Billings case see Richard H. Frost, *The Mooney Case.* For the Scottsboro case see Dan T. Carter, *Scottsboro: A Tragedy of the American South.*
On community organizing see David Footman, *Red Prelude*, for a description of the Russian Narodnicks. For the United States see Saul Alinsky, *Reveille for Radicals* and *Rules for Radicals.*
On confrontations see Kirkpatrick Sale, *SDS.* For a description of typical examples at Cornell and Stanford universities see Irving Louis Horowitz and William H. Friedland, *The Knowledge Factory: Student Power and Academic Politics in America*, "Five Years of Confrontation at Cornell," Case Study 1.

Chapter 15: Revolutionary Warfare

There are a number of standard works on revolutionary warfare. For Friedrich Engels see *Engels as a Military Critic.* For Trotsky see his *Military Writings.* Mao's writings are scattered but are brought together in a single volume *Selected Military Writings.* A collection of work from a variety of writers will be found in William J. Pomeroy (ed.), *Guerrilla Warfare and Marxism.* An important book by Vo Nguyen Giap, *People's War, People's Army* reveals the approach to military revolutionary strategy in Vietnam. On Cuba and Latin America see Che Guevara, *Guerrilla Warfare*; Regis Debray presents his distinct conception of vanguardist warfare in *Revolution in the Revolution?* On urban guerrilla warfare see Abraham Guillén, and Carlos Marighela, *For the Liberation of Brazil.* For a view projecting the character of military forces after the socialist transformation see Jean Jaurès, *L'Armée Nouvelle.*
On the Spanish Civil War of 1936-39 see Leon Trotsky, *The Spanish Revolution*; Hugh Thomas, *The Spanish Civil War*; P. Broué and E. Témine, *The Revolution and Civil War in Spain.*
The main military writings of Mao Zedong on which we have drawn include: "The Struggle in the Chingkang Mountains," "On Correcting Mistaken Ideas in the Party," "A Single Spark Can Start a Prairie Fire," "Problems of Strategy in China's Revolutionary War," "Problems of Strategy in Guerrilla War Against Japan," "On Protracted War," "Problems of War and Strategy," "On Production by the Army for Its Own Support and on the Importance of the Great Movements for Rectification and for Production." All are found in his *Selected Military Writings* and in the four volumes of his *Selected Works.*

Chapter 16: Future Arrangements

Discussion of the future is widely scattered through the writings of both Marx and Engels. For major sources see their *The German Ideology*, and Marx, *Economic and Philosophical Manuscripts, Critique of the Gotha Program.* Karl Marx, *Selected Writings in Sociology and Social Philosophy*, T. B. Bottomore (ed.), devotes Part V to selections on future society. See also Engels's "Introduction" to Marx's *The Civil War in France* for his discussion on the dictatorship of the proletariat.

On the utopians see Charles Nordhoff, *The Communistic Societies of the United States*; Frank E. Manuel (ed.), *Utopias and Utopian Thought*. For Engels's attack on the utopians see his *Socialism: Utopian and Scientific*.

On the Chinese Cultural Revolution see Joan Robinson, *The Cultural Revolution in China*; Jean Esmein, *The Chinese Cultural Revolution*; Victor Nee with Don Layman, *The Cultural Revolution at Peking University*; E. L. Wheelwright and Bruce McFarlane, *The Chinese Road to Socialism*. For articles on the Cultural Revolution mainly by bourgeois scholars consult *China Quarterly*.

On the communist phase see especially V. I. Lenin, *The State and Revolution*; Michael P. Lerner, *The New Socialist Revolution*.

References

In citing classical works by Marx, Engels, Lenin, Trotsky, Mao, et al., we have provided, wherever possible, citations to chapters, sections, paragraphs (where numbered) so that readers may utilize any editions availble. References for quotations will be given for the specific edition cited in the Bibliography, giving the place of publication, publisher, and date of publication. Our specific citations here are in the following sequence: author, date of publication, page number(s).

Introduction

xiii   "The sentence employed"   Lenin, *What Is to Be Done?* Chapter 2, Section B. Vol. I, 1970: 151.

Introduction to Part One

1   "The most indubitable"   Trotsky, *The History of the Russian Revolution*, "Preface," 1937: xvii.

Chapter 1

6   "Men make their own"   Marx, *The Eighteenth Brumaire of Louis Bonaparte* in Marx and Engels, 1968: 97.

6   The dialectical aspect   On the dialectic see Marx and Engels, *The German Ideology*, Part I, Section 1.

6   *forces of production*   Marx, "Preface to *A Contribution to the Critique of Political Economy*" in Tucker, 1972: 4–5.

7   "In the development"   Marx and Engels, *The German Ideology*, quoted in Bottomore and Rubel, 1964: 64.

8   "The history of all"   Marx and Engels, *The Communist Manifesto*, Part I, 1968: 35–36.

9   "is not the satisfaction"   Marx, 1964*b*: 125.

219

10	"because beyond certain limits"	Marx, *Capital*, Vol. 3, Chapter 15, Section 3, 1967: 250–251.
11	*immiseration*	Marx, *Economic and Philosophical Manuscripts*, First Manuscript, "Wages of Labor," in Bottomore, 1964: 69–84.
11	"In a society"	Ibid., 72–73.
11	*absolute* or *relative decline*	Ibid.
11	In *Capital*, however	Marx, *Capital*, Vol. 3, Part III.
11	In his notes to *Capital*	Marx, *The Grundrisse*, McLellan, 1971: 94–96; see also Nicolaus, 1969.
12	"Competition simply"	C. Pecqueuer, *Theorie nouvelle d'economie sociale et politique*, quoted by Marx in *Economic and Philosophical Manuscripts*, First Manuscript, Bottomore, 1964: 97–98.
13	"The real limitation"	Bottomore and Rubel, 1964: 144; *Capital*, Vol. 3, 1967: 250.
13	THE PROLETARIAT	Marx, "Introduction to the Contribution to the Critique of Hegel's *Philosophy of Right*," Tucker, 1972: 18–23; see also *The Communist Manifesto*, "Proletarians and Communists," 1968: 46–53.
13	"Communism is for"	Marx, *The German Ideology*," in Tucker, 1972: 126.
13	This awareness of *class*	Marx, "Introduction to the Contribution to the Critique of Hegel's *Philosophy of Right*," Tucker, 1972: 18–23; Bendix and Lipset, 1953.
14	As enterprises got	For a well-developed argument that the process continues in modern capitalism see Braverman, 1974.
14	"has played"	Marx and Engels, *The Communist Manifesto*, "Bourgeois and Proletarians," 1968: 37–40.
14	"expropriate the expropriators"	*Capital*, Vol. 1., Part 8, 1967: 763.

Chapter 2

17	1. Tribal ownership	Marx and Engels, *The German Ideology*, "Feuerbach," 1947: 9–16.
17	Franco-Prussian war	See "First Address of the General Council of the International Workingmen's Association on the Franco-Prussian War" and "Second Address . . ." in Marx, *The Civil War in France* in Marx and Engels, 1968: 263–273.
17	Civil War in the United States	Marx and Engels, *The Civil War in the United States*.
18	"Anyone who says"	Engels quoted in Labedz, "Introduction," 1962: 9.
18	"The worst thing"	Engels, *The Peasant War in Germany*, Chapter 6, 1926: 135, emphasis in the original.
18	stages of development	*The German Ideology*, "Feuerbach," Section 3, 1947: 73.
18	"the practical workers"	Engels, "Supplement to the Preface of 1870 for the Third Edition of 1875" of *The Peasant War in Germany* in Marx and Engels, 1968; 250.
18	"While the democratic"	Marx, "Address to the Central Council of the Communist League," Tucker, 1972: 367, 373.
19	"The complete victory"	Lenin, *Two Tactics of Social-Democracy in the Democratic Revolution*, "Epilogue," Section 2, Vol. 1, 1970: 554.

19   "the revolutionary-democratic"   Ibid., Section 6, Vol. 1, 1970: 483.

19   "From the democratic"   Lenin, "Social Democracy's Attitude toward the Peasant Movement," cited by Liebman, 1970: 68–69.

21   "The task of arming"   Trotsky, "Results and Prospects" in Trotsky, 1969: 61.

21   "the proletariat in power"   Quoted by Deutscher, Vol. 1, 1965: 71; also see "Results and Prospects," Trotsky, 1969: 71.

22   In Mao Zedong   For a short summary of Mao on the stages of the revolutionary process see Schram, 1969: 67–69.

22   Attacking Trotsky   See Mao, "Win the Masses . . ." Vol. 1, 1967:290

22   massacred the Shanghai workers   Isaacs, 1951: Chapter 11.

22   "protracted war"   Mao, "On Protracted War." Vol. 2.

23   "and we are for"   Mao, "Win the Masses . . ." Vol. 1: 290.

23   "the new-democratic"   Mao, "The Chinese Revolution and the Chinese Communist Party." Vol. 2; 326.

23   "a dictatorship"   Ibid., 327.

Chapter 3

24   "went there to find"   Che Guevara, "Exception or Vanguard," in Gerassi, 1968: 134.

24   "The small-holding peasants"   Marx, *The Eighteenth Brumaire*, in Marx and Engels, 1968: 171–172.

25   "The essence of"   Lenin, "Conclusion" from *The Agrarian Programme of Social-Democracy* . . . in *Selected Works* (1943). Vol. 3: 278.

25   As early as 1920   For a discussion of early Bolshevik orientations toward China see Whiting, 1953.

26   *Analytic Problems*   Shanin, 1966, provides an excellent discussion of some of the conceptual difficulties with the peasantry.

26   "The idiocy of rural life"   Mark and Engels, *The Communist Manifesto*, 1968: 39.

28   *The Disruptions*   Lenin, *Imperialism*. Vol. 1, 1970: 594–647.

28   Traditional social and economic   On the disruptions to peasant economies see Luxemburg, 1968: Chapters 27–29; on markets and trade in China see Lattimore, 1940.

28   "The process of"   Mitrany, 1951: 77.

29   Before dealing with   Lenin, *Imperialism*; see also his "Critical Remarks on the National Question" in Lenin, 1968. For a good summary of the marxist discussion of the national question see Davis, 1967.

30   "When the native"   Fanon, 1968: 52.

30   "The most serious"   Memmi, 1965: 91–93.

31   "he is not an animal"   Fanon, 1968: 52.

31   "And it is clear"   Ibid., 61.

32   Lenin recognized   Lenin, "The Agrarian Question in Russia at the End of the 19th Century." In *Selected Works* (1943), Vol. 1: 21, 61*ff*. See also his *The Development of Capitalism in Russia*. In *Selected Works* (1943). Vol. 1: Chapters 3–4.

32   "The poor peasants"   Mao, "Report of an Investigation of the Peasant Movement in Hunan." Vol. 1: 32–33.

| 32 | According to this analysis | See the discussion in Schram, 1969, Section C of the "Introduction:" 45-56 on Mao's writings in 1926-27 on peasant-based revolutions. For an excellent analysis of Mao's action in mobilizing the middle peasants as against what he claimed was the revolutionary potential of poor peasants see Alavi, 1965. |

Chapter 4

36	Mary Inman	Inman, 1940.
37	"Our experience in"	Berkeley-Oakland Women's Union, 1974: 74-75.
37	"The industrial reserve army"	Marx, 1967, Vol. 1, Chapter 25, Section 3.
38	The labor movement has a long history	For the history of blacks in the United Mine Workers see Gutman, 1968. For other essays on blacks and American labor see Jacobson, 1968.
39	The Socialist Party of the United States	On the Socialist Party and Negroes see Allen, 1974: Chapter 7.
39	The Industrial Workers of the World	On the IWW and Negroes see Allen, 1974: 191-195.
39	With the formation of the Communist Party	On the CP and Negroes see Record, 1951; Allen, 1974: Chapter 7.
40	"had the misfortune"	Allen, 1974: 221-222.
40	Marcus Garvey	Cronin, 1969; Vincent, 1972.
41	Malcolm X	Malcolm X, 1966.
42	an *internal colony*	On internal colonialism see Blauner, 1972: Chapter 3.
42	"We now see"	Huey Newton, *The Black Panther*, June 5, 1971.
42	"the people see"	Ibid.
43	"there is not going"	Cleaver, 1969.
43	"Those who are"	Colorado chapter, *The Black Panther*, June 27, 1970.
43	Tomás Almaguer	Almaguer, 1975.
46	"whether or not"	Mao Zedong, "The Orientation of the Youth Movement," Vol. 2, 1967: 246.
46	"Come mothers and fathers"	Bob Dylan, "The Times They Are a' Changing," Columbia Records.
46	"We are all outlaws"	The Jefferson Airplane, "We Can Be Together," *Volunteers*.
47	"A basic far-reaching"	Roussopolous, 1970.
47	"institutions like the"	Klonsky, 1968.
47	One analysis that exemplifies	Rowntree, 1968.
47	"total employment"	Ibid., 32. In 1967 the 10% figure still held, Reich and Finkelhor, 1972: 393-394.
48	"the character of"	Rowntree, 1968: 34.
48	"It is the 'know-how' "	Ibid., 38.
48	"They share an occupation"	Horowitz and Friedland, 1972: 123.
49	"Young white people"	Hayden, 1970: 166.

Chapter 5

| 53 | "Capital is itself" | Marx, *The Grundrisse*, (McLellan) 1971: 142-143. |
| 54 | "end of ideology" | This notion developed its label from the title of a |

54	C. Wright Mills	book by Daniel Bell (1960). For a critique of the concept, see Waxman, 1968. See his *White Collar*, 1953, especially Chapters 4 and 13.
56	Andre Gorz outlined	Gorz, 1965.
56	"The modern working class"	Mallet, 1965.
58	"has become a"	Kerr, 1963:
58	two distinct functions	For a fuller development of this argument, see Gintis, 1970: 13–43.
58	*The Expanded Proletariat*	For a discussion of the changing character of the U.S. working class see Oppenheimer, 1972.
59	"The fundamental institutions"	Gintis, 1970: 26
59	Gramsci	See Gramsci, 1970, 1971.
60	"modern capitalism"	Gilbert, n.d.

Introduction to Part II

| 63 | "In what relation" | Marx and Engels, *The Communist Manifesto*, Part 2, "Proletarians and Communists," 1968: 46. |

Chapter 7

All entries to this chapter except the first are from Lenin's *What is to Be Done* (abbreviated as *What Is*) and *One Step Forward, Two Steps Back* (abbreviated as *One Step*). Citations for *What Is* and *One Step* are from the 1970 edition of Lenin's *Selected Works*, 1970, Vol. 1, 119–454.

73	With a police force	Edeen, 1960: 276.
74	"to build up"	*What Is*, Chapter 5, Part B: 247.
75	"only on the basis"	Karl Kautsky quoted by Lenin, ibid., Chapter 2, Part B: 150.
75	"socialist consciousness"	Ibid., 150.
75	"to vagueness and vacillation"	*One Step*, Section I: 322.
76	"precisely because"	Ibid., 319.
76	"tail ender"	Ibid., 320.
76	"Now we have"	Ibid., Section O: 407.
76	"produce from"	*What Is*, Chapter 4, Section D: 220.
76	democratic centralism	See *What Is*, Chapter 4, Section E; also Lenin, "The Organization of the Party," in Vol. 1, 1970: 564–572.
77	"perverting the"	Lenin paraphrasing Kautsky in *One Step*, Section Q: 433.
77	"Democracy does not"	Kautsky quoted by Lenin in ibid.: 433–434.
77	"In its struggle"	Ibid., Section R: 446.
77	"unity of organization"	Ibid., Section Q: 423.
77	"it is a bad business"	*What Is*, Chapter 4, Section C: 215.
77	"without the 'dozen' "	Ibid., 215.
77	"the number of"	Ibid., 217.
78	"there can be no talk"	*One Step*, Section I: 319.
78	"boundlessly devoted"	*What Is*, Chapter 4, Section D: 225.
78	"through its ideological unification"	*One Step*, Section R: 446.

Chapter 8

82	*The German Social-Democratic*	See Russell, 1965; Landauer, Vol. 1, 1959; 365; Cole, 1960: 249.
82	During the period 1878–	Cole, 1960: 249.
86	At its peak	Weinstein, 1969: *passim*; Cole, 1960: 809.
87	"To kow-tow to"	Eugene Victor Debs, "Danger Ahead," in Radosh, 1971: 52.
87	"as useless as"	Debs quoted by Weinstein, 1969: 32.
87	"the state or"	Constitution of the Socialist Party quoted in Kipnis, 1952: 106.
88	"I confess to"	Debs, "Sound Socialist Tactics," in Radosh, 1971: 42.
88	"The Socialist Party"	Debs, "Working Class Politics," in Radosh, 1971: 27.
89	"mechanical-bureaucratic	Luxemburg, 1971a: 64.
89	"ultra-centralism"	Luxemburg, 1971b: 286.
89	"to give the cue"	Luxemburg, 1971a: 54.
89	"Organizational Questions"	Luxemburg, 1971b: 283–306.
90	"Nothing will deliver"	Ibid., 302.
90	"We must frankly"	Ibid., 306.
90	"The 'discipline' which"	Ibid., 291.
91	"the product of"	Ibid., 293.
91	"no single act"	Luxemburg, 1971a: 52.
91	"Whether they stand"	Ibid., 79.
91	"the class instinct"	Ibid., 67.
91	"a year of revolution"	Ibid.
91	"model organization"	Ibid., 103.
91	"a more rigorous application"	Luxemburg, 1971b: 304.
92	"The Spartacus League"	Ibid., 375–376.

Chapter 9

94	"turn the International"	Bakunin quoted by Carr, 1937: 440.
94	"We do not wish"	Quoted in Woodcock, 1962: 229.
95	This meant that	Cf., Carr, 1937: 453.
95	"our conception"	Kropotkin, "Modern Science and Anarchism," in Horowitz, 1964: 165–166.

Chapter 10

100	"I'm going head-on"	Charles Sherrod quoted in Zinn, 1965: 227.
100	"to show Negroes"	Ibid., 113.
101	In addition to	Ibid., 10–11.
101	Local people chose	Ibid., 267–268.
101	The anticentralization spirit	Ibid., 216.
102	100,000 members	Sale, 1974: 664.
102	"share in those"	SDS, *The Port Huron Statement*, 1962: 7; see also Teodori, 1969: 167.
102	"the need to create"	Tom Hayden in Jacobs and Landau, 1966: 35.

102	"expected to operate"	SDS Constitution, *New Left Notes*, June 26, 1967.
103	In 1967,	SDS Constitution, *New Left Notes*, July 10, 1967.
104	"land, bread"	*"Black Panther Party—Platform and Program,"* Appendix A in Major, 1971: 287.
105	"That is a lot"	Eldridge Cleaver, "The Black Man's Stake in Vietnam" in Foner, 1970: 103.
105	"the Vanguard Party must"	Huey Newton, "The Correct Handling of a Revolution," in Foner, 1970: 41.
105	"This is the genius"	Alprentice Carter, "The Genius of Huey Newton," in Foner, 1970: 28.
105	"There are basically three ways"	Huey P. Newton, in Foner, 1970: 42.
106	"a cadre organization"	Bernadine Dohrn, et al., 1969.
106	"a centralized organization"	Ibid.
106	"The development of"	Ibid.
106	"demand total"	Shin'ya Ono, 1969.
106	Internally, changing	Anonymous, "Revolution in the 70's," *The Fire Next Time*, January 30, 1970.
107	"People who live together"	Anonymous, "Inside the Weather Machine," *Rat*, February 6, 1970.
107	After some brief experiments	Anonymous, "Weather Letter," *Rat*, July 15, 1970.
107	"great possibilities for"	Anonymous, "Weather Letter," *Rat*, July 15, 1970.

Chapter 11

118	"The strategic task"	Trotsky, 1973a: 74–75.
119	"It is easier"	Ibid., 128–129.
120	If somewhat complex and difficult	One attempt at such implementation will be found in the concept of "socialist reforms" developed by Gorz, 1973: Chapter 3, 135–177.
123	"Some people say"	Mao, "We Must Learn to Do Economic Work," Vol. 3, 1967: 193–194. See also "Production is also Possible in the Guerrilla Zones," Vol. 3: 197–200; and "On Production by the Army for Its Own Support . . .", Vol. 3: 275–279.
123	"If you want to know"	Mao, "On Practice," Vol. 1, 1967: 300.

Chapter 12

131	PROGRAMS AND SLOGANS	See Lenin, "On Slogans," Vol. 2, 1970: 200–206.
131	*minimum* and *maximum* programs	See the discussion of the Erfurt program of German social-democracy in Schorske, 1955: 4–6; Laidler, 1968: 233–236.
132	"All power to the Soviets"	The Bolsheviks did not use this slogan continuously. Between the March and November revolutions Lenin despaired for some time of using the soviets as the transitional revolutionary instrument. As Bolshevik strength increased in the soviets, the slogan was revived.
137	Henry David Thoreau	See "Civil Disobedience" in Thoreau, 1962: 85–104.
137	"Abolitionists should"	Ibid., 93–94.

137	Mahatma Gandhi	See, for example, Fischer, 1950; Payne, 1969.
137	Martin Luther King, Jr.	"Pilgrimage to Nonviolence," in Lynd, 1966: 391–392.
138	"We need to"	Dellinger, 1971: 84.
138	"Under 'normal' conditions	Trotsky, *Their Morals and Ours*, in Deutscher 1965: 336–337.
139	"I *am* for"	Malcolm X, 1966: 367.

Chapter 13

143	Invented by factory workers	See Jones, 1964, for a description of the Akron sit-down strikes.
148	"The conception of a democracy"	Braverman, 1974: 445.
148	General Motors Vega plant	See Rothschild, 1974.
152	"There will not"	Quoted in Laidler, 1968: 97.
152	"Kapp Putsch"	See Fischer, 1948: Chapter 5; Anderson, 1945: Chapter 13.
153	"such power behind it"	Sorel, 1950: 152.
153	Engels argued	Engels, "The Bakuninists at Work: Notes on the Spanish Uprising in the Summer of 1873," in Marx and Engels, 1939.
153	Russian revolution of 1905	Trotsky, 1972; Schwarz, 1967.
153	"Tear the workers"	Quoted in Deutscher, Vol. 1, 1965a: 110–111.
154	"The power of the strike"	Deutscher, 1964: 52; see also Trotsky, 1972: 252.
154	"the economic struggle"	Luxemburg, 1971a: 49.
154	"schoolmaster"	Ibid., 52.

Chapter 14

| 166 | "Do show yourself" | Quoted in Zinn, 1965: 19–20. |
| 166 | "individual vocal dissension" | Davidson, 1967. |

Chapter 15

169	"The Communists . . . openly"	Marx and Engels, *The Communist Manifesto*, final paragraph, 1968: 63.
170	"Weapons are an important"	Mao, "On Protracted War," Paragraph 48, Vol. 2, 1967: 143–144.
170	"The first condition"	Mao, "Problems of Strategy in China's Revolutionary War," Chapter 5, Section 3, Vol. 1, 1968: 216.
170	"Everywhere the National"	Ibid., 217.
170	"we should tell"	Ibid., 210.
171	"a vast sea"	Mao, "On Protracted War," Paragraph 66, Vol. 2, 1967: 154.
171	"The people are"	Giap, 1968, Section 2: 49.
171	Political mobilization,	Mao, "On Protracted War," Paragraph 67, Vol. 2, 1968: 155.
171	"outadministering" the imperialists	Ahmad, 1965.
172	"We must lead"	Mao, "Be Concerned with the Well-Being of the

174	Engels saw	Masses, Pay Attention to Methods of Work," Vol. 1, 1968: 147–148. Engels, "Introduction," to Marx, 1964*a*: 21–25; also included as "Barricade Tactics" in Pomeroy, 1968: 68–72.
174	Similarly, Mao Zedong	Mao, "Problems of War and Strategy," Section 5, 1967: 230. See also Mao's analysis of the "Characteristics of China's Revolutionary War," Section 2 of "Problems of Strategy in China's Revolutionary War," 1967: 196–197.
175	Tupamaros	Nuñez, 1970; Gerassi, 1970; see also *Tricontinental*, Nos. 9, 10, and 17.
175	In China, for example,	There is an extensive literature on rebellions in China, particularly on the Taiping and "Boxer" rebellions. See, for example, Wright, 1962; Jen, 1973; Purcell, 1963.
175	temper of urban populations	Hobsbawm, "The City Mob," 1965: Chapter 7.
175	Spartacus	For a fictional treatment of the Spartacan rebellion, see Koestler, 1947.
175	The Age of Revolution	See Hobsbawm, 1969.
176	two types of warfare	Lenin, "Guerrilla Warfare," in Pomeroy, 1968: 84–94; see especially page 87.
176	*Protracted Warfare*	A good overall treatment of Chinese communism reflecting the critical view of a bourgeois scholar is found in Schwartz, 1961.
177	Mao deplored "guerrilla-ism"	Mao, "Problems of Strategy in China's Revolutionary War," Chapter 3, Section 3, Vol. 1, 1967: 199, and Chapter 5, Section 3: 214–215, Chapter 5, Section 7: 243.
177	*base areas*	Mao, "Problems of Strategy in Guerrilla War against Japan," Chapter 6, Vol. 2, 1967: 93–102.
177	*mobility in small groups*	Mao, "On Protracted War," paragraphs 91–96, Vol. 2, 1967: 170–174.
177	"The enemy advances"	Mao, "A Single Spark Can Start a Prairie Fire," Vol. 1, 1967: 124; "Problems of Strategy in China's Revolutionary War," Chapter 5, Section 3, Vol. 1, 1967: 213.
177	"As the Red Army"	Ibid., 243.
178	"the strategic bases"	Mao, "Problems of Strategy in Guerrilla War against Japan," Chapter 6, Vol. 2, 1967: 93.
178	two stages	Ibid., Chapter 6, Section 2: 96–97.
178	"when large numbers"	Ibid.
178	Mao further	Ibid., 98–99.
178	"without organization"	Ibid., 99.
179	". . . the Chinese Red Army"	Mao, "On Correcting Mistaken Ideas in the Party," Vol. 1, 1967: 106.
179	"The army is not only"	Mao, "Turn the Army into a Working Force," Vol. 4, 1969: 337–338.
179	Mao listed	Mao, "On Production by the Army for Its Own Support and on the Importance of the Great Movements for Rectification and for Production," Vol. 3, 1967: 277–278.
179	"deviations"	Mao, "Problems of Strategy in China's Revolutionary War," Chapter 5, Section 1, Vol. 1, 1967: 205.

180	"Our strategy is"	Ibid., Chapter 5, Section 6: 237.
180	"Fight when"	Ibid., Chapter 5, Section 7: 241.
180	"Injuring all"	Ibid., Chapter 5, Section 9: 248.
180	"We should strike"	Ibid., Chapter 5, Section 5: 231.
180	"it is inadvisable"	Ibid., Chapter 5, Section 7: 241.
180	Mao outlined three stages	"On Protracted War," Paragraphs 35-50, Vol. 2, 1967: 136-145.
181	"Where a government"	Guevara, 1969: 2.
181	"The revolutionary guerilla"	Debray, 1967: 41.
181	"three golden rules"	Ibid., 42.
181	"guerilla warfare is"	Guevara, 1969: 3-4.
183	"The urban guerilla"	Marighela, 1971: 63.
183	"(1) The physical liquidation"	Ibid., 66.
184	"The government's chances"	Ibid., 76.
184	"It is fundamental"	"Thirty Questions to a Tupamaro," quoted in Nuñez, 1970: 30.

Chapter 16

190	From Robert Owen's	For Robert Owen, see Harvey, 1949. For Charles Fourier and other French utopian socialists see Manuel, 1962.
190	Almost all died	On the longevity of utopian experiments see Kanter, 1972.
190	From Proudhon to Bakunin	In addition to the anarchist sources suggested in readings for Chapter 9, see Apter and Joll, 1972, for a discussion of modern-day anarchist thinking.
190	Marx believed that	Marx and Engels, *The German Ideology*, "Feuerbach," Section 1a, 1947: 23-27; *The Communist Manifesto*, Part III, Section 3, "Critical-Utopian Socialism and Communism," 1968: 59-62.
191	period of transition	See, for example, Marx, *Critique of the Gotha Program*, Section 4.
192	"in communist society"	Marx and Engels, *The German Ideology*, "Feuerbach," Section 1a, 1947: 22.
192	"From each according"	Marx, *Critique of the Gotha Program*, Section 1, 1968: 325.
193	"rectification"	Rue, 1966: 273-275; Selden, 1971: 188-210.
194	". . . the Commune was"	Engels, "Introduction" to Marx, *The Civil War in France*, 1968: 216.
194	*Critique of the Gotha*	Section 4, 1968: 331.
195	Because it is organized	Cf. Marx and Engels, *The German Ideology*, "Feuerbach," Section 2c, 1947: 67-68.
196	"Workingmen's wages"	See "Introduction" to *The Civil War in France*, 1968: 262; Lenin, *The State and Revolution*, Chapter 6, Section 2, Vol. 2, 1970.
198	ratios approximating 3.5 to 1	For Cuba, see MacEwen, 1975: 123. For China, see Wheelwright and McFarlane, 1970: 134-136.
199	"Who says organization"	Michels, 1968.
200	International Typographical Union	Lipset, et al., 1956.

200	*Overcoming the Difference*	The issue is formulated here in classical marxian terminology. For a more current formulation advocating the de-differentiation of the division of labor see Agger, 1978.
200	The problem emerged	On the "scissors crisis" in Russia that concerned the question of rural-urban separation see Deutscher, Vol. 2, 1965*b*: Chapters 2 and 4; see also Cohen, 1975: Chapter 6.
200	The contrast in China	Schiller, 1962: 331–350.
204	"one hundred flowers"	Mao, "On the Correct Handling of Contradictions among the People," 1971, Section 8: 462.

Bibliography

All sources referred to in the suggested source readings and references have been included in the bibliography.

Agger, Robert E. 1978. *A Little White Lie: Institutional Divisions of Labor and Life.* New York, Elsevier.

Ahmad, Eqbal. 1965. "Revolutionary Warfare: How to Tell When the Revolutionaries Have Won." *Nation*, Aug. 30, 95-100.

Alavi, Hamza. 1965. "Peasants and Revolution." In John Saville and Ralph Miliband (eds.), *The Socialist Register 1965.* New York, Monthly Review Press.

Alinsky, Saul D. 1969. *Reveille for Radicals.* New York, Vintage.

_____ . 1972. *Rules for Radicals: A Practical Primer for Realistic Radicals.* New York, Vintage.

Allen, Robert L. 1974. *Reluctant Reformers: Racism and Social Reform Movements in the United States.* Washington, D. C., Howard University Press.

Almaguer, Tomas. 1975. "Class, Race, and Chicano Oppression." *Socialist Revolution*, No. 25, July-September: 71-99.

Alperovitz, Gar. 1972. "Socialism as a Pluralist Commonwealth." In Richard C. Edwards, Michael Reich, and Thomas Weisskopf (eds.), *The Capitalist System: A Radical Analysis of American Society.* Englewood Cliffs, N.J. Prentice-Hall.

Ameringer, Oscar. 1940. *If You Don't Weaken.* New York, Henry Holt.

Amin, Samir. 1974. *Accumulation on a World Scale: A Critique of the Theory of Underdevelopment.* New York, Monthly Review Press.

Anderson, Evelyn. 1945. *Hammer or Anvil: The Story of the German Working Class Movement.* London, Victor Gollancz.

Anonymous. 1970. "Inside The Weather Machine." *Rat.* February 6.

Anonymous. 1970. "Revolution in the '70's." *The Fire Next Time.* Also published in Jacobs, 1970. January 30.

_____ . 1970. "Weather Letter." *Rat.* Also published in Jacobs, 1970. July 15.

Anweiler, Oskar. 1974. *The Soviets: The Russian Workers, Peasants, and Soldiers Councils, 1905-1921.* New York, Pantheon.

Apter, David E., and James Joll (eds.). 1972. *Anarchism Today.* New York, Doubleday Anchor.

231

Baran, Paul A. 1970. "On the Political Economy of Backwardness." In Robert I. Rhodes (ed.),
    Imperialism and Development: A Reader. New York: Monthly Review Press: 285–301.
Baron, Samuel H. 1963. *Plekhanov: The Father of Russian Marxism.* Stanford, Stanford
    University Press.
Barry, Eldon. 1965. *Nationalization in British Politics: The Historical Background.* Stanford,
    Calif. Stanford University Press.
Bebel, August. 1971. *Women Under Socialism.* New York, Schocken.
Bell, Daniel. 1960. *The End of Ideology.* New York, Free Press.
Bendix, Reinhard, and Seymour Martin Lipset. 1953. "Karl Marx' Theory of Social Classes."
    In Bendix and Lipset (eds.) *Class, Status and Power.* Glencoe, Ill. Free Press.
Benson, C. Randolph. 1971. *Thomas Jefferson as Social Scientist.* Rutherford, N.J., Fairleigh
    Dickenson University Press.
Berkeley-Oakland Women's Union. 1974. "The 'Principles of Unity' of the Berkeley-Oakland
    Women's Union," *Socialist Revolution,* Vol. 4, No. 1: 74–75.
Berkman, Alexander. 1929. *What Is Communist Anarchism?* New York, Vanguard.
Bernstein, Eduard. 1970. *Evolutionary Socialism.* New York, Schocken.
Bernstein, Irving. 1970. *Turbulent Years: A History of the American Workers 1933–1941.*
    Boston, Houghton Mifflin.
Blauner, Robert. 1964. *Alienation and Freedom: The Factory Worker and His Industry.*
    Chicago, University of Chicago Press.
———. 1972. *Racial Oppression in America.* New York, Harper & Row.
Bottomore, T. B. (ed). 1964. *Karl Marx: Early Writings.* New York, McGraw-Hill.
———, and Maximilien Rubel (eds.). 1964. *Karl Marx: Selected Writings in Sociology and
    Social Philosophy.* New York, McGraw-Hill.
Brandt, Conrad, Benjamin Schwartz, and John K. Fairbank (eds.). 1959. *A Documentary
    History of Chinese Communism.* Cambridge, Harvard University Press.
Braverman, Harry. 1974. *Labor and Monopoly Capital.* New York, Monthly Review Press.
Brecher, Jeremy. 1975. *Strike!* Greenwich, Conn., Fawcett.
Broué, P., and E. Témine. 1974. *The Revolution and Civil War in Spain.* Cambridge, Mass.,
    MIT Press.
Carr, E. H. 1937. *Michael Bakunin.* New York, Vintage.
Carter, Dan T. 1971. *Scottsboro: A Tragedy of the American South.* New York, Oxford Uni-
    versity Press.
Chodorow, Nancy. 1979. "Mothering, Male Dominance, and Capitalism." In Zillah Eisenstein
    (ed.), *Capitalist Patriarchy,* New York: Monthly Review Press: 83–106.
Cleaver, Eldridge. 1969. "An Open Letter to Stokely Carmichael." *Ramparts.* September.
Coates, Ken, and Tony Topham. 1974. *The New Unionism: The Case for Workers' Control.*
    Baltimore, Penguin Books.
Cohen, Stephen F. 1975. *Bukharin and The Bolshevik Revolution.* New York, Vintage.
Cohn-Bendit, Daniel and Gabriel. 1968. *Obsolete Communism: The Left-Wing Alternative.*
    New York, McGraw-Hill.
Cole, G. D. H. 1960. *A History of Socialist Thought: Vol. 3, Part I, The Second Interna-
    tional 1889–1914.* London, Macmillan.
Commons, John R. 1918. *History of Labor in the United States.* New York, Macmillan.
Cox, Oliver C. 1964. *Capitalism as a System.* New York, Monthly Review Press.
Cronin, E. David. 1969. *Black Moses: The Story of Marcus Garvey and The Universal Negro
    Improvement Association.* Madison, University of Wisconsin Press.
Crook, Wilfrid H. 1960. *Communism and The General Strike.* Hamden, Conn., Shoe String
    Press.
Cruse, Harold. 1967. *The Crisis of the Negro Intellectual.* New York, William Morrow.
Dancis, Bruce. 1975. "Socialism and Women in the United States, 1900–1917." *Socialist Rev-
    olution.* No. 27.
Davidson, Carl. 1967. "Toward Institutional Resistance." *New Left Notes,* November 13.
    Also published in Wallerstein and Starr, 1971.
Davis, Horace B. 1967. *Nationalism and Socialism: Marxist and Labor Theories of National-
    ism to 1917.* New York, Monthly Review Press.
Debray, Regis. 1967. *Revolution in the Revolution?* New York, Grove.

De Caux, Len. 1971. *Labor Radical: From the Wobblies to the CIO.* Boston, Beacon Press.

Dellinger, Dave. 1971. *Revolutionary Nonviolence.* Garden City, N.Y., Anchor.

Deutscher, Isaac (ed.). 1964. *The Age of Permanent Revolution: A Trotsky Anthology.* New York, Dell.

Deutscher, Isaac. 1965*a. The Prophet Armed: Trotsky 1879-1921.* Vol. I. New York, Vintage.

_____ . 1965*b. The Prophet Unarmed: Trotsky 1921-1929.* Vol. 2. New York, Vintage.

_____ . 1965*c. The Prophet Outcast: Trotsky 1929-1940.* Vol. 3. New York, Vintage.

Dixon, Marlene. 1969. *Why Women's Liberation.* San Francisco, Bay Area Radical Education Project.

Dohrn, Bernadine, et al. 1969. "You Don't Need a Weatherman To Know Which Way The Wind Blows," *New Left Notes.* June 18. Also published in Jacobs, 1970.

Dolgoff, Sam (ed.). 1972. *Bakunin on Anarchy.* New York, Alfred A. Knopf.

Dubofsky, Melvyn. 1969. *We Shall Be All: A History of the IWW.* Chicago, Quadrangle.

Dunbar, Roxanne. 1974. *Female Liberation as The Basis for Social Revolution.* Boston, New England Free Press.

Edeen, Alf. 1960. "The Civil Service: Its Composition and Status." In Cyril E. Black (ed.), *The Transformation of Russian Society.* Cambridge, Mass., Harvard University Press: 274-292.

Edwards, Richard C., Michael Reich, and Thomas E. Weisskopf (eds.). 1978. *The Capitalist System: A Radical Analysis of American Society.* Englewood Cliffs, N.J., Prentice-Hall. 2nd Edition.

Ehrenreich, Barbara. 1975. "Speech at the National Conference on Socialist Feminism," *Socialist Revolution, 5,* 4: 89.

Ehrenreich, Barbara, and John. 1977. "The Professional-Managerial Class." *Radical America, 11,* 2, March-April: 7-31.

Ehrman, Herbert B. 1969. *The Case That Will Not Die: Commonwealth vs. Sacco and Vanzetti.* Boston, Little, Brown.

Einaudi, Mario, et al. 1955. *Nationalization in France and Italy.* Ithaca, N.Y., Cornell University Press.

Eisenstein, Zillah. 1979. *Capitalist Patriarchy and the Case For Socialist Feminism.* New York: Monthly Review Press.

Emmanuel, Arghiri. 1972. *Unequal Exchange: A Study of the Imperialism of Trade.* New York: Monthly Review Press.

Engels, Friedrich. 1926. *The Peasant War in Germany.* New York, International Publishers.

_____ . 1959. *Engels As A Military Critic.* Manchester, England, Manchester University Press. With an introduction by W. H. Chaloner and W. O. Henderson.

_____ . 1939. "The Bakuninists at Work: Notes on the Spanish Uprising in the Summer of 1873." In Marx and Engels, *Revolution in Spain:* 211-236.

_____ . 1968. "The Peasant Question in France and Germany." In Marx and Engels, *Selected Works:* 633-650.

_____ . 1968. *Socialism: Utopian and Scientific.* In Marx and Engels, *Selected Works:* 379-434.

Esmein, Jean. 1973. *The Chinese Cultural Revolution.* Garden City, N.Y., Doubleday Anchor.

Evans, Sara. 1979. *Personal Politics: The Roots of Women's Liberation in the Civil Rights Movement and the New Left.* New York: Knopf.

Fanon, Frantz. 1968. *The Wretched of the Earth.* New York, Grove.

Farman, Christopher. 1972. *The General Strike, May 1926.* London, Rupert Hart-Davis.

Feuer, Lewis. 1969. *The Conflict of Generations.* New York, Basic Books.

Firestone, Shulamith. 1971. *The Dialectic of Sex: The Case for Feminist Revolution.* New York, Bantam.

Fischer, Louis. 1950. *The Life of Mahatma Gandhi.* New York, Harper.

Fischer, Ruth. 1948. *Stalin and German Communism.* Cambridge, Mass., Harvard University Press.

Flacks, Richard. 1967. "The Liberated Generation: An Exploration of the Roots of Student Protest." *Journal of Social Issues, 23,* 3: 52-75.

Foner, Philip S. (ed.). 1970. *The Black Panthers Speak.* Philadelphia, J. B. Lippincott.

Footman, David. 1968. *Red Prelude*. London, Barrie and Cresset.

Forman, James. 1972. *The Making of Black Revolutionaries*. New York, Macmillan.

Frank, Andre Gunder. 1969. *Capitalism and Underdevelopment in Latin America*. New York: Monthly Review Press.

Froelich, Paul. 1972. *Rosa Luxemburg: Ideas in Action*. London, Pluto Press.

Frost, Richard H. 1968. *The Mooney Case*. Stanford, Calif., Stanford University Press.

Gardiner, Jean. 1979. "Women's Domestic Labor." In Zillah Eisenstein (ed.), *Capitalist Patriarchy*, New York: Monthly Review Press: 173–189.

Gerassi, John (ed.). 1968. *Venceremos: The Speeches and Writings of Che Guevara*. New York, Touchstone-Clarion.

Gerassi, Marysa. 1970. "Uruguay's Urban Guerrillas." *New Left Review*. July–August.

Giap, Vo Nguyen. 1968. *People's War, People's Army*. New York, Bantam.

Gilbert, Dave. n.d. *Consumption: Domestic Imperialism*. Ithaca, N.Y., Cornell Students for a Democratic Society and the Glad Day Press.

Gintis, Herbert. 1970. "The New Working Class and Revolutionary Youth." *Socialist Revolution*. May–June.

Glaberman, Martin. 1980. *Wartime Strikes: The Struggle against the No Strike Pledge in the UAW during World War II*. Detroit: Bewick.

Goldman, Emma. 1911. *Anarchism and Other Essays*. New York, Mother Earth Publishing Association.

Gorz, Andre. 1964. *Strategy For Labor*. Boston, Beacon Press.

_____ . 1965. "Capitalist Relations of Production and the Socially Necessary Labor Force." *International Socialist Journal*. August.

_____ . 1973. *Socialism and Revolution*. New York, Doubleday Anchor.

Gramsci, Antonio. 1970. *The Modern Prince and Other Writings*. New York, International Publishers.

_____ . 1971. *Prison Notebooks*. New York, International Publishers.

_____ . n.d. *Soviets in Italy*. Nottingham, England, Institute for Workers' Control.

Guerin, Daniel. 1970. *Anarchism*. New York, Monthly Review Press.

Guevara, Che. 1969. *Guerilla Warfare*. New York, Vintage.

Guillén, Abraham. 1973. *Philosophy of the Urban Guerilla: The Revolutionary Writings of Abraham Guillen*. Donald C. Hodges, ed. New York, William Morrow.

Gutman, Herbert G. 1968. "The Negro and the United Mine Workers of America." In Julius Jacobson (ed.), *The Negro and the American Labor Movement*. Garden City, N.Y., Doubleday Anchor.

Hartman, Heidi. 1979. "Capitalist Patriarchy and Job Segregation by Sex." In Zillah Eisenstein (ed.), *Capitalist Patriarchy*, New York: Monthly Review Press: 206–247.

Harvey, Rowland Hill. 1949. *Robert Owen: Social Idealist*. Berkeley, University of California Press.

Hayden, Tom. 1970. *Trial*. New York, Holt, Rinehart and Winston.

Hobsbawm, E. J. 1965. *Primitive Rebels*. New York, Norton.

_____ . 1969. *The Age of Revolution*. New York, Praeger.

Hoffman, Abbie ("Free"). 1968. *Revolution For The Hell Of It*. New York, Dial.

_____ . 1969. *Woodstock Nation*. New York, Vintage.

Horowitz, Irving L. (ed.). 1964. *The Anarchists*. New York, Dell.

_____ . 1968. *Radicalism and the Revolt Against Reason: The Social Theories of Georges Sorel*. Carbondale, Ill., Southern Illinois University.

_____ , and William H. Friedland. 1972. *The Knowledge Factory: Student Power and Academic Politics in America*. Carbondale, Ill., Southern Illinois University.

Howe, Irving (ed.). 1965. *The Basic Writings of Trotsky*. New York, Vintage.

Hunnius, Gerry, G. David Carson, and John Case (eds.). 1973. *Workers' Control: A Reader on Labor and Social Change*. New York, Vintage.

Inman, Mary. 1940. *In Woman's Defense*. Los Angeles, Committee to Organize the Advancement of Women.

Isaacs, Harold R. 1951. *The Tragedy of the Chinese Revolution*. Stanford, Calif., Stanford University Press.

Jacobs, Harold (ed.). 1970. *Weatherman*. Berkeley, Calif., Ramparts Press.

Jacobs, Paul, and Saul Landau. 1966. *The New Radicals: A Report With Documents.* New York, Vintage.

Jacobson, Julius (ed.). 1968. *The Negro and the American Labor Movement.* Garden City, N.Y., Doubleday Anchor.

Jaurès, Jean. 1910. *L'Armée nouvelle.* Paris, Rouf.

Jen Yu-wen. 1973. *The Taiping Revolutionary Movement.* New Haven, Conn., Yale University Press.

Johnstone, Monty. 1967. "Marx and Engels and the Concept of the Party." In John Saville and Ralph Miliband (eds.), *The Socialist Register 1967.* New York, Monthly Review Press.

Jones, Alfred Winslow. 1964. *Life, Liberty, and Property.* New York, Octagon.

Kanter, Rosabeth Moss. 1972. *Commitment and Community: Communes and Utopias in Sociological Perspective.* Cambridge, Mass., Harvard University Press.

Kedward, Roderick. 1971. *The Anarchists.* New York, American Heritage.

Kerr, Clark. 1963. *The Uses of the University.* Cambridge, Mass., Harvard University Press.

Kipnis, Ira. 1952. *The American Socialist Movement 1897-1912.* New York, Columbia University Press.

Klonsky, Mike. 1968. "Toward A Revolutionary Youth Movement." *New Left Notes.* December 23.

Koestler, Arthur. 1947. *The Gladiators.* New York, Macmillan.

Kornbluh, Joyce (ed.). 1964. *Rebel Voices: An I.W.W. Anthology.* Ann Arbor, University of Michigan.

Krimerman, Leonard, and Lewis Perry (eds.). 1966. *Patterns of Anarchy.* Garden City, N.Y., Anchor.

Kropotkin, P. A. 1970. *Selected Writings on Anarchism and Revolution.* Martin Miller (ed.). Cambridge, Mass., MIT Press.

Labedz, Leopold (ed.). 1962. *Revisionism: Essays on the History of Marxist Ideas.* New York, Frederick Praeger.

Laidler, Harry. 1968. *History of Socialism.* New York, Thomas Y. Crowell.

Landauer, Carl. 1959. *European Socialism: A History of Ideas and Movements.* Berkeley, University of California.

Larrowe, Charles. 1972. *Harry Bridges: The Rise and Fall of Radical Labor in the U.S.* New York, Lawrence Hill.

Lasswell, Harold D., and Dorothy Blumenstock. 1939. *World Revolutionary Propaganda: A Chicago Study.* New York, Alfred A. Knopf.

Lattimore, Owen. 1940. *Inner Asian Frontiers of China.* New York, American Geographical Society.

Lenin, V. I. 1943. *Selected Works.* 12 volumes. New York, International Publishers.

———. 1943. *The Agrarian Programme of Social-Democracy in the First Russian Revolution, 1905-1907* in *Selected Works*, Vol. 3: 157-286.

———. 1943. "The Agrarian Question in Russia at the End of the 19th Century," *Selected Works*, Vol. 1: 13-91.

———. 1943. *The Development of Capitalism in Russia*, in *Selected Works*, Vol. 1, 93-259.

———. 1968. "Critical Remarks on the National Question." In Lenin, *National Liberation, Socialism and Imperialism.* New York: International Publishers: 12-44.

———. 1968. "Guerilla Warfare." In Pomeroy, 84-94.

———. 1970. *Selected Works.* 3 volumes. Moscow, Progress Publishers. Unless otherwise noted, all of Lenin's works cited are found in this edition.

———. *Imperialism: The Highest Stage of Capitalism.* Vol. 1, 667-768.

———. "Lessons of the Revolution." Vol. 2, 207-221.

———. "Marxism and Insurrection." Vol. 2, 380-384.

———. "On Slogans." Vol. 2, 200-206.

———. *One Step Forward, Two Steps Back.* Vol. 1, 273-454.

———. "The Reorganization of the Party." Vol. 1, 564-572.

———. *The State and Revolution.* Vol. 2, 283-376.

———. "The Tasks of the Proletariat in the Present Revolution." Vol. 2, 41-47.

———. *Two Tactics of Social-Democracy in the Democratic Revolution.* Vol. 1, 459-563.

_____ . *What Is to Be Done?* Vol. 1, 119-217.

Lerner, Michael P. 1973. *The New Socialist Revolution.* New York, Dell.

Levine, Norman. 1975. *The Tragic Deception: Marx Contra Engels.* Santa Barbara, ABC-Clio.

Liebman, Marcel. 1970. "Lenin in 1905: A Revolution that Shook a Doctrine." *Monthly Review.* April.

Lipset, Seymour Martin, Martin A. Trow, and James S. Coleman. 1956. *Union Democracy.* Glencoe, Ill., Free Press.

Luxemburg, Rosa. 1968. *The Accumulation of Capital.* New York, Monthly Review Press.

_____ . 1971a. *The Mass Strike, The Political Party, and The Trade Unions and the Junius Pamphlet.* New York, Harper & Row.

_____ . 1971b. *Selected Political Writings.* Dick Howard (ed.). New York, Monthly Review Press.

Lynd, Staughton (ed.). 1966. *Nonviolence in America: A Documentary History.* Indianapolis, Bobbs-Merrill.

MacEwen, Arthur. 1975. "Incentives, Equality, and Power in Revolutionary Cuba." *Socialist Revolution.* No. 23, April: 117-130, 138-143.

Major, Reginald. 1971. *A Panther is a Black Cat.* New York, William Morrow.

Malcolm X. 1966. *The Autobiography of Malcolm X.* New York, Grove.

Mallet, Serge. 1965. "Socialism and the New Working Class." *International Socialist Journal.* April.

Manuel, Frank E. 1962. *The Prophets of Paris.* Cambridge, Mass., Harvard University Press.

_____ , (ed.). 1966. *Utopias and Utopian Thought.* Boston, Houghton Mifflin.

Mao Zedong. 1963. *Selected Military Writings.* Peking, Foreign Languages Press.

_____ . 1971. *Selected Readings From the Works of Mao Tse-tung.* Peking, Foreign Languages Press.

_____ . 1967 and 1969. *Selected Works.* 4 Vols. Vols. 1-3, 1967: Vol. 4, 1969. Peking, Foreign Languages Press. All of Mao's works cited in this book, except as noted, are available in *Selected Works.* Many are also available in his *Selected Military Writings* and in the one-volume *Selected Readings From the Works of Mao Tse-tung.*

_____ . "Analysis of Classes in Chinese Society." Vol. 1: 13-21.

_____ . "Be Concerned with the Well-Being of the Masses, Pay Attention to Methods of Work." Vol. 1: 147-152.

_____ . "The Chinese Revolution and the Chinese Communist Party." Vol. 2: 305-334.

_____ . "On Contradiction." Vol. 1: 311-347.

_____ . "On the Correct Handling of Contradictions Among the People." In *Selected Readings From the Works of Mao Tse-tung:* 432-479.

_____ . "On Correcting Mistaken Ideas in the Party." Vol. 1: 105-116. Also available in *Selected Military Writings.*

_____ . "On Production by the Army for Its Own Support and on the Importance of the Great Movements for Rectification and for Production." Vol. 3: 275-279. Also available in *Selected Military Writings.*

_____ . "On Protracted War." Vol. 2: 113-194. Also available in *Selected Military Writings.*

_____ . "The Orientation of the Youth Movement." Vol. 2: 241-249.

_____ . "Problems of Strategy in China's Revolutionary War." Vol. 1: 179-254. Also available in *Selected Military Writings.*

_____ . "Problems of Strategy in Guerrilla War Against Japan." Vol. 2: 79-112. Also available in *Selected Military Writings.*

_____ . "Problems of War and Strategy." Vol. 2: 219-235. Also available in *Selected Military Writings.*

_____ . "Production is also Possible in the Guerrilla Zones." Vol. 3: 197-200.

_____ . "Report on an Investigation of the Peasant Movement in Hunan." Vol. 1: 23-59.

_____ . "A Single Spark Can Start A Prairie Fire." Vol. 1: 117-128. Also available in *Selected Military Writings.*

_____ . "Spread the Campaigns to Reduce Rent, Increase Production and 'Support the Government and Cherish the People' in the Base Areas." Vol. 3: 131-135.

———. "The Struggle in the Chingkang Mountains." Vol. 1: 73–104. Also available in *Selected Military Writings.*

———. "Turn the Army into a Working Force." Vol. 4: 337–339. Also available in *Selected Military Writings.*

———. "We Must Learn to do Economic Work." Vol. 3: 189–195.

———. "Win the Masses in Their Millions for the Anti-Japanese National United Front." Vol. 1: 285–294.

Marighela, Carlos. 1971. *For the Liberation of Brazil.* Baltimore, Penguin.

Marx, Karl. 1964a. *The Class Struggles in France, 1848–50.* New York, International Publishers.

———. 1964b. *Early Writings.* Edited by T. B. Bottomore. New York, McGraw-Hill.

———. 1964b. *Economic and Philosophical Manuscripts.* Published in *Early Writings,* T. B. Bottomore (ed.). New York, McGraw-Hill.

———. 1964c. *Selected Writings in Sociology and Social Philosophy.* Edited by T. B. Bottomore and M. Rubel. New York, McGraw-Hill.

———. 1966. *Critique of the Gotha Programme.* New York, International Publishers. Also published in Marx and Engels, *Selected Works,* 1968: 315–335.

———. 1967. *Capital.* 3 Volumes. New York, International Publishers.

———. 1968. *The Civil War in France.* In Marx and Engels, *Selected Works*: 252–313.

———. 1968. *The Eighteenth Brumaire of Louis Napoleon.* In Marx and Engels, *Selected Works*: 95–180.

———. 1971. *The Grundrisse.* Edited by David McLellan. New York, Harper & Row.

———. 1972. "Introduction to the Contribution to the Critique of Hegel's *Philosophy of Right.*" In Tucker, 11–23.

———. 1972. "Preface to *A Contribution to the Critique of Political Economy.*" In Tucker, 3–6.

———. 1973. *On the First International.* Edited by Saul K. Padover. New York, McGraw-Hill.

Marx, Karl, and Friedrich Engels. 1939. *Revolution in Spain.* New York, International Publishers.

———. 1947. *The German Ideology.* New York, International Publishers.

———. 1961. *The Civil War in the United States.* New York, Citadel.

———. 1968. *Selected Works.* 1 Volume. New York, International Publishers.

———. 1968. *The Communist Manifesto.* In *Selected Works*: 31–63.

McAfee, Kathy and Myrna Wood. n.d. *Bread and Roses.* San Francisco, Bay Area Radical Education Project.

McLellan, David (ed.). 1971. *The Grundrisse.* By Karl Marx. New York, Harper & Row.

Memmi, Albert. 1965. *The Colonizer and the Colonized.* New York, Orion.

Menashe, Louis. 1973. "Vladimir Ilyitch Bakunin: An Essay on Lenin." *Socialist Revolution.* No. 18, November–December: 9–54.

Michels, Robert. 1968. *Political Parties: A Sociological Study of the Oligarchical Tendencies of Modern Democracy.* New York, Free Press.

Mills, C. Wright. 1953. *White Collar: The American Middle Classes.* New York: Oxford University Press.

Mitchell, Juliet. 1973. *Women's Estate.* New York, Vintage.

Mitrany, David. 1951. *Marx Against the Peasant.* Chapel Hill, University of North Carolina Press.

Nee, Victor, with Don Layman. 1969. *The Cultural Revolution at Peking University.* New York, Monthly Review Press.

Nettl, J. P. 1969. *Rosa Luxemburg.* New York, Oxford University Press.

Newton, Huey. 1974. *Revolutionary Suicide.* New York, Ballentine.

Nicolaus, Martin. 1969. "The Unknown Marx." In *The New Left Reader,* edited by Carl Oglesby. New York, Grove.

Nordhoff, Charles. 1961. *The Communist Societies of the United States.* New York, Hillary House.

Nuñez, Carlos. 1970. *The Tupamaros: Urban Guerillas in Uruguay.* New York, Times Change Press.

Ono, Shin'ya. 1969. "You Do Need a Weatherman to Know which Way the Wind Blows." *Leviathan*. December. Also published in Jacobs, 1970.

Oppenheimer, Martin. 1972. "What is the New Working Class?" *New Politics*, Vol. 10, No. 1, Fall: 29–43.

Padover, Saul K. (ed.). 1973. *Karl Marx on the First International*. New York, McGraw-Hill.

Paige, Jeffrey M. 1975. *Agrarian Revolution: Social Movements and Export Agriculture in the Underdeveloped World*. New York: Free Press.

Payne, Robert. 1969. *The Life and Death of Mahatma Gandhi*. New York, E. P. Dutton.

Pomeroy, William J. (ed.). 1968. *Guerilla Warfare and Marxism*. New York, International Publishers.

Poulantzas, Nicos. 1975. *Classes in Contemporary Capitalism*. London, New Left Books.

Preis, Art. 1972. *Labor's Giant Step: Twenty Years of the CIO*. New York, Pathfinder.

Purcell, Victor. 1963. *The Boxer Uprising*. Cambridge, England, The University Press.

Radosh, Ronald (ed.). 1971. *Debs*. Englewood Cliffs, N.J., Spectrum.

Rayback, Joseph. 1966. *A History of American Labor*. New York, Free Press.

Record, Wilson. 1951. *The Negro and the Communist Party*. Chapel Hill, University of North Carolina Press.

Reich, Michael. 1972. "The Development of the Wage-Labor Force." In Edwards, Reich, Weisskopf, 1978: 179–185.

Reich, Michael, and David Finkelhor. 1972. "The Military Industrial Complex: No Way Out." In Edwards, Reich, and Weisskopf, 1978: 393–406.

Robinson, Joan. 1970. *The Cultural Revolution in China*. Harmondsworth, England, Penguin.

Rosaldo, Michele Zimbalist. 1974. "Women, Culture, and Society: A Theoretical Overview." In Michele Zimbalist Rosaldo and Louise Lamphere (eds.), *Women, Culture, and Society*, Stanford: Stanford University Press: 17–42.

Rothschild, Emma. 1974. *Paradise Lost: The Decline of the Auto-industrial Age*. New York, Vintage.

Roussopoulos, Dimitri. 1970. "Toward A Revolutionary Youth Movement." *Our Generation*. Montreal. June–July.

Rowbotham, Sheila. 1973. *Woman's Consciousness, Man's World*. London: Penguin.

Rowntree, John and Margaret. 1968. "Youth As A Class." *International Socialist Journal*. February.

Rubin, Gayle. 1975. "The Traffic in Women: Notes on the 'Political Economy' of Sex." In Rayna R. Reiter (ed.). *Toward an Anthropology of Women*, New York: Monthly Review Press.

Rubin, Jerry. 1970. *Do It!* New York, Simon and Schuster.

———. 1971. *We Are Everywhere*. New York, Harper & Row.

Rue, John E. 1966. *Mao Tse-tung in Opposition, 1927–1935*. Stanford, Calif., Stanford University Press.

Russell, Bertrand. 1965. *German Social Democracy*. New York, Simon and Schuster.

Russell, Frances. 1962. *Tragedy at Dedham: The Story of Sacco and Vanzetti*. New York, McGraw-Hill.

Sale, Kirkpatrick. 1974. *SDS*. New York, Vintage.

Schiller, Otto. 1962. "The Agrarian Systems in the Soviet Union and Communist China: A Comparison." In Kurt London (ed.), *Unity and Contradiction: Major Aspects of Sino-Soviet Relations*. New York, Praeger.

Schorske, Carl. 1955. *German Social Democracy 1905–1917*. Cambridge, Mass., Harvard University Press.

Schram, Stuart. 1969. *The Political Thought of Mao Tse-tung*. New York, Praeger.

———. 1971. "Mao Tse-tung and the Theory of the Permanent Revolution, 1958–69." *China Quarterly*. No. 46, April–June: 221–244.

Schwartz, Benjamin I. 1961. *Chinese Communism and The Rise of Mao*. Cambridge, Mass., Harvard University Press.

Schwarz, Solomon M. 1967. *The Russian Revolution of 1905*. Chicago, University of Chicago Press.

Seale, Bobby. 1970. *Seize the Time*. New York, Vintage.

Selden, Mark. 1971. *The Yenan Way in Revolutionary China*. Cambridge, Mass., Harvard University Press.

———. "SDS Constitution." *New Left Notes*. July 1, 1966; June 26, 1967; July 10, 1967.

Selznick, Philip. 1952. *The Organizational Weapon: A Study of Bolshevik Strategy and Tactics*. New York, McGraw-Hill.

Shaffer, Robert. 1979. "Women and the Communist Party, USA, 1930-1940." Socialist Review, No. 45, May-June: 73-118.

Shanin, Teodor. 1966. "The Peasantry as a Political Factor." *The Sociological Review, 14*, 1, March: 5-27.

Shannon, David. 1967. *The Socialist Party of America*. Chicago, Quadrangle.

Sorel, Georges. 1950. *Reflections on Violence*. Glencoe, Ill., Free Press.

Students for a Democratic Society. 1962. *The Port Huron Statement*. Chicago, Students for a Democratic Society.

Sturmthal, Adolf. 1972. *Comparative Labor Movements: Ideological Roots and Institutional Development*. Belmont, Calif., Wadsworth.

Teodori, Massimo. 1969. *The New Left: A Documentary History*. Indianapolis, Bobbs-Merrill.

Thomas, Hugh. 1961. *The Spanish Civil War*. New York, Harper & Row.

Thompson, E. P. 1963. *The Making of the English Working Class*. New York, Vintage.

Thoreau, Henry David. 1962. *Thoreau: Walden and Other Writings*. Edited by Joseph Wood Krutch. New York, Bantam.

Trotsky, Leon. 1937. *The History of the Russian Revolution*. New York, Simon and Schuster.

———. 1965. *Their Morals and Ours*. In Deutscher, 1965: 331-341.

———. 1969. *The Permanent Revolution and Results and Prospects*. New York, Merit.

———. 1971. *Military Writings*. New York, Pathfinder.

———. 1972. *1905*. New York, Vintage.

———. 1973a. *The Spanish Revolution*. New York, Pathfinder.

———. 1973b. *The Transitional Program For Socialist Revolution*. New York, Pathfinder.

Tucker, Robert C. (ed.). 1972. *The Marx-Engels Reader*. New York, W.W. Norton.

U.S. Bureau of the Census. 1974. *Statistical Abstracts of the United States*. Washington, D.C.; U.S. Government Printing Office.

———. 1980. *Statistical Abstracts of the United States*. Washington, D.C.; U.S. Government Printing Office.

Vincent, Theodore G. 1972. *Black Power and the Garvey Movement*. Berkeley, Ramparts Press.

Wallerstein, Immanuel, and Paul Starr (eds.). 1971. *The University Crisis Reader*. New York, Vintage.

Waxman, Chaim I. 1968. *The End of Ideology Debate*. New York, Touchstone-Clarion.

Webb, Sidney and Beatrice. 1965. *Industrial Democracy*. New York, Augustus M. Kelley.

Weinstein, James. 1969. *The Decline of Socialism in America 1912-1925*. New York, Vintage.

———. 1970. "The IWW and American Socialism." *Socialist Revolution*. September-October.

———. 1975. *Ambiguous Legacy: The Left in American Politics*. New York, New Viewpoints.

Wheelwright, E. L., and Bruce McFarlane. 1970. *The Chinese Road to Socialism*. New York, Monthly Review Press.

Whiting, Allen S. 1953. *Soviet Politics in China 1917-1924*. New York, Columbia University Press.

Woodcock, George. 1962. *Anarchism: A History of Libertarian Ideas and Movements*. Cleveland, World.

Wright, Mary C. 1962. *The Last Stand of Chinese Conservatism*. Stanford, Calif., Stanford University Press.

Zinn, Howard. 1965. *SNCC: The New Abolitionists*. Boston, Beacon.

Index

organization, 162–64; confrontation, 164–68; consciousness raising, 36, 127, 135–36, 172; in general society, 156–68; general strike, 152–55; historical context, 113–24; increasing participation, 127–28; legality and morality in, 136–39; Lenin's view of, 117, 123; Mao's approach to, 120–23, 170–72; Marx on, 114–16, 123, 131, 136; nationalization, 145–46; periods of inactivity, 157; at point of production (*see* Point of production); programs, 131–32; slogans, 131–33; soviets (*see* Soviets); study groups, 133–36; theory, practice, and issues, 123–39; Trotsky's transitional program for, 117–20, 123; undermining the system, 128–29; warfare as (*see* Revolutionary warfare); workers' control in, 145–49

Revolutionary syndicalism, 96–97
Revolutionary theory, xi–xiv, 5, 6, 67; new groups in, 34–50; of organization (*see* Organization theories)
Revolutionary Union, 102
Revolutionary warfare, 169–85; consciousness in, 172; guerrilla (*see* Guerrilla warfare); insurrectionary, 173–76; popular support of, 169–73; protracted, 174, 176–80; recruitment for, 173; undermining the system, 173
Revolutions of 1848, ix, 95, 113, 175; French, 173, 175; German, 18
Rewards, equality and inequality of, 197–99
Richardson, Gloria, 101
Roman Empire, 8–9; rebellion of Spartacus, 175
Roosevelt, Franklin D., 40
Rousseau, Jean Jacques, 95
Rowntree, John, 47–48
Rowntree, Margaret, 47–48
Ruling class, preventing development of, 199–200
Rumania, foreign investment and standard of living, 29*n*
Rural-urban relationships, 200–201
Russia (czarist): anarchist organizations in, 97; enterprises in, compared with U.S., 20, *table,* 20; foreign investments, 27; foreign investments and standard of living, 29*n*; general strike, 1905, 153–54; proletariat in, 19–22; terrorism in, 73; underground activity in, 157; urban population growth in 19th century, 20; vanguard party in, 73–79 (*see also* Soviet Union)

Russian Revolution of 1905, 2, 16, 18, 19, 21, 85, 91, 114, 117, 118, 149, 153–54, 173, 174, 175
Russian Revolution of 1917, xi, 2, 16, 25, 33, 78, 114, 117, 118, 149, 150; analysis of, 173–74, 176, 192–93, 208, 209

Sacco, Nicola, 159, 160
Saint-Simon, Henri, ix, 189
Sandinistas, 182
San Francisco, general strike (1934), 152
Scottsboro Boys, 158, 159
Seale, Bobby, 104
Sex-gender system, 37
Sexism, 36–38
Slogans, 131–33
Social-Democratic Party, German, 71, 72, 82–86; Luxemburg's criticism of, 90–92; in 1912, 82–83
Social-Democratic Party, Russian, 76–77
Socialism: Chinese and Russian compared, 208–9; early, 189–90; "feudal," 115; Marx's prediction of future, 187, 189–92, 194–97; reformism in, 74
Socialist Party of the United States, 86–89, 98, 133; blacks and, 39; feminist movement and, 35–36; groups in, 86; unions and, 87
Socialist Workers Party, 133
Social systems, positive and negative aspects of, 6–7
Sonvillier Circular, 94–95
Sorel, Georges, 153
Southern Christian Leadership Conference, 40
Soviets (councils), 118, 149–52, 195; origin and development of, 149–51
Soviet Union, 191; bureaucracy in, 199, 206; mobilization in, 114; repression of individualism in, 203–4; Stalin's rule of, 78; Trotsky's transitional mobilization program for, 117–20; turn toward Asia, 34; in World War II, 145
Spain: revolutionary syndicalism in, 96; working class in, 15
Spartacus, 175
Spartacus League, 91–92
Stages of development (theories of), 3, 15–23; marxian, 15–19; social relationships in, 17; Trotskian, 20–22
Stalin, Joseph, 78, 122, 193, 209; Mao's attitude toward, 22; Stalin-Hitler Pact, 145
State: bourgeois, future destruction of, 191, 193–97; functions of, 128; seizure and transformation of power, 128–29

About the Authors

William H. Friedland is Professor of Community Studies and Sociology at the University of California, Santa Cruz. The founding chairperson of the Department of Community Studies, Friedland has been at Santa Cruz since 1969. Prior to that time, he was on the faculty of Cornell University. Before beginning his career, he was involved with the labor movement, serving as Assistant Education Director of the Michigan CIO Council and International Representative in the engineering department of the United Automobile Workers Union.

Amy Barton is currently completing her doctoral degree in sociology at the University of California, Santa Cruz; she has worked extensively with the author on research on agriculture. Bruce Dancis is completing his dissertation in history at Stanford University. Michael Rotkin is the field studies coordinator of the Community Studies Program and, at the time of publication, the mayor of Santa Cruz; he, too, is completing a dissertation (in the History of Consciousness) at Santa Cruz. Michael Spiro is completing a master's thesis in ethnomusicology at the University of Washington.